Simone Knox · Kai Hanno Schwind

Friends

A Reading of the Sitcom

Simone Knox
University of Reading
Reading, Berkshire, UK

Kai Hanno Schwind
Kristiania University College
Oslo, Norway

ISBN 978-3-030-25428-5   ISBN 978-3-030-25429-2   (eBook)
https://doi.org/10.1007/978-3-030-25429-2

© The Editor(s) (if applicable) and The Author(s) 2019

This work is subject to copyright. All rights are solely and exclusively licensed by the Publisher, whether the whole or part of the material is concerned, specifically the rights of translation, reprinting, reuse of illustrations, recitation, broadcasting, reproduction on microfilms or in any other physical way, and transmission or information storage and retrieval, electronic adaptation, computer software, or by similar or dissimilar methodology now known or hereafter developed.

The use of general descriptive names, registered names, trademarks, service marks, etc. in this publication does not imply, even in the absence of a specific statement, that such names are exempt from the relevant protective laws and regulations and therefore free for general use.

The publisher, the authors and the editors are safe to assume that the advice and information in this book are believed to be true and accurate at the date of publication. Neither the publisher nor the authors or the editors give a warranty, expressed or implied, with respect to the material contained herein or for any errors or omissions that may have been made. The publisher remains neutral with regard to jurisdictional claims in published maps and institutional affiliations.

This Palgrave Macmillan imprint is published by the registered company Springer Nature Switzerland AG
The registered company address is: Gewerbestrasse 11, 6330 Cham, Switzerland

For Cas and the Fonz (my little lobster)
—Simone Knox

For Linus
—Kai Hanno Schwind

Acknowledgements

First and foremost, we owe a debt of gratitude to our interviewees, Marta Kauffman, Kevin S. Bright, James Burrows and John Shaffner for engaging with our questions, providing insights and giving us their valuable time. Special thanks go to John Shaffner for his kind support and permission to use the photograph of the model box. We are grateful to Molly Arkin, Karen Marsh and Chris Connor for making the interviews possible, and to Line Engelsås at Nordiske Seriedager in Oslo, and in particular Mari Lundefaret Steinrud for introducing us to Marta Kauffman. We also thank our friends and colleagues for their thoughts, kind support and critical engagement with our project, in particular: Anna Amalie Blomeyer, Ingrid Brekke, Sven Buchholz, Gary Cassidy, Tamara Courage, Jon Inge Faldalen, Mahmud Farjami, Shweta Ghosh, Thomas Giertsen, Lara Herring, Ruchi Kher Jaggi, Anders Larsson, Delphi May, Adam O'Brien, Lisa Purse, Gry Rustad, Johanna Steiner, Änne Troester, Anna Varadi and Katrin Wiegand. We are grateful to the organisers and participants of the 'State of Play: Television Scholarship in "TVIV"' *Critical Studies in Television* Conference (Edge Hill University, September 2018) and the Intermedia/Interarts Workshop 'China & the UK' (University of Reading, May 2019) for their interest in and feedback on our research for this book. We also thank the Sewing Circle, organised by Douglas Pye, for the engaged discussion in February 2019. We thank our students, who over the years have confirmed that *Friends* is still a relevant show to watch. We are grateful to Lina Aboujieb and the team at Palgrave Macmillan for their enthusiasm for this project.

Simone Knox would like to thank: my friends, especially Tamara and Reina-Marie, for putting up with me while I was busy with *Friends*; Kai for all the laughing and (digital) hugging; and Cas for love, patience and countless dinners.

Kai Hanno Schwind would like to thank: my *Friends* friends—Viktor Weimer, Malin Moe and Johanna Steiner—for introducing and experiencing the series with me at different stages of my life; Simone Knox for your precision, stamina, friendship and for giving me that Mockolate bar; and Ståle Norum for patiently coping with my obsessions.

Contents

1 **Introduction: The One where They Take Stock and Identify the Strategy of Intimacy**   1
The One with the Backlash   4
The One with the Scholarship—Or (Relative) Lack Thereof   7
The One with All the 'Quality TV'   9
The One with Genre and Authorship   11
The One where They're Reflecting on Their Methodology   14
The One with All the Intimacy: From Structure of Feeling to Strategy   17
The One with All the Chapter Outlines   22
Bibliography   27

2 **The One with All the Laughing and the Hugging: Specificity of Humour and Comedic Types**   35
The One where They're Feeling Humour: Comedic Sensibility and Tonality   37
The One about Sitcom and Humour   40
The One where They Look from the Pitch to the Pilot: A Comedic Typology   45

Contents

	The One with Rachel Green: 'So here she is, trained for nothing' (Kauffman and Crane 1993)	47
	The One with Monica Geller: 'For all her toughness, she has a real maternal side' (Kauffman and Crane 1993)	50
	The One with Phoebe Buffay: 'She's sweet, flaky, a waif, a hippie' (Kauffman and Crane 1993)	55
	The One with Ross Geller: 'He really really really doesn't want to be single' (Kauffman and Crane 1993)	58
	The One with Joey Tribbiani: 'He really thinks he's God's gift to women' (Kauffman and Crane 1993)	62
	The One with Chandler Bing: 'He's the droll observer of everybody else's life' (Kauffman and Crane 1993)	66
	The One with the Group Identity, Comedic Dialogue and the Laugh Track	68
	Conclusion	74
	Bibliography	79
3	**The One where They Tame the Three-Headed Monster: Foregrounding Holistic Performance**	83
	The One with David Schwimmer and Jennifer Aniston: Performing Ross and Rachel	87
	The One with the Leather Pants: David Schwimmer and Physical Comedy	93
	The One with the Hollywood Guest Stars: Wrestling with the Three-Headed Monster	102
	The One with Rachel and Joey: Matt LeBlanc and Emotionally Truthful Performance	110
	Conclusion	115
	Bibliography	120
4	**The One where They Look at Monica's Apartment: Style, Space, Set Design**	125
	The One with the Iconic Space: Set Design and Texture	129
	The One with the Couch: Multi-Camera Sitcom and Creative Engagement with Space	139
	The One with the Diachronic Space: Layers and Patterns	148

The One with Multi-Camera Sitcom's Regime of Looking In and Rupture	153
Conclusion	161
Bibliography	163

5 The One with the Emblematic Problematic Fave: *Friends* and the Politics of Representation — 169

The One with the Paratextual Patterns	170
The One where They Emphasise the Importance of Context and Tone	173
The One with the Dominant Whiteness	176
The One where Aisha Tyler Plays a White Woman on *Friends*	180
The One where Aisha Tyler Doesn't Play a White Woman on *Friends*	187
The One with Representation, Performance and Tone	191
The One where They Come Full Circle on Intimacy: Re-evaluating *Friends* and the Genre of Sitcom	200
Conclusion	209
Bibliography	214

6 The One with the Orbit of Failure: The *Joey* Spin-Off, Other Adaptations and the Global Reception of *Friends* — 223

The One where the *Joey* Spin-off Doesn't Work	227
The One with *Coupling*: Cultural Proximity, National Specificities and a Lack of Intimacy in Transnational Media Spaces	234
The One with the Conceptualisation of the Television Format	235
The One where *Coupling* Gets Lost in Transnational Media Space	238
The One with *Friends* Across the Globe: Narrative Transparency and Reception	245
The One where They Get Lost in Translation: The German Dubbing of *Friends*	250

    The One with the Unofficial International Adaptations:
    Iran and China   259
    Conclusion   266
    Bibliography   269

7 Conclusion: The One where They'll Still Be There for You—Reflections on *Friends*' Place in Television Culture for Its 25th Anniversary   277
    The One with Continuity and Transformation   281
    The One where They Look Ahead   284
    Bibliography   289

Index   291

List of Figures

Fig. 2.1	First episode, first scene: Joey (Matt LeBlanc), Monica (Courteney Cox), Phoebe (Lisa Kudrow) and Chandler (Matthew Perry) in 'The One where Monica Gets a Roommate' (1.1)	51
Fig. 2.2	'Are you saying that you don't wanna get with this?': a sick Monica (Courteney Cox) tries to seduce Chandler in 'The One with Rachel's Sister' (6.13)	54
Fig. 2.3	Premature umbrella popping: Rachel (Jennifer Aniston) and Ross (David Schwimmer) in 'The One where Monica Gets a Roommate' (1.1)	61
Fig. 2.4	Fake foreskin: Joey's (Matt LeBlanc) legs frame the image as the director (Scott Adsit) and the casting director (Mo Gaffney) get a surprise in 'The One with Ross and Monica's Cousin' (7.19)	65
Fig. 2.5	Group comedic sensibility: Joey (Matt LeBlanc), Chandler (Matthew Perry), Rachel (Jennifer Aniston) and Monica (Courteney Cox) in 'The One with all the Embryos' (4.12)	69
Fig. 2.6	Fat Monica (Courteney Cox) in 'The One where the Stripper Cries' (10.11)	76

List of Figures

Fig. 3.1	'Drunk' performance: Rachel (Jennifer Aniston) tries to get over Ross in 'The One where Ross Finds Out' (2.7)	90
Fig. 3.2	Ross struggles with his leather pants: David Schwimmer in 'The One with All the Resolutions' (5.11)	96
Fig. 3.3	Ross continues to struggle with his leather pants: David Schwimmer in 'The One with All the Resolutions' (5.11)	98
Fig. 3.4	Ross struggles with his leather pants no more: David Schwimmer in 'The One with All the Resolutions' (5.11)	99
Fig. 3.5	Brad Pitt watches as David Schwimmer fills the pause in 'The One with the Rumour' (8.6)	107
Fig. 3.6	'I'm gonna be moving out, man!': Joey (Matt LeBlanc) gets hurt in 'The One where Ross Hugs Rachel' (6.2)	112
Fig. 3.7	Emotionally truthful performance: Rachel (Jennifer Aniston) and Joey (Matt LeBlanc) in 'The One where Joey Tells Rachel' (8.16)	115
Fig. 4.1	Model box for Monica's apartment by John Shaffner	136
Figs. 4.2 and 4.3	Hug-and-roll: Ross's (David Schwimmer) agreement with Rachel (Jennifer Aniston) is shown to be insincere to Chandler (Matthew Perry) in 'The One with the Jam' (3.3)	143
Fig. 4.4	Watching friends with *Friends*: 'The One with the Prom Video' (2.14)	147
Fig. 4.5	Ross (David Schwimmer) and Rachel (Jennifer Aniston) break up in 'The One with the Morning After' (3.16)	157
Fig. 4.6	Moment of rupture: Chandler (Matthew Perry) in 'The One with the Secret Closet' (8.14)	158
Fig. 5.1	Glowing skin: Ross (David Schwimmer) and Charlie (Aisha Tyler) in 'The One in Barbados, Part 2' (9.24)	189
Fig. 5.2	Looking stunned: Charlie (Aisha Tyler) and Ross (David Schwimmer) in 'The One after Joey and Rachel Kiss' (10.1)	194

Fig. 5.3	Evoking the Wicked Witch: Emily (Helen Baxendale) in 'The One with Joey's Dirty Day' (4.14)	205
Fig. 5.4	Sharing a look: Charlie (Aisha Tyler), Ross (David Schwimmer), Chandler (Matthew Perry), Monica (Courteney Cox) and Phoebe (Lisa Kudrow) in 'The One after Joey and Rachel Kiss' (10.1) (set lights visible due to DVD aspect ratio)	207
Fig. 6.1	Unfamiliar surroundings: Michael (Paulo Costanzo), Joey (Matt LeBlanc) and Gina Tribbiani (Drea de Matteo) in *Joey* ('Joey and the Student', 1.2)	230
Figs. 7.1 and 7.2	June (Elisabeth Moss) in *The Handmaid's Tale* ('Unwomen', 2.2) enjoys Monica (Courteney Cox) in 'The One with Phoebe's Uterus' (4.11)	278
Fig. 7.3	Courteney Cox's Instagram snapshot (May 2019): the *Friends* cast on the plane trip to Las Vegas before the pilot aired (1994)	286

1

Introduction: The One where They Take Stock and Identify the Strategy of Intimacy

In his review of one of the 1994/1995 US television season's new situation comedies, critic Ken Tucker comments that: 'Because the show looks and behaves like so many other sitcoms, the originality at [its] center […] comes as something of a surprise' (1994). According to him, while the new NBC show harbours some clichés, it is distinguished by 'sharp writing, and a crack ensemble cast' (ibid.). Tucker's review concludes: 'It's just another sitcom, but even so, *Friends* is pretty irresistible. A-' (ibid.). That penultimate, unprophetic comment—that *Friends* is 'just another sitcom'—plays on our minds nearly a quarter-century later, as we queue up for the 2018 Friendsfest interactive touring exhibition. Filled with the benefit of hindsight, we think: Of course, he is not wrong—but could he *be* any more wrong?

Friends was, of course, 'just another sitcom', indeed, just one of several new programmes that would begin broadcasting in the autumn of 1994. The date of its premiere, 22 September 1994, was ringed by the start of a number of new shows in the US prime-time television schedule, such as the sitcoms *All-American Girl* (ABC 1994–1995), *Me and the Boys* (ABC 1994–1995), *Something Wilder* (NBC 1994–1995), *The Boys Are Back* (CBS 1994–1995) and *Wild Oats* (Fox 1994). Its autumn 1994 brethren from other genres furthermore included action-adventure drama *Fortune Hunter* (Fox 1994), family drama *Party of Five* (Fox 1994–2000), telefantasy *Touched By an Angel* (CBS 1994–2003), teen drama *My So-Called Life* (ABC 1994–1995) and medical dramas *Chicago Hope* (CBS 1994–2000) and *ER* (NBC 1994–2009). As the years pertaining to these programmes' original broadcast runs reflect, the 1994/1995 intake would find varying levels of success: many would be cancelled quickly, some would run for a few years and very few would achieve a high profile within the competitive television landscape.

However, it would be multi-camera situation comedy *Friends* (1994–2004) that would go on to become a cornerstone of NBC's Must-See TV scheduling strategy (achieving 20+ million viewers for each of its ten season premieres) and the most binge-watched television show of 2018, according to a study based on the behaviour of 12 million registered users worldwide (Spangler 2018). It is thus not surprising that it would be *Friends* for whose streaming rights Netflix paid WarnerMedia roughly $100 million to retain for another year in late 2018 (Lee 2018), even though the programme is still readily available via linear television. (It will shift from Netflix US to WarnerMedia's new streaming service HBO Max from 2020.) It would be *Friends* that would receive a global profile, shown in countries that include Australia, China, Egypt, France, Germany, Greece, India, Japan, Norway, the Philippines, Spain and the UK. It would be *Friends* whose ratings in the latter—despite the show having been available via constant reruns across different British channels for years and the popularity of its DVD box set—would see an actual year-on-year increase on Comedy Central UK in 2015 (Sweney 2015). It would be *Friends* that would become a multi-billion-dollar franchise, whose strong tie-in merchandise market would find its perhaps most vivid embodiment in the Mockolate bars on sale at the Friendsfest gift shop.

In addition to its multi-billion-dollar commercial success, the series has also achieved considerable critical recognition. It has won numerous awards, including six Emmys, a Golden Globe and six People's Choice Awards, and featured in a number of 'best TV series of all time' lists compiled by, among others, the Writers Guild of America. Its cultural impact has been significant, launching catchphrases that range from the oft-repeated 'How *you* doin'?' and 'We were on a break!'—the latter,

Judy Kutulas has argued, 'has become an intertextual symbol' (2018, 1182)—to the more obscure 'Pivot!' and 'Paper! Snow! A Ghost!' It has influenced the English language through its characters' use of the word 'so' to add emphasis (Tagliamonte and Roberts 2005), and has furthermore served as a language-learning tool for non-anglophone viewers (see, e.g., Learn English with TV Series 2016). It inspired a popular hairstyle, The Rachel, and its theme song, 'I'll Be there for You', is instantly recognized by millions. It has become a cultural touchstone within the broader cultural media landscape, referenced in sitcoms including *Curb Your Enthusiasm*, *Peep Show*, *The Office—An American Workplace* and *Unbreakable Kimmy Schmidt*; in drama series like *Law & Order*, *The Handmaid's Tale* and *Weeds*; in feature films such as *What Women Want* and *The Terminal*; in plays such as Caryl Churchill's *Seven Jewish Children: A Play for Gaza* (2009); and in music videos such as Jay-Z's *Moonlight* (2017). (We will take note of *Friends*' influence on television culture, specifically the sitcom genre, further below.)

The wide-ranging, if not eclectic, nature of the list above provides some support for Anne Marie Todd's point that *Friends* 'quickly became more than a show: "it was an explanation and exploration of what it meant to come of age in the 1990s"' (2011, 856). That *Friends* has become more than even the latter is already implied by the list above, but more forcefully confirmed by the Friendfest in the UK (which began in 2015 and has grown in size for each annual iteration), the replica Central Perk cafes opened in Beijing (Lim 2013) and Egypt, the three-dimensional *Sims* model of Monica's apartment (Romano 2014) and the forthcoming *Friends: The Tribute Musical* (announced by Ticketmaster in early 2019). Clearly, *Friends* has achieved a longevity for its fans that far outstrips its ten seasons. Matt Hills has argued that fandom 'provide[s] a cultural space for types of knowledge and attachment' (2002, xi), and both of these, as well as fandom's performative nature, are evident in the popularity of *Friends*-themed quiz nights—one held at Samfunnet Bislet in Oslo on 6 February 2019, featured teams named 'The I Hate Rachel Club', 'Ugly Naked Girls', 'Pivot!!!' and several 'Miss Chanandler Bong', reflecting *Friends*' status as a reference show—as well as the 'The One where Everyone Drinks' improvisation performances based on different translated *Friends* scripts, hosted at various locations in Norway by Teater Pappvin since 2018. Considerable, ongoing fan investment is furthermore manifest in the innumerable Facebook and Instagram fan accounts that feature daily posts for a programme whose finale aired in the USA almost exactly three months after Facebook was founded.

Indisputably, *Friends* is one of the most significant programmes in the history of television and media culture.

The One with the Backlash

Such considerable and long-lasting commercial success, cultural influence and investment by fans has since the mid-2010s been running in parallel to the equally considerable criticism *Friends* has been receiving for its representation of different identities. Following Jonathan Gray's argument that engaging with paratexts 'promises to tell us how a text creates meaning in popular culture and society more generally' (2010, 26), it is worth registering that the current criticism of *Friends* is distinguished by the breadth of discourses within which this critical paratextual framing has been articulated, as the following brief overview will demonstrate.

Cosmopolitan's '11 actually pretty shocking things Friends couldn't get away with today' (Baxter-Wright 2017) is one example of the numerous clickbait pieces that capitalise on the show's continuing high profile, seeking to attract online readers with a list of offending materials that are captured via screenshots, memes and clips, and framed by a cursory discussion. Ostensibly intersectional, such lists gravitate towards splitting *Friends*' representational failings into separate categories, without actually exploring the ways in which different aspects of identity meaningfully inform one another (Crenshaw 1989). Such tendencies are also evident in *The Independent*'s 'Friends: 10 times the classic sitcom was problematic'. One of many newspaper articles devoted to criticising the show, it offers the following commentary:

> Perhaps it was a sign of the times or a lack of self-awareness on the part of the writers, but many of the storylines, situations and characters on

Friends were problematic. [...] Storylines laced with homophobia, sexism, borderline emotional abuse and sexual harassment are portrayed as punchlines. The lack of diversity within its 10 seasons is inexcusable and embarrassing. [...] Recently, *Friends* was added to Netflix in the UK, and millennials were astounded by the problematic elements that persisted for 10 seasons. (Kaplan 2018)

Those 'problematic elements' were not only picked up by younger British viewers: indeed, as part of a course titled 'Gender, Race and Popular Culture' taught at Queen's University at Kingston, Canadian students in 2016 set up the blog criticalinsightintofriends.wordpress.com to share their thoughts on what they identified as the show's poor representation of different sexual orientations as well as racial discrimination. There is also no shortage of commentary by a range of demographics on Twitter about the various ideological shortcomings of the show, at times articulated in terms of who is the 'worst *Friends* character'.

Issues concerning representation have certainly been explored by those who already watched the show during its initial broadcast run. The now defunct *Slate Represent* podcast featured a recurring 'Pre-Woke Watching' segment, in which guests discussed the popular screen culture they used to enjoy but have come to view with some critical distance. In March 2017 Panoply's Valerie Woodward Srinivasan discussed with host Aisha Harris *Friends* in terms of the questionable representation of LGBTQ+ issues she had come to identify. She commented that the programme's acquisition by Netflix was 'when I think a lot of people started re-watching it and kind of realising that it was problematic in ways that we didn't realise probably the first time that we saw it' (*Slate Represent* 2017).

Journalist Kelsey Miller, who like many viewers has rewatched *Friends* over the years because it 'was always there, one way or another' (2018a, 11), in her recent book refers to a number of issues concerning diversity and inclusion. She pays specific attention to the Lyle v. Warner Brothers Television Productions sexual harassment lawsuit, brought by Amaani Lyle, a former writers' assistant on *Friends* and one of the few women of colour to have worked on the show. Josh Heuman notes that one of the claims pursued by her pertained to her 'dismissal in retaliation for her criticisms of the show's lack of onscreen diversity' (2016, 196). This lawsuit was ultimately rejected by the California Supreme Court in 2006, with Justice Chin expressing in his concurring opinion that:

> This case has very little to do with sexual harassment and very much to do with core First Amendment free speech rights. The writers of the television show, *Friends*, were engaged in a *creative process* – writing adult comedy – when the alleged harassing conduct occurred. The First Amendment protects creativity. (Lyle v. Warner Brothers Television Productions 2006, emphasis in original)

Rightly pointing out that this lawsuit was not widely known because of scant news coverage—remarkably, the innumerable webpages devoted to *Friends* notwithstanding, the lawsuit has yet to receive a Wikipedia entry—Miller (2018b) in a subsequent online article goes as far as to suggest that the ruling set back the #MeToo movement by years.

Recent criticism of *Friends* has also extended to the creative industries, with a particular focus on issues of race and ethnicity. A 2016 *Saturday Night Live* 'Weekend Update' segment, co-hosted by Colin Jost and Michael Che, featured Vanessa Bayer impersonating 'Rachel from Friends'. Bayer at one point asked Jost 'What's that?' while pointing at Che, who explained to Jost that: 'She's on *Friends*; she's never seen a black person, Colin.' In the *Unbreakable Kimmy Schmidt* episode 'Kimmy is Bad at Math!' (1.8), the Vietnamese character Dong Nguyen (Ki Hong Lee) mentions his 'favourite show *Six White Complainers*. I believe in America it's called *Friends*!' Jay-Z's 2017 *Moonlight* featured a remake of moments from 'The One where No One's Ready' (3.2) and the fountain shots from the opening credits, with Jerrod Carmichael cast as Ross, Tiffany Haddish as Phoebe, Lil Rel Howery as Joey, Issa Rae as Rachel, Lakeith Stanfield as Chandler and Tessa Thompson as Monica, offering a literalised commutation test to viewers. Directed by Alan Yang, the video's combination of a close match with the original (in terms of set design, costuming, camera and dialogue) and all-black cast vividly draws attention to the dominant whiteness of *Friends*.

So, across different discourses, *Friends* has been noted for its difficult track record in terms of both its process and product, as the above demonstrates with some collective heft.

The One with the Scholarship—Or (Relative) Lack Thereof

For a quarter of a century, *Friends* has had significant cultural impact, attracted considerable fan investment and sparked rising criticism and controversy. This makes it only more striking that rather little scholarship exists on the series. With the exception of Katherine Dillion (2009) and Lisa Marie Marshall (2007), there is no book-length study of *Friends*; and the latter is an unpublished Ph.D. thesis, and the former an ethnographic study of viewers in Egypt, with a sociological intention to use 'the show as a lens or looking glass with which to view women from another cultural group' (Dillion 2009, 169) and facilitate discussions about changing social trends and attitudes. In this way, Dillion's work is representative of a number of studies from other scholarly fields in which *Friends* figures as a means to an end for the research. Television scholarship, and specifically key titles on sitcom, have paid some (Mills 2005), passing (Mills 2009; Savorelli 2010) and scant (Morreale 2003; Dalton and Linder 2016) attention to the programme. Where the series has been explored in some depth, the focus has tended to rest on its politics of representation, and earlier scholarship here, chiefly manifest in the form of a handful of articles (Sandell 1998; Kessler 2006; Rockler 2006a, b; Chidester 2008), has argued that the programme reinforces hegemonic discourses on a number of levels, which chimes with the rising paratextual criticism noted above. (There are, of course, further exceptions, such as Nancy San Martín's [2003] study of the series' function within the NBC Must-See TV schedule, Stuart Bell's [2016] Ph.D. thesis, part of which considers *Friends*' use of narrative closure, and Kutulas's [2018] exploration of the programme in relation to genre.)

The most significant and consolidated contribution to scholarly debates on *Friends* to date is the 2018 *Television & New Media* special issue, which considers a number of aspects, including set design (Thompson 2018), but whose focus lies ultimately with representation. Here, for example, Hannah Hamad considers *Friends* as 'an unacknowledged and structuring ur-text of millennial post-feminist media culture' (2018, 694). She discusses how there is potential within the text to challenge normative notions of gender through, for example, the characterisation of Monica or Joey's enjoyment of his man bag. However, ultimately, Hamad argues, such potential is withdrawn from, as the series 'conceded to the inherent conservatism of the sitcom genre' (ibid., 698): Monica 'embodies and articulates a discourse of neo-traditionalism that is centered on (white) heteronormative love, and the fetishization of the domestic sphere' (ibid., 695), while Joey is resituated via 'homophobic and transphobic jokes […] within the semiotic landscape of hegemonic masculinity' (ibid., 701).

While the existing academic engagement with the programme has made a productive contribution to television studies, we cannot help but notice the overall absence of in-depth television scholarship on what is one of the most significant programmes in television history. This becomes especially detectable when you cast even a quick glance at the literature available on other US television shows that ran during the 1990s, such as *Buffy the Vampire Slayer* or *The Sopranos*, or indeed television shows that ran during the 1990s, are linked to the genre of sitcom and set in New York City, such as *Seinfeld*, *Sex and the City* and, to a lesser extent, *Will & Grace*. It is worth reflecting on this further. Scholarship on sitcom has tended to acknowledge a traditional neglect of the genre within academia, but the literature has been expanding and consolidating for some time—but not yet in ways that reflect *Friends*' central role within the genre landscape. In his discussion of 'invisible television', Brett Mills notes that 'how television is talked about and the programmes that are analysed, discussed and taught, lead to a normalised understanding of what television is, what it is constituted of, what it does, who it is for and what is done with it' (2012, 1). Given *Friends*' hyper-visibility in cultural discourses, what may have fostered its relative invisibility in television scholarship thus far, and what broader gains stand to be made from engaging with the programme in more depth?

The One with All the 'Quality TV'

We will begin to address the question above by focusing first on issues of prestige and legitimacy, and exploring how the historical development of television studies may help illuminate the fact that *Friends* has not held a central place in scholarly discourses on television, both in general and—its acclaim within the television industry notwithstanding—in terms of debates on 'quality' television. As Paul Attallah (2003) has noted, the notion of 'unworthiness' has long hung over television, and sitcom in particular, and this has undoubtedly contributed to the fact that academic engagement with sitcom took some time to expand in scope and depth. Scholarship during the 1980s recognised a shift towards quality—here figured in terms of the label of 'relevance'—in 1970s situation comedies, with multi-camera MTM productions *The Mary Tyler Moore Show* and *Rhoda*, and the Norman Lear-produced *All in the Family* and *Maude* understood as revivifying the genre through greater sophistication in scripts, liberal themes and more complex characters (Feuer et al. 1984). While *Friends* can be matched to such characteristics, the focus of debates concerning quality were shifting into a different direction by the time of its first appearance on NBC schedules.

In the 1990s and 2000s—which saw both *Friends*' first broadcast run and a period of flourish for anglophone television studies—scholarly debates on television paid much attention to issues of quality; as Jason Jacobs noted at the beginning of the twenty-first century, 'the historical development of television's dramatic efforts has reached a point where issues of excellence are pressing to an extent that has not been before' (2001, 432). In their work to lay bare the processes of legitimation that have repeatedly sought to distinguish certain kinds of drama over 'ordinary', 'old' and/or feminised mass programming, Michael Z. Newman and Elana Levine point out that:

> discourses of legitimation are premised upon cultural hierarchies and hierarchies of all kinds require the denigration of some to justify the elevation of others. In the case of television, it is not other media that suffer this denigration. Rather, it is certain kinds of television that are denigrated, dismissed, or ignored. (2012, 36)

The programmes not denigrated, dismissed or ignored by press, critic and scholarly discourses around the turn of the millennium were predominately US television series, especially those shown on the US premium cable channel HBO or marked by the 'HBO effect'. As networks and other cable channels shifted towards high-production profile programming, 'serious' dramas like *The Sopranos* found unprecedented acclaim for combining an aesthetically ambitious *mise-en-scène* with dense storytelling and a serialised focus on characterisation, in ways that produce intense and discriminating spectatorial involvement.

Sitcom was not excluded from the 'quality debate', but the focus here remained firmly on the rise of the single-camera sitcom in the early 2000s, with shows such as *Arrested Development* and *Community* employing production methods noted for their invested use of camera and post-production. Often eye-catching, such sitcoms received much interest and acclaim within press, critic and academic discourses: *30 Rock* received 103 Emmy Award nominations, winning the award for Outstanding Comedy Series for its first three seasons. In their 2016 combined top 100 list of 'greatest American shows of all time', critics Alan Sepinwall and Matt Zoller Seitz included *Arrested Development* at number 15 and *Community* at number 54. (*Friends* was ranked 56th.) Jeremy Butler (2010) has framed single-camera sitcoms such as *Scrubs* in terms of the 'resurrection' of the genre.

What the dramatic and comedic shows that featured prominently in the 'quality debate' have in common is that their use of style links to notions of the 'cinematic'. This points to traditional conceptions of television as a medium of relay, whereby the (supposedly) aesthetically conservative essence of television is frequently positioned in contrast to a more adventurous interest in style in cinema. That quality television was increasingly being understood in terms of its proximity to cinema is indicated by HBO's (in)famous 1990s promotional tagline 'It's not TV. It's HBO', which rather preoccupied scholarship on television for some time, at times with a lack of critical reflection. While it bears out a number of production links to cinema—it was shot in Hollywood, with some creative personnel with experience in film, and marked by an early interest 'to make it look like a movie', as noted by executive producer Kevin S. Bright—with its multi-camera production style, 'cinematic' is not one of the first adjectives that come to mind when describing *Friends*. It is certainly televisual—'It's not HBO. It's TV'—and not in the sense of televisuality as put forward in John T. Caldwell's (1995) discussion of how US television in the 1980s shifted towards a cultivation of and preoccupation with style. First broadcast in a time period in which 'it has become axiomatic that quality television aims for an association with cinema' (Chamberlain and Ruston 2007, 17), *Friends* would not find ready admission into scholarly (and critics') debates about 'quality' television. If TV is seen as an unworthy medium, sitcom as an unworthy genre and multi-camera sitcom as an unworthy exponent of that genre, then *Friends* is unworthy indeed. Its original broadcast ran somewhat in parallel to the prestige ascribed to HBO-style drama series and single-camera sitcoms; and while television scholarship (e.g. Jaramillo 2013) has since increasingly taken issue with the term 'cinematic' as an under-defined, uninterrogated placeholder marked by an essentialism that does critical engagement with television no favours, it seems to us that there is still some catching up to do with *Friends* by the field.

There is, of course, another sitcom set in New York that ran during the 1990s on NBC that did get ascribed with notions of prestige and received much more scholarly attention, notwithstanding the fact that it is also a multi-camera production; and that is *Seinfeld*. This brings our discussion to issues of legitimacy in relation to genre and authorship.

The One with Genre and Authorship

One reason why *Friends* has not received that much scholarly recognition is that it has not been understood as an innovative contribution to the genre. The show has here suffered from comparison with its contemporary *Seinfeld*, which has been generally understood as somewhat 'radical' because of its reputation for being a show about 'nothing', with 'no hugging, no learning'. This is quite distinct from *Friends*, in which hugging abounds, and which, as Kevin S. Bright sees it, 'is fundamentally about relationships' and offers 'a little bit of a tutorial' on how to conduct friendships. Such a perception is perhaps caused or reinforced by the fact that *Friends* has been so influential on the sitcom genre.

Its basic set-up seems very familiar now: a group of twenty-something friends in New York, Ross (David Schwimmer), Monica (Courteney Cox), Rachel (Jennifer Aniston), Chandler (Matthew Perry), Joey (Matt LeBlanc) and Phoebe (Lisa Kudrow). Storylines explore, as per co-creators Marta Kauffman and David Crane's original pitch, 'sex, love, relationships, careers … a time in your life when everything is possible, which is really exciting and really scary. […] And it's about friendship, because when you're young and single in the city, your friends are your family' (1993).

As Kutulas points out, to feature a 'constructed family not linked by a workplace' (2018, 1176) and an ensemble cast with equally important main characters were significant innovations at the time, which set up a 'blueprint' for subsequent flat-sharing sitcoms such as, most prominently, *How I Met Your Mother*, *The Big Bang Theory*, *New Girl* and *Happy Endings*. (Kutulas further discusses the ways in which *Friends* influenced such programmes as *Scrubs* and *The Office—An American Workplace*.) So, *Friends* may appear as a somewhat conventional sitcom because its approach to storytelling has been so impactful. Jane Feuer has argued that 'the sitcom develops by reacting to and against previous sitcoms' (1992, 151), and this of course also applies to *Friends*, whose complex relationship to genre is marked by lineages such as the trope of the woman who moves to the city (on the heels of a broken engagement), which it borrows from *The Mary Tyler Moore Show*, as well as the fact that *Friends* draws quite strongly on soap opera in terms of its serialised storytelling and focus on relationships. So, there is much about *Friends* that may seem familiar, but which represents no less of a productive inflection of its genre for that. Moreover, while its approach to storytelling has not been included in debates on narrative complexity (Mittell 2006), Kutulas (2018) highlights that *Friends* should further be considered as making a contribution to sitcom through its use of origin stories and alternative storylines. A degree of intertextuality is also detectible in genre-specific parodies, such as the visual references to the Spaghetti Western in Joey's stand-off with the Hombre Man in episode 2.2. (While such stylistic flourishes tend to appear in earlier episodes, they certainly complicate any views of *Friends* as possessing a transparent style.)

Such textual characteristics and specificities at least hint at the possibility of an auteurial presence, and here it is interesting to consider that *Friends* has generally not been understood within scholarship as an authored show in the way that *Seinfeld* has. Indeed, much of the existing literature makes scant or no mention of Marta Kauffman, David Crane or Kevin S. Bright—let alone later showrunners such as Wil Calhoun, Shana Goldberg-Meehan or Scott Silveri—despite their names' regular appearance in the end credits and their Hitchcockian cameos in episodes such as 2.13. While Kauffman and Crane were only showrunners throughout the series' first three seasons, the programme's set-up and key creative choices (including the granular level of prop choice) are informed by a strong specificity grounded in the shared lived experience of the key creative personnel, as Kauffman, Bright and John Shaffner confirm. (As Kauffman notes, she and David Crane used to be part of a close-knit group of 'six best friends living in New York' and this informed their early discussions about the show.) Perhaps one reason why *Friends* has not been considered as authored is that its key creatives have spoken very openly about restrictions imposed upon them by Standards and Practices; for example, Marta Kauffman has recalled for us how in the first season, 'we couldn't say the word "nipple" and so we ended up using the word "nippular", which I thought was actually funnier'. This openness and *Friends*' close engagement with the high-profile 'Who's Gonna Drink the Diet Coke?' promotional campaign that culminated in January 1996 discursively contrasts with the attention paid to Jerry Seinfeld's and Larry David's 'uncompromising' auteurial vision. The latter is noted for turning down requests for a *Friends–Seinfeld* cross-over episode and to participate in NBC's 'Blackout Thursday' promotional stunt (Burns and Schildhause 2015)—which (the considerably much less established) *Friends* did, on 3 November 1994, with 'The One with the Blackout' (1.7).

Another reason may concern the number of inconsistencies in the storytelling and *mise-en-scène*—such as the dates of characters' birthdays, whether Chandler can indeed cry, that Rachel and Chandler's previous acquaintance (as established in later flashbacks) is not apparent in the pilot, or the 'numerous fenestral realities' (Waring 2016) concerning the kitchen window—frequently shared on social media. Such irregularities reflect the myriad of creative personnel (including several showrunners) involved in the production of a show with 236 episodes as much as they do a considerable fan interest into the fictional world created within those episodes. In her thoughtful contribution to the 'quality debate', Sarah Cardwell proposes that what she calls good television offers 'interpretive richness and endurance (i.e. the capacity to sustain repeated viewings and concomitant interpretive revisions), stylistic coherence, and thematic seriousness or importance' (2007, 34). We think that *Friends* could and should be considered good television: its occasional inconsistencies notwithstanding, the programme is marked by a high level of craft invested in the construction and development of its fictional world, which, as the chapters in this book will show, bears out repeated viewing and indeed detailed scrutiny. Here, we do not mean so much the 'Easter eggs' made available for attentive viewers, such as the Magna Doodle in Joey and Chandler's apartment or Central Perk's chalkboard menu, which the production team invested into before digital technology made such details more easily detectable for viewers. Nor do we mean such authorial tropes as the thematic preoccupation with food and eating. What interests us most is how significant creative decisions pertaining to set design, humour and performance affect the programme's sensibility and underpin its considerable popularity. As they reflect the input of a number of creative personnel, these decisions highlight the importance of considering *Friends* as authored television, which in turn helps to bestow long overdue legitimacy.

The One where They're Reflecting on Their Methodology

As we have outlined above, there is a nexus of reasons why *Friends* has not been ascribed with notions of prestige within scholarly discourses in the way that other (multi-camera) sitcoms have. This points to the need for closer and multipronged engagement with the show. Here, our methodological approach is weighted towards close textual analysis informed by consideration of relevant production, genre, industry, reception and socio-cultural contexts. We have found textual analysis that embraces the specificity of detail to be curiously absent from much of the existing scholarly literature on *Friends*, which has tended to be focused on narrative and dialogue, without taking much notice of how the use of style and performance operates and informs meaning. Following the calls within television studies for closer attention to audio-visual forms as fundamental to meaningful critical engagement (Jacobs and Peacock 2013), we rewatched all 236 episodes with a viewing protocol designed to pay attention to particular aspects, such as the use of style, humour, performance and representation.

This longitudinal study deepened our understanding of how *Friends* works as an overall composition (Smart 2012) and reminded us that its textual identity is not fixed or stable. (For example, the stylistic flourishes noted earlier tend to disappear after the first couple of seasons, similar to other series, such as *Sex and the City*; and while the visual access to the fictional world appears consistent, the programme repeatedly intercuts between different takes in which the cameras may be repositioned. Moreover, our study is based on the 15th anniversary box set, and there are a number of textual differences between the various box sets.) Lucy Fife Donaldson rightly notes that 'the reward for this kind of detailed approach goes beyond simply an in-depth knowledge of one particular' (2016, 4) programme; and yet we were struck—given that we had watched the show on countless previous occasions—by how much more there was still to be discovered about *Friends*, particularly in terms of fully discerning patterns (concerning, e.g., the use of space and humour) that we had (at best) only partially registered before.

Such patterns reflect the work and achievements of a myriad of creative collaborators, whose knowledge and experiences we intended to capture through original interviews where possible and feasible. We conducted interviews with co-creator, co-showrunner and writer Marta Kauffman (via email, 7 June 2019) and executive producer and director Kevin S. Bright (via Skype, 17 April 2019), whose remit included post-production. We spoke with director James Burrows (via phone, 7 May 2019), whose multi-camera directing credits include *Cheers* (which he co-created), *Frasier*, *Will & Grace* and *The Big Bang Theory*. We interviewed John Shaffner (via Skype, 29 January 2019)—his official credit for *Friends* is art director, because as he explained to us, 'Warner Bros had a policy to not give the credit production designer to people in multi-camera'—whose work as a production designer includes *Dharma*

& Greg, *Mike & Molly* and *The Big Bang Theory*, and who served as Chairman and CEO of the Academy of Television Arts & Sciences. (Quotes in the book are taken from these interviews, unless otherwise indicated.)

Whilst the process of securing interviews is marked by chance and fortune, the mix of above-the-line and below-the-line personnel is intentional, as is the presence of creative roles other than writer, which has traditionally been privileged in discourses on television authorship as the locus of the creation of meaning. Our objective has been to produce new knowledge about and emphasise the importance of craft and process, as well as the range of creative inputs that have made crucial contributions to *Friends*' enduring appeal and the broader television landscape. In particular, James Burrows is a seminal figure, and in-depth scholarly engagement with his work as a director is sorely overdue. Moreover, sitcom and other genres have been influenced by the work of creative practitioners like John Shaffner for decades, who thus also deserve much more scholarly recognition.

Our Skype and phone interviews employed a semi-structured approach, whereby open questions were supplemented with relevant follow-up questions, thus allowing both the development of a stronger narrative line within the questions and the ability 'to *probe* beyond the answers and thus enter into a dialogue with the interviewee' (May 2011, 134, emphasis in original). Interviews are marked by issues of subjectivity and memory, producing 'interpretative and richly interpretable' (Williams 2008, 134) material. This interpretative quality is perhaps only furthered in the case of individuals working in the creative industries; after all such 'practitioners are storytellers by trade' (Mills 2008, 152). However, whilst information obtained from interviewing cannot be treated as unproblematically usable evidence, as Heather Sutherland has noted, 'oral history should not be tarnished as a lesser source' (2010, 160). Indeed, interviewing can (and should) meaningfully inform other sources and discourses, and Donald Ritchie's view that 'as a result of [...] blind spots, oral history can develop information that might not have appeared in print' (2003, 26) strikes us as useful given the extent to which even creative practitioners with high profiles such as those at the helm of Bright/Kauffman/Crane Productions have been neglected within existing scholarship. All of our interviewees are 'exclusive informants' (Bruun 2016) because their significant professional involvement in *Friends* provides them with irreplaceable knowledge that could not be obtained via alternative means, and into which we wanted to gain insights in order to inform and complement our own scholarly analysis.

The One with All the Intimacy: From Structure of Feeling to Strategy

With two rich resources at our disposal, namely a long-running television series and several practitioner interviews, we are very aware that the analysis in the chapters to come cannot possibly achieve comprehensiveness. Indeed, our discussion favours critical depth over scope. As the first book-length television scholarship study of *Friends*, our focus lies with the programme's particular sensibility which we detect and consider crucial to its (continuing) popularity. When we have mentioned to friends and acquaintances that we are writing a book on this series, we have often received affirmative comments about the timelessness of the show. Linked in complex ways (that are beyond the scope of this book) to 1990s nostalgia (see Andersen 2015), this timelessness is debatable: *Friends* has visually indisputably aged, most strikingly in terms of the technology present and absent on-screen. Moreover, the socio-cultural context of its time of creation is detectable, Gwen Ihnat (2014) has argued, especially in terms of the disillusionment of Generation X in relation to authority figures, embodied by the friends' often unhelpful parents, experiences of professional frustration and uncertainty about the future (the latter is especially articulated in the early seasons). And paratextual criticism is quick to point out that some of the programme's representations have not aged well.

At the same time, the show, as Bright confirms, moved to reduce its pop-cultural references quite early on and is 'not about politics, not about current events, not about many things that get dated'. (The show's original broadcast run took place in a socio-political context that encompassed the O. J. Simpson trial, the Clinton–Lewinsky scandal and the Iraq War, all of which remain firmly absent from *Friends'* fictional world.) This is why the few exceptions that do explicitly place the show in its historical context are so striking, such as when in episode 'The One with Chandler's Work Laugh' (5.12) Joey tries to persuade Ross to come to the cinema to see *You've Got Mail* (1998). This is an odd moment to watch nowadays, because that film *feels* so much older than *Friends*, offering a reminder that this episode first aired in early 1999. Similarly, the on-screen dedication of the episode 'The One after "I Do"' (8.1) to 'the people of New York City' in acknowledgment of 9/11—an event that saw the show's ratings improve, as US viewers were drawn, Bright notes, to the comfort it provides—temporarily disrupts the series' contemporaneity. This timeless quality is clearly influenced by the show's ongoing presence on television, laptop, tablet and smartphone screens—unlike *You've Got Mail*, *Friends* has never really not been on.

But perhaps, its perceived timelessness also speaks to the 'deep connection' (2018, 1182) Kutulas observes between *Friends* and its viewers, which the show engenders through several means. Bright as well as Kutulas (2018) and Todd (2011) refer to the show in terms of 'comfort food' television, and these strong connotations of emotional well-being possibly hold another reason for its relative neglect within scholarship. In his discussion of 'invisible television', Mills further writes:

> As we are academics, so we are audiences. It is unsurprising that we commonly choose to write about those programmes that we find interesting, or addictive, or pleasurable. Indeed, it is often the case that it is those interests that spark our desire to work as academics in the first place. And it is that enthusiasm which commonly informs our teaching and becomes an impetus to our work as a whole. (2012, 5)

Knowing many scholars who enjoy *Friends*, we think the reverse could be applied to the series: perhaps scholars also reserve some programmes for their leisure, to wind-down after a long day's teaching, researching and/or administrative duties. Perhaps *Friends* is academic 'comfort food' television. Be that as it may, the term 'comfort food' to us does not sit well with the complexity of *Friends'* textual identity, especially the fact that its humour works in complex ways, as one of our chapters in this book will explore. (This is already reflexively suggested by the online videos that show extracts from *Friends* with the laugh track removed, such as the video that uses 'The One with Unagi' [6.17]: it is quite unsettling to watch Ross seek advice from a self-defence instructor on how to attack women without the non-diegetic laughter [see sboss 2013].) Because of this lack of nuance, we wish to avoid the use of the label 'comfort food', and instead draw on the notion of intimacy.

Intimacy has been explored across different disciplines and debates, as Lauren Berlant (1998) outlines, with need for 'more cases, more narratives, more attempts to bring to expression the ways attachments make worlds and world-changing fantasies' (1998, 288), including in relation to the medium of television. The significance of intimacy for television was first raised by Horace Newcomb in his seminal *TV: The Most Popular Art*, in which he proposed that the medium is marked by three distinguishing features, namely intimacy, continuity and history, which are informed by and speak to the smallness of the television screen, the medium's domestic context, as well as 'the economic necessities of television production' (1974, 249). Helen Wheatley (2016) rightly points out that intimacy 'belongs' to television no more than spectacle does to cinema, but it nevertheless holds significance for television and, as our analysis will show, productive potential for engaging with multi-camera sitcom, and *Friends* in particular.

Intimacy and multi-camera sitcom might not seem like the most obvious or natural bedfellows, given the theatricality and heightened quality frequently associated with the latter. Indeed, Newcomb's analysis made repeated references to the use of close-ups as one major way to achieve intimacy, able to offer to viewers 'faces, reactions, explorations of emotions' (1974, 245–246). This could seem to raise problems for understanding multi-camera sitcoms as (at least potentially) marked by intimacy, given the relative absence of close-ups. However, Newcomb himself argued for intimacy being achieved in multi-camera sitcoms such as *Maude* through the emphasis on character relationships and the viewers' familiarity with the characters over time. He further paid attention to how the use of audio-visual forms can convey a concern with intimacy. Newcomb noted that there are 'shows and series that develop the idea of intimacy as a conceptual tool' (ibid., 250), and *Friends*, we want to argue and subsequent chapters will seek to demonstrate, is such a show. (The programme's notion of intimacy does not appear to diminish when it is being watched online, linking to Glen Creeber's point that 'the internet produces an intensely *intimate* screen' [2013, 121, emphasis in original].) *Friends*' emphasis on intimacy may have contributed to its relative neglect within television scholarship, which, as Kristyn Gorton argued in the 2000s, 'continues to overlook or disregard the value of emotion or sentiment within programmes' (2006, 72). If and when emotion and emotional engagement are critically valued, then this emphasis on intimacy can be understood as making an important claim for the series' consideration as good television.

Earlier in our research, we were inclined to conceive of this notion of intimacy marking *Friends* in terms of a structure of feeling, building on Ien Ang's pioneering work, in which she—herself drawing on Raymond Williams (1977)—explores how *Dallas* cultivates a tragic structure of feeling:

> It is emotions which count in a structure of feeling. Hence emotions form the point of impact for a recognition of a certain type of structure of feeling in *Dallas*; the emotions called up are apparently what remain with the [viewers] most. […] What we can deduce from this is the notion that in life emotions are always being stirred up, i.e. that life is characterized by an endless fluctuation between happiness and unhappiness […]. This structure of feeling can be called the *tragic* structure of feeling; tragic because of the idea that happiness can never last forever but, quite the contrary, is precarious. In the tragic structure of feeling emotional ups and downs occupy a central place[.] (1985, 45–46, emphasis in original)

There is much here that is useful for thinking through how in the intimate structure of feeling in *Friends*, feelings of closeness, familiarity, attachment and warmth occupy a central space. However, while intimacy is a 'complex of meanings which […] viewers can read from' (ibid., 61) *Friends*, we have come to recognise—especially through our interviews with the creative practitioners who were instrumental in the look and feel of the show—that the term 'structure of feeling' in itself does perhaps not quite capture the full extent to which notions of intimacy are inscribed into the programme, especially through creative choices concerning humour, performance and set design.

As our interview testimonies reflect, the strong level of intimacy is informed by the core creative team's shared 'deep affection for the material' and 'mutual emotional feelings about the city', as articulated by Shaffner, as well as the specificity of the core creative team's experience of young adulthood in New York, as Bright recalled for us. Such specificity is, of course, carefully balanced against the presence of what can be understood as universal elements that draw on widely recognisable genre tropes and storytelling archetypes. Such universality, which one of the chapters will further explore, helps to minimise the series' 'cultural discount', which Colin Hoskins and Rolf Mirus have defined as follows:

> A particular programme rooted in one culture, and thus attractive in that environment, will have a diminished appeal elsewhere as viewers find it difficult to identify with the style, values, beliefs, institutions and behavioural patterns of the material in question. (1988, 500)

Especially through the thematic focus on 'the time when your friends are your family', as Kauffman sums it up, which was of personal significance to the core creative team, *Friends* avoids being so culturally specific that viewers outside the demographic of its core character group—young adults living in New York around the turn of the millennium—would find it difficult to fully access its fictional world. Through a careful negotiation of specificity and universality, whereby the programme is neither bland and interchangeable nor inaccessible and exclusionist, viewers are encouraged to become intimately attached to the show. Consequently, we find it helpful and appropriate to think of *Friends* in terms of a strategy of intimacy, for this better reflects the intention shared by the core creative team to speak to their lived experience of living in New York as twenty-somethings, of creating characters that viewers could (and would) emotionally invest into (especially through an approach to performance rooted in realism), and of carefully balancing the comedic and dramatic elements of storytelling located within a fictional world that is both resonant and easily accessible.

The One with All the Chapter Outlines

As a point of departure for our close reading of the series, Chapter 2 addresses the specificities of the humour in *Friends*. Surprisingly, whilst in most scholarly accounts frequently referred to as a comedic show or with brief references to irony (e.g. Hamad 2018; Cobb 2018), *Friends*' discourses of humour are often not unpacked in any further detail. We argue that understanding and contextualising the humour in the programme is vital for any further analysis, as it is situated at the heart of its narrative, performance and aesthetic discourses; but, also, *Friends* is a show about humour. We begin by offering a more structural approach by exploring and contextualising the series as part of a larger canon of American sitcoms and a more theoretical framework of humour theory. We also discuss the scholarly approaches to 'sitcom as genre' in the influential works by, among others, Brett Mills (2005, 2009). This theoretical approach illustrates to what extent sitcom can be a site of confirmation of hegemonic values and/or critique. *Friends*, as sitcom, we argue, offers both, and enables a paratextual engagement between the programme and its audience which is clearly facilitated through its distinct humour.

Informed by our interviews with Marta Kauffman and Kevin S. Bright, we offer a typology of the six main characters of the programme as distinct 'comedic types' which allow the series to address a considerable variety of humouristic themes, comic situations and types of comedic performances. We then argue that *Friends*' humour is moreover characterised by a group quality and ensemble dynamic in which individual jokes and gags almost always serve a larger narrative 'agenda'. Based on close analysis of several moments and sequences, in particular the first scene of the first episode, the chapter shows how densely woven *Friends*' humour actually is and that its distinct comedic sensibility helps to facilitate its strategy of intimacy.

Chapter 3 explores the specificities of *Friends*' approach to performance. Casting and performance are undoubtedly of considerable importance to *Friends*, but previous scholarly work on sitcom has not paid much attention to the intricacies and challenges of a successful sitcom performance. Where it has done so, it has usually understood the multi-camera shooting style (with its wider framing and physical distance between camera and actor) in terms of a lack of interest in character psychology. Our argument is that *Friends*' success is closely informed by the fact that its core cast does not follow the performative, heightened style of acting frequently associated with multi-camera sitcom. Informed by Stanislavskian terminology (Stanislavski 2013 [1937]), we undertake close analysis of scenes involving Jennifer Aniston, David Schwimmer and Matt LeBlanc. We engage with the nuanced specificities of these distinctly holistic performances, which are grounded in realism and naturalism and support the series' overall strategy of intimacy.

We illuminate the particularities of multi-camera performance by considering the struggles experienced by some of the guest actors of the show. Here, we focus on Brad Pitt's guest appearance in the eighth season, examining how an award-winning actor associated with film acting, which is usually afforded more prestige, unsuccessfully grapples with the 'three-headed monster' that is multi-camera production. We pay attention to how *Friends* engages with matters concerning star image (Dyer 1998) when it comes to Pitt, but more so as concerns Bruce Willis's guest appearance in the sixth season, articulating the viewing pleasures on offer when the renowned Hollywood 'hard man' screeches 'Chicken Boy'. The chapter concludes by reflecting on how *Friends*' particular approach to the determinants of television acting (Pearson 2010) facilitates the successful performances by its core cast.

Chapter 4 explores *Friends*' strategy of intimacy in relation to issues of style. Taking as our point of departure existing debates concerning the 'zero-degree' aesthetics of multi-camera sitcom (Butler 2010), we propose that multi-camera may achieve an aesthetics of intimacy through the use of set design, camera and editing. In the case of Monica's apartment, one of the most iconic sets in television history, intimacy is constructed through an emphasis on rich texture and the particular placement of the couch, which furthermore enables a creative engagement with space for the performers. Our discussion not only pays attention to the use of space in *Friends* at individual moments within the programme, but also diachronically, uncovering how notions of intimacy are reinforced through carefully managed change in terms of the set design, as well as through an accumulation of meaning in its layered, thickened spaces for long-term viewers.

Our analysis of the use of cameras and editing demonstrates that multi-camera sitcom offers a mode of address and relationship to viewers that has thus far not received the recognition it deserves: this concerns a regime of looking in, which offers an intimate, immersive viewing experience. This is reflexively highlighted by a moment within *Friends* that ruptures the usual texture of multi-camera sitcom and reveals the fourth wall. Informed particularly by our interview with John Shaffner as well as comparative attention to the use of set design in other relevant sitcoms, we suggest that multi-camera sitcom is productively understood as facilitating the potential for a style that is different to 'cinematic' single-camera production—yet no less complex for that—requiring and rewarding detailed attention. Resonating with Jason Jacobs's (2000) argument that early television needs to be understood as more than photographed stage plays, the chapter offers a critical framework for engaging with televisual aesthetics that is 'not dependent on the supposed superiority of other forms' (Mills 2013, 61) and thus makes an important contribution to scholarship on sitcom and television more broadly.

Chapter 5 is interested in exploring the fact that, in the age of 'peak television' and a contemporary moment marked, as Wesley Morris notes, by such discursive tensions as the Trump administration and #MeToo, *Hamilton* on Broadway and 'white nationalists on the march even as confederate statues are being toppled' (2018), so much energy is being expended into critiquing a sitcom that began a quarter century ago. This is not the first backlash the series has received: a (by now largely forgotten) push-back also happened in response to the core cast's cultural overexposure and the Diet Coke advertising campaign in 1996. However, the backlash that *Friends* has been receiving in recent years is much more pronounced, and it is certainly not groundless: the programme's politics of representation are, to use that ubiquitous word, problematic on a number of levels. The chapter begins by reflectively exploring the backlash, identifying some interesting patterns within it and pertinent questions raised by it. Our close analysis then focuses on issues of race, and specifically the representation of Charlie Wheeler, played by Aisha Tyler.

With *Friends* so readily available on contemporary screens, Charlie Wheeler may appear in close proximity and yet also far removed from acclaimed black female characters in shows with much more diverse story worlds, such as Tracee Ellis Ross in *Black-ish* or Issa Rae in *Insecure*. However, as per the core of the chapter's argument, the representations within *Friends* (and any other programme) need to be engaged with by paying careful attention to both context and tone (Pye 2007). Through this emphasis, the chapter avoids a binary tendency Beretta E. Smith-Shomade has identified within some television criticism to frame 'Black women's representations either as regressive/denigrative or as potentially enabling real-life women to resist hegemonic positioning' (2002, 3). Instead, the chapter unpicks the complex ways in which Tyler's Charlie maps onto existing frameworks relevant to the representation of black women, and how her presence operates within the aesthetics of representation and the wider storytelling project of the show. Paying attention to intersection of race and class, our close analysis uncovers a considerable tonal ambiguity within a particular scene in episode 10.1, produced by Aisha Tyler's performance and Kevin S. Bright's work. The chapter draws to a close by reflecting on why it is that *Friends* has become such a key site for ardent debates about representation, linking this back to the programme's strategy of intimacy and suggesting that the latter works in complex ways in relation to the series' politics of representation, just as sitcom as a genre has a far from straightforward relationship to hegemonic discourses.

Chapter 6 looks beyond *Friends* to consider the show's various intertextual brethren, whose different degrees of failure help to illuminate the appeal and success *Friends* has been receiving around the globe. Our interview with Kevin S. Bright, who was involved in the ill-fated spin-off *Joey* as executive producer, informs our analysis of this short-lived programme, as well as our intervention into scholarly conceptualisations of what constitutes 'failure' and how this theoretical approach could, and should, trigger more precise scholarly research. We move on to an analysis of the short-lived US format adaptation of the British sitcom *Coupling*, which, in turn, was influenced by *Friends*. We employ this case study for a more general reflection on the challenges of transnational format adaptation, in which television formats have to be considered as more complex and layered products of popular entertainment than previous scholarship has quite managed to. This may subvert and indeed should challenge established conceptions of terms and dynamics such as 'creative borrowing' and 'cultural appropriation'.

We then explore the reception of *Friends* in such diverse cultural contexts as India, Egypt and Germany. Discussing previous studies based on Scott Robert Olson's (1999) useful narrative transparency strategy, we gain insights into the ways in which audiences with different socio-cultural backgrounds read the programme, and what issues may arise from audio-visual translations for non-anglophone viewers. As we are going to show with our analysis of the German dubbing of *Friends*, certain appropriations of the source text can lead to serious and problematic alterations and even change a programme's comedic sensibility, tonality and, eventually, also appeal. We conclude our conceptualisation of *Friends* as a global television format by exploring two of several 'unofficial' adaptations, namely the Iranian show *Eshgh Ta'til Nist* which has sought to recreate Monica and Rachel's apartment to a noticeable level of similarity, and the Chinese sitcom *iPartment*, which was accused of plagiarism and 'stealing' jokes from *Friends* and other American sitcoms. Finally, we argue that *Friends* successfully reconciles the ambiguous (if not sceptical) views of international audiences (as propagating American values and a capitalist agenda) with a universal appeal and cultural flexibility, which has helped it become possibly the most significant global sitcom in the history of television.

The book's conclusion begins to offer our final reflections on the show and its place in present and future television culture by attending to an intertextual reference to *Friends* within a television show that in many ways could not be more different from it, namely *The Handmaid's Tale* (Hulu, 2017–present). The contrast between the multi-camera sitcom and the dystopian thriller allows us to conclude our considerations of *Friends*' strategy of intimacy and moreover to think through the ways in which the programme complicates notions of the 'then and now' and discourses of continuation and transformation. Summing up the key contribution the book seeks to make to television scholarship, the conclusion finishes by reflecting on *Friends*' 25th anniversary in September 2019.

Bibliography

Andersen, Kurt. 2015. The Best Decade Ever? The 1990s, Obviously. *The New York Times*. https://www.nytimes.com/2015/02/08/opinion/sunday/the-best-decade-ever-the-1990s-obviously.html. Accessed 22 April 2019.

Ang, Ien. 1985. *Watching Dallas: Soap Opera and the Melodramatic Imagination*. London: Methuen.

Attallah, Paul. 2003. The Unworthy Discourse: Situation Comedy in Television. In *Critiquing the Sitcom: A Reader*, ed. Joanne Morreale, 91–115. Syracuse: Syracuse University Press.

Baxter-Wright, Dusty. 2017. 11 Actually Pretty Shocking Things Friends Couldn't Get Away with Today. *Cosmopolitan*. https://www.cosmopolitan.com/uk/entertainment/a38817/11-times-friends-sexist-homophobic/. Accessed 14 April 2019.

Bell, Stuart. 2016. 'Don't Stop': Re-thinking the Function of Endings in Narrative Television. Unpublished PhD thesis, University of Glasgow.

Berlant, Lauren. 1998. Intimacy: A Special Issue. *Critical Inquiry* 24 (2): 281–288.

Bruun, Hanne. 2016. The Qualitative Interview in Media Production Studies. In *Advancing Media Production Research. Shifting Sites, Methods, and Politics*, ed. Chris Paterson et al., 131–146. Basingstoke: Palgrave.

Burns, Ashley and Chloe Schildhause. 2015. The Story of Larry David, 'Seinfeld,' and 'The Fastest No in Show Business'. *Uproxx*. https://uproxx.com/tv/seinfeld-larry-david-nbc-festivus-christmas/. Accessed 22 April 2019.

Butler, Jeremy G. 2010. *Television Style*. New York and London: Routledge.

Caldwell, John T. 1995. *Televisuality: Style, Crisis, and Authority in American Television*. New Brunswick: Rutgers University Press.

Cardwell, Sarah. 2007. Is Quality Television Any Good? Generic Distinctions, Evaluations and the Troubling Matter of Critical Judgement. In *Quality TV: Contemporary American Television and Beyond*, ed. Janet McCabe and Kim Akass, 19–34. London: I.B. Tauris.

Chamberlain, Daniel, and Scott Ruston. 2007. 24 and Twenty-First Century Quality Television. In *Reading 24: TV Against the Clock*, ed. Steven Peacock, 13–24. London: I.B. Tauris.

Chidester, Phil. 2008. May the Circle Stay Unbroken: *Friends*, the Presence of Absence, and the Rhetorical Reinforcement of Whiteness. *Critical Studies in Mass Communication* 25 (2): 157–174. https://doi.org/10.1080/15295030802031772.

Cobb, Shelley. 2018. 'I'd Like Y'all to Get a Black Friend': The Politics of Race in Friends. *Television & New Media* 19 (8): 708–723. https://doi.org/10.1177/1527476418778420.

Creeber, Glen. 2013. *Small Screen Aesthetics: From TV to the Internet*. London: Palgrave Macmillan.

Crenshaw, Kimberlé. 1989. Demarginalizing the Intersection of Race and Sex: A Black Feminist Critique of Antidiscrimination Doctrine, Feminist Theory and Antiracist Politics. *University of Chicago Legal Forum 1989* (1): 139–167.

Dalton, Mary M., and Laura R. Linder (eds.). 2016. *The Sitcom Reader: America Re-viewed, Still Skewed*. Albany: State University of New York Press.

Dillion, Katherine. 2009. *Friends Watching Friends: American Television in Egypt*. Newcastle upon Tyne: Cambridge Scholars Publishing.

Dyer, Richard. 1998. *Stars*, 2nd ed. London: BFI.

Feuer, Jane. 1992. Genre Study and Television. In *Channels of Discourse, Reassembled: Television and Contemporary Criticism*, 2nd ed, ed. Robert C. Allen, 138–160. Chapel Hill: University of North Carolina Press.

Feuer, Jane, Paul Kerr, and Tise Vahimagi (eds.). 1984. *MTM: 'Quality Television'*. London: BFI.

Fife Donaldson, Lucy. 2016. Series Spaces: Revisiting and Re-evaluating Inspector Morse. *Journal of Popular Television* 4 (1): 3–28. https://doi.org/10.1386/jptv.4.1.3_1.

Gorton, Kristyn. 2006. A Sentimental Journey: Television, Meaning and Emotion. *Journal of British Cinema and Television* 3 (1): 72–81. https://doi.org/10.3366/JBCTV.2006.3.1.72.

Gray, Jonathan. 2010. *Show Sold Separately: Promos, Spoilers, and Other Media Paratexts*. New York, London: New York University Press.

Hamad, Hannah. 2018. The One with the Feminist Critique: Revisiting Millennial Postfeminism with Friends. *Television & New Media* 19 (8): 692–707. https://doi.org/10.1177/1527476418779624.

Heuman, Josh. 2016. What Happens in the Writers' Room Stays in the Writers' Room? Professional Authority. *Lyle v. Warner Bros. Television & New Media* 17 (3): 195–211. https://doi.org/10.1177/1527476415594887.

Hills, Matt. 2002. *Fan Cultures*. London: Routledge.

Hoskins, Colin, and Rolf Mirus. 1988. Reasons for the US Dominance of the International Trade in Television Programmes. *Media, Culture and Society* 10 (4): 499–515. https://doi.org/10.1177/016344388010004006.

Ihnat, Gwen. 2014. How *Friends* Changed the Sitcom Landscape. *AV/TV Club*. https://tv.avclub.com/how-friends-changed-the-sitcom-landscape-1798271378. Accessed 22 April 2019.

Jacobs, Jason. 2000. *The Intimate Screen: Early British Television Drama*. Oxford: Oxford University Press.

Jacobs, Jason. 2001. Issues of Judgement and Value in Television Studies. *International Journal of Cultural Studies* 4 (4): 427–447. https://doi.org/10.1177/136787790100400404.

Jacobs, Jason, and Steven Peacock. 2013. Introduction. In *Television Aesthetics and Style*, ed. Jason Jacobs and Steven Peacock, 1–20. New York and London: Bloomsbury.

Jaramillo, Deborah L. 2013. Rescuing Television from 'The Cinematic': The Perils of Dismissing Television Style. In *Television Aesthetics and Style*, ed. Jason Jacobs and Steven Peacock, 67–75. New York and London: Bloomsbury.

Kaplan, Ilana. 2018. Friends: 10 Times the Classic Sitcom Was Problematic. *The Independent*. https://www.independent.co.uk/arts-entertainment/films/friends-netflix-sitcom-problem-sexism-men-joey-phoebe-chandler-ross-rachel-a8168976.html. Accessed 14 April 2019.

Kauffman, Marta, and David Crane. *Insomnia Café* Pitch. 7 December 1993.

Kessler, Kelly. 2006. Politics of the Sitcom Formula: Friends, Mad About You and the Sapphic Second Banana. In *The New Queer Aesthetic on Television: Essays on Recent Programming*, ed. James R. Keller and Leslie Stratyner, 130–146. Jefferson: McFarland.

Kutulas, Judy. 2018. Anatomy of a Hit: Friends and Its Sitcom Legacies. *The Journal of Popular Culture* 51 (5): 1172–1189. https://doi.org/10.1111/jpcu.12715.

Learn English with TV Series. 2016. Learn English with TV Series: Friends. YouTube. https://www.youtube.com/watch?v=cslyPxzMLWg&fbclid=IwAR2H_A77LSJafnF5V2N0vovF30Mw9jaIZL-SBG0WsXa7I0QNqRUejQfhu54. Accessed 22 April 2019.

Lee, Edmund. 2018. Netflix Will Keep 'Friends' in a $100 Million Deal. *The New York Times*. 5 December, B5.

Lim, Louisa. 2013. *All Things Considered*. NPR. 23 January.

Marshall, Lisa Marie. 2007. 'I'll Be There for You' if You Are Just Like Me: An Analysis of Hegemonic Social Structures in 'Friends'. Unpublished PhD thesis, Graduate College of Bowling Green State University.

May, Tim. 2011. *Social Research: Issues, Methods and Process*, 4th ed. Maidenhead: Open University Press.

Miller, Kelsey. 2018a. *I'll Be There For You: The One About Friends*. London: HQ.

Miller, Kelsey. 2018b. The Ruling in This 'Friends' Lawsuit Set Back the #MeToo Movement By Years—Now The Woman at the Center of It Speaks Out. *Bustle*. https://www.bustle.com/p/the-ruling-in-this-friends-lawsuit-set-back-the-metoo-movement-by-years-now-the-woman-at-the-center-of-it-speaks-out-12636045. Accessed 14 April 2019.

Mills, Brett. 2005. *Television Sitcom*. London: BFI.

Mills, Brett. 2008. After the Interview. *Cinema Journal* 47 (2): 148–153. https://doi.org/10.1353/cj.2008.0009.

Mills, Brett. 2009. *The Sitcom*. Edinburgh: Edinburgh University Press.

Mills, Brett. 2012. Invisible Television: The Programmes No-One Talks About Even Though Lots of People Watch Them. *Critical Studies in Television* 5 (1): 1–16. https://doi.org/10.7227/CST.5.1.3.

Mills, Brett. 2013. What Does It Mean to Call Television 'Cinematic'? In *Television Aesthetics and Style*, ed. Jason Jacobs and Steven Peacock, 57–66. London: Bloomsbury.

Mittell, Jason. 2006. Narrative Complexity in Contemporary American Television. *The Velvet Light Trap* 58: 29–40. https://doi.org/10.1353/vlt.2006.0032.

Morreale, Joanne (ed.). 2003. *Critiquing the Sitcom: A Reader*. Syracuse: Syracuse University Press.

Morris, Wesley. 2018. Should Art Be a Battleground for Social Justice? The Morality Wars. *The New York Times*. https://www.nytimes.com/interactive/2018/10/03/magazine/morality-social-justice-art-entertainment.html. Accessed 22 April 2019.

Newcomb, Horace. 1974. *TV: The Most Popular Art*. Garden City: Anchor Books.

Newman, Michael Z., and Elana Levine. 2012. *Legitimating Television: Media Convergence and Cultural Status*. New York and London: Routledge.

Olson, Scott Robert. 1999. *Hollywood Planet: Global Media and the Competitive Advantage of Narrative Transparency*. Mahwah and London: Lawrence Erlbaum.

Pearson, Roberta. 2010. The Multiple Determinants of Television Acting. In *Genre and Performance: Film and Television*, ed. Christine Cornea, 166–183. Manchester: Manchester University Press.

Pye, Douglas. 2007. Movies and Tone. In *Close Up 02*, ed. John Gibbs and Douglas Pye, 1–80. London: Wallflower Press.

Ritchie, Donald A. 2003. *Doing Oral History: A Practical Guide*, 2nd ed. Oxford: Oxford University Press.

Rockler, Naomi R. 2006a. 'Be Your Own Windkeeper': Friends, Feminism, and Rhetorical Strategies of Depoliticization. *Women's Studies in Communication* 29 (6): 244–264.

Rockler, Naomi R. 2006b. Friends, Judaism, and the Holiday Armadillo: Mapping a Rhetoric of Postidentity Politics. *Communication Theory* 16 (4): 453–473. https://doi.org/10.1111/j.1468-2885.2006.00278.x.

Romano, Andrea. 2014. Superfan Perfectly Recreates 'Friends' for 'The Sims 4'. MashableUK. https://mashable.com/2014/09/08/friends-in-sims/?europe=true. Accessed 22 April 2019.

Sandell, Jillian. 1998. I'll Be There for You: Friends and the Fantasy of Alternative Families. *American Studies* 39 (2): 141–155.

San Martín, Nancy. 2003. 'Must See TV': Programming Identity on NBC Thursdays. In *Quality Popular Television: Cult TV, the Industry and Fans*, ed. Mark Jancovich and James Lyons, 32–47. London: BFI.

Savorelli, Antonio. 2010. *Beyond Sitcom: New Directions in American Television Comedy*. Jefferson, NC: McFarland.

sboss. 2013. Friends—No Laugh Track 2 (Ross Attacks Women). YouTube. https://www.youtube.com/watch?v=DgKgXehYnnw. Accessed 22 April 2019.

Slate Represent. 2017. #33: Unpacking Jordan Peele's 'Get Out'. *Slate*.

Smart, Billy. 2012. The Case of *Juliet Bravo*: You Have to Watch All of a Series to Truly Understand a Series. *CSTOnline*. https://cstonline.net/the-case-of-juliet-bravo-you-have-to-watch-all-of-a-series-to-truly-understand-a-series-by-billy-smart/. Accessed 22 April 2019.

Smith-Shomade, Beretta E. 2002. *Shaded Lives: African-American Women and Television*. New Brunswick and London: Rutgers University Press.

Spangler, Todd. 2018. 'Friends,' 'Grey's Anatomy' Were Most Binge-Watched TV Shows of 2018, Study Finds. *Variety*. https://variety.com/2018/digital/news/friends-greys-anatomy-most-binge-watched-2018-1203094184/. Accessed 22 April 2019.

Stanislavski, Constantin. 2013 [1937]. *An Actor Prepares*. London and New York: Bloomsbury.

Sutherland, Heather. 2010. 'It Ought to Be a Dream': Archives and Establishing the History of BBC Light Entertainment Production, 1975–87. *Critical Studies in Television* 5 (2): 154–170. https://doi.org/10.7227/CST.5.2.18.

Sweney, Mark. 2015. Friends Repeats to Stay on Comedy Central in UK after New Deal. *The Guardian*. https://www.theguardian.com/media/2015/aug/12/friends-repeats-comedy-central-uk. Accessed 22 April 2019.

Tagliamonte, Sali, and Chris Roberts. 2005. So Weird; So Cool; So Innovative: The Use of Intensifiers in the Television Series *Friends*. *American Speech* 80 (3): 280–300. https://doi.org/10.1215/00031283-80-3-280.

Thompson, Lauren Jade. 2018. 'It's Like a Guy Never Lived Here!': Reading the Gendered Domestic Spaces of Friends. *Television & New Media* 19 (8): 758–774. https://doi.org/10.1177/1527476418778414.

Todd, Anne Marie. 2011. Saying Goodbye to Friends: Fan Culture as Lived Experience. *The Journal of Popular Culture* 44 (4): 854–871. https://doi.org/10.1111/j.1540-5931.2011.00866.x.

Tucker, Ken. 1994. TV Show Review: Winning 'Friends'. *Entertainment Weekly*. https://ew.com/article/1994/10/21/tv-show-review-winning-friends/. Accessed 22 April 2019.

Waring, Olivia. 2016. There Was Something Really Weird Going on with Monica's Apartment in Friends—But Did You Spot It? *Metro*. http://metro.co.uk/2016/03/04/there-was-something-really-weird-going-on-with-monicas-apartment-in-friends-but-did-you-spot-it-5731671/. Accessed 22 April 2019.

Wheatley, Helen. 2016. *Spectacular Television: Exploring Televisual Pleasure*. London and New York: I.B. Tauris.

Williams, Linda Ruth. 2008. Speaking of Soft Core. *Cinema Journal* 47 (2): 129–135. https://doi.org/10.1353/cj.2008.0013.

Williams, Raymond. 1977. *Marxism and Literature*. Oxford: Oxford University Press.

Television

All-American Girl (1994–1995), USA: ABC.
All in the Family (1971–1979), USA: CBS.
Arrested Development (2003–2006, 2013–present), USA: Fox, Netflix.
Black-ish (2014–present), USA: ABC.
Buffy the Vampire Slayer (1997–2003), USA: The WB/UPN.
Cheers (1982–1993), USA: NBC.
Chicago Hope (1994–2000), USA: CBS.
Community (2009–2014, 2015), USA: NBC, Yahoo! Screen.

Coupling (2000–2004), UK: BBC2.
Coupling (2003), USA: NBC.
Curb Your Enthusiasm (2000–present), USA: HBO.
Dallas (1978–1991), USA: CBS.
Dharma & Greg (1997–2002), USA: ABC.
ER (1994–2009), USA: NBC.
Eshgh Ta'til Nist (2015, عشق تعطیل نیست), Iran: شبکه نمایش خانگی / Home Broadcasting Media.
Fortune Hunter (1994), USA: Fox.
Frasier (1993–2004), USA: NBC.
Friends (1994–2004), USA: NBC.
Happy Endings (2013–2013), USA: ABC.
How I Met Your Mother (2005–2014), USA: CBS.
Insecure (2016–present), USA: HBO.
iPartment (爱情公寓, 2009–2014), USA: Jiangxi TV, Dragon TV.
Joey (2004–2006), USA: NBC.
Law & Order (1990–2010), USA: NBC.
Maude (1972–1978), USA: CBS.
Me and the Boys (1994–1995), USA: ABC.
Mike & Molly (2010–2016), USA: CBS.
My So-Called Life (1994–1995), USA: ABC.
New Girl (2011–2018), USA: Fox.
Party of Five (1994–2000), USA: Fox.
Peep Show (2003–2015), UK: Channel 4.
Rhoda (1974–1978), USA: CBS.
30 Rock (2006–2013), USA: NBC.
Saturday Night Live (1975–present), USA: NBC.
Scrubs (2001–2008, 2009–2010), USA: NBC, ABC.
Seinfeld (1989–1998), USA: NBC.
Sex and the City (1998–2004), USA: HBO.
Something Wilder (1994–1995), USA: NBC.
The Big Bang Theory (2007–2019), USA: CBS.
The Boys Are Back (1994–1995), USA: CBS.
The Handmaid's Tale (2017–present), USA: Hulu.
The Mary Tyler Moore Show (1970–1977), USA: CBS.
The Office—An American Workplace (2005–2013), USA: NBC.
The Sopranos (1999–2007), USA: HBO.
Touched by an Angel (1994–2003), USA: CBS.

Unbreakable Kimmy Schmidt (2015–2019), USA: Netflix.
Weeds (2005–2012), USA: Showtime.
Wild Oats (1994), USA: Fox.
Will & Grace (1998–2006, 2018–present), USA: NBC.

Film

Ephron, N. (1998). *You've Got Mail*. USA: Warner Bros.
Meyers, N. (2000). *What Women Want*. USA: Paramount Pictures.
Spielberg, S. (2004). *The Terminal*. USA: DreamWorks Pictures.

2

The One with All the Laughing and the Hugging: Specificity of Humour and Comedic Types

When executive producer and director Kevin S. Bright reflected on shooting the wedding scene between Ross and Emily in episode 4.24 ('The One with Ross's Wedding, Part 2') in our interview, he recalled a particular moment on the London set:

> During the rehearsal, Kenneth Branagh […] visited the set and is standing behind me. And I have six monitors in front of me as I'm running six cameras in this scene. It's the scene in the church. And he taps me on the shoulder and says: 'Can I just ask you one question? How do you know where to look?'

This anecdote by one of the key members of the creative personnel involved in the production of *Friends* illustrates two points. First, the production of a multi-camera sitcom is (at least) as challenging and attention-demanding as any of its single-camera brethren. And, second, facilitating humour within the production context of situation comedy requires an extensive overview of the actual 'situation' and a meticulous attention to detail.

Unfortunately, a similar attention to the details of *Friends*' humour and comedic approach has, for the most part, been absent in scholarly research, both on sitcom genre in general and the show in particular. Brett Mills (2005, 2009) addresses some of the specificities of *Friends'* humour, and Antonio Savorelli (2010) pays some attention to the programme's ability to extract humour from darker themes, such as character deaths and divorces. More recently, studies focusing on distinct epistemological and methodological approaches from the realms of linguistics have emerged, such as a master's dissertation analysing Chandler's and Phoebe's character humour strategies based on the violation of Grice's conversational maxims (Smilauerová 2012). It strikes us as odd, that a situation comedy as influential and continually lauded for its humour as *Friends* has not been the subject of a more holistic analysis of its approach to humour and comedic style. We believe that understanding the series' specific intertextual framework of humour, as well as its distinct comedic sensibility and tonality, is vital for *Friends'* strategy of intimacy that we have identified in the introduction to this book. This is why, in this opening chapter, we will take a more structural approach to the comedic style(s) and humour(s) of *Friends* and pay attention to various aspects of the actual mechanics of the comedy at work. We will do so by exploring the multiple ways in which the written dialogue corresponds to and is enhanced by the approaches to comedic performance by its main cast, as well as analysing how distinctive diegetic and non-diegetic elements shape how the humour of the series may 'feel' to an audience.

Furthermore, we will render and categorise the series' core characters as distinct 'comedic types', each of them characterised by a specific sense of humour addressed by the programme's narrative, while simultaneously facilitating an ensemble-based comedic style. This interaction, we will argue, facilitates an emotional investment into the characters, which enables an intimate approach to the series' narrative and visual aesthetics that exceeds traditional expectations towards multi-camera sitcoms. As such, it might explain why Chandler, Joey, Monica, Phoebe, Rachel and Ross have come to mean so much to so many viewers and, more significantly, why *Friends* still ranks among the most relevant reference shows in the age of TVIV (Jenner 2016).

Before undertaking close analysis of selected scenes and comedic moments across the ten seasons of the series, we have to introduce a few key terms relevant for our analysis and seek out to contextualise *Friends* within previous scholarship on sitcom in particular and, more generally, theorisations within the interdisciplinary field of humour research.

The One where They're Feeling Humour: Comedic Sensibility and Tonality

'Perhaps I know best why it is man alone who laughs; he alone suffers so deeply that he had to invent laughter' (Lippitt 1992, 41)—so claimed Nietzsche in his usual cheerfulness, expressing the notion that humankind alone seems to be able to produce and perceive humour. From Aristotle's musings in the *Poetics* (2016) to Chandler Bing claiming that 'You have to stop the Q-tip when there is resistance' ('The One with Ross's New Girlfriend', 2.1), the possibilities to approaching humour seem endless. Theories of humour have focused on an intricate analysis of what humour is and how it works, as well as what 'having a sense of humour' implies and what kinds of 'comedic persona' different individuals might subscribe to. Humour can be located at the centre of social interaction and its targets represent what is of vital concern to a society and the individual, thus making it a fundamental subject of interest.

To date, we can identify three main theories of humour and laughter, namely 'superiority theory', 'relief theory' and 'incongruity theory' which have been established, developed and refined across a variety of academic disciplines (Kuipers 2008). To summarise 'the classics' briefly: the 'superiority theory', ascribed to Plato and Aristotle and developed by Thomas Hobbes (see Morreal 1983) claims that humour and laughter are induced by social power relations, mostly through laughing at individuals who are either considered superior or inferior in terms of social ranking and mandate. The 'incongruity theory' originated in the works of Immanuel Kant—who wrote that laughter 'is an affection arising from the sudden transformation of a strained expectation into nothing' (2012 [1790], first part, sec. 54)—and refined by Arthur Schopenhauer (2014 [1818]) and others, states that all humour is based on the perception or recognition of incongruity: something which does not fit our ordinary accepted behaviour, customs and patterns. Finally, the 'relief theory' (postulated, e.g., by Herbert Spencer (1860), and further developed by Sigmund Freud (1990 [1905])) claims that humour and laughter are socially acceptable forms of relieving the tension caused by suppressed fears and feelings.

Indeed, Freud was among the first to combine several aspects of the three classical approaches and stress the importance of social relationships as well as taboos for the dynamics of humour and laughter. However, a broad spectrum of theorisations of the phenomenon humour is available across an array of academic disciplines. From the 'obvious' candidates of sociology and philosophy, via psychology, anthropology, literary and media studies to education, medical science and even computer science, many fields have tried to come up with an explanation as to why we find certain things funny and what it means to do so (see Raskin 2008). For the purpose of this analysis, we conceptualise humour as first and foremost a phenomenon of social interaction: 'Humor is a form of communication, a question of taste, a marking of social boundaries' (Kuipers 2006, 10). Though true, focusing on the aspect of demarcation alone is to consider only one side of the dichotomy of social interaction through humour, for, as other sociologists have also argued, 'to laugh, or to occasion laughter through humor and wit, is to invite those present to come close' (Coser 1959, 172). We are taking our cue from observations of such notions of 'closeness' as well as humour being 'not solely amusement; it can bring people closer to each other' (Kuipers 2006, 4); it is here we see humour at play in facilitating intimacy towards a group of fictional sitcom characters such as the core group in *Friends*.

However, when applying humour theory in this way, we have to differentiate between the analysis of jokes and other humour-related phenomena and contexts, such as comedy in general and situation comedy in particular. After all, our discussion is not preoccupied with a micro-level analysis of how jokes are semantically and linguistically constructed, but explores the more complex relationships of how humour, through its mediatisation into television comedy, works within (and also outside) the boundaries of the generic conventions of sitcom. *Friends*, as a sitcom, responds to a number of elements which are inherent to the genre (more on that below), and which scholars such as Brett Mills (2005, 2009) discuss, based on the categories proposed by Nick Lacey (2000). These categories include setting, character, narrative, iconography, style and stars (ibid., 137). What they do not address, however, is the distinct way a comedic programme interacts on a para-psychological level with its viewers; in other words, how it manages to engage with them, how exactly it makes them laugh and how it makes them feel. Furthermore, it seems to us, that besides prevalent notions of taste, audiences particularly connect with the specific ways and tonalities through which sitcoms present their characters and narratives and negotiate their socio-cultural contexts. Gry Rustad and Kai Hanno Schwind (2017) propose the useful categories of 'cold' and 'warm' with regards to a sitcom's comedic 'temperature'. Discussing the tonality of one of *Friends*' 1990s contemporaries, they argue that '*Seinfeld* is […] drenched in postmodern ironic apathy where the humour is first and foremost observationally distanced, highly judgemental and very often serves as an end in itself' (ibid., 140).

Applying this concept to *Friends*, we suggest that the series can be regarded as a 'warm sitcom', adopting an approach of immersive tonal intimacy facilitated to a significant degree through its humour. Exactly how this immersion through tonality is achieved will be the subject of the close analysis in this chapter; however, in order to illuminate this dynamic and to conceptualise this process of how *Friends* as a sitcom handles its distinct approach to humour, it is useful to draw on the notion of comedic sensibility. This points to the presence of what may be simultaneously within and outside the text, and hints at a paratextual process which might facilitate (or prevent) intimacy. In other words, a comedic sensibility is what an audience quickly recognises and responds to in any television programme with a 'comedic impetus' (Mills 2005). It is at play when we perceive the humour of a sitcom as, for instance, 'silly', 'kind' or 'cynical'; and it describes the process of how a humorous programme establishes and frames its intrinsic sense of humour and comedic trajectory. As such, different comedic sensibilities are informed by the historicity and generic development of situation comedy itself, which we are going to address in the following section.

The One about Sitcom and Humour

The work of French philosopher Henri Bergson on humour seems particularly suitable as an epistemological historical point of departure for an analysis of a sitcom such as *Friends*. In his seminal study, *Laughter: An Essay on the Meaning of the Comic*, he considers the comic element in 'situations' and 'words': 'Assuming that the stage is both a magnified and simplified view of life, we shall find that comedy is capable of furnishing us with more information than real life on this particular part of the subject. [...] Now, comedy is a game, a game that imitates life' (Bergson 2008[1911], 37). In other words, just as the stage is life in a nutshell, humour and comedy offer a useful framework to comprehend life, which brings us to the conceptualisation of sitcom. For, it is the 'situation' in sitcom that represents a reduced (and simplified) canvas of real life, providing a stage for the characters and actions to take place on. Indeed, the structural core of sitcom seems to consist of the Bergsonian terms 'situations' and 'words', and the theatrical staging of a multi-camera sitcom, often with an actual audience present and audible, underlines the suitability of Bergson's approach.

Adding yet another layer of meaning to the epistemological relationship of 'humour' and 'the situation', Simon Critchley quotes an excerpt from Trevor Griffiths's 1975 play *Comedians*:

> A real comedian – that's a daring man. He *dares* to see what his listeners shy away from, fear to express. And what he sees is a sort of truth about people, about their situation, about what hurts or terrifies them, about what's hard, above all, about what they *want*. A joke releases the tension, says the unsayable, any joke pretty well. But a true joke, a comedian's joke, has to do more than release tension, it has to *liberate* the will and the desire, it has to *change the situation*. (Griffiths in Critchley 2002, 9–10, emphases in original)

Exploring this discursive relationship of the comic and the situation, in a broader, perhaps more philosophical sense, then, posits our analysis and discussion of *Friends* as situation comedy. Here, 'words' and 'situations', in the Bergsonian sense, have to be negotiated and reconciled with the critical contexts and industrial frameworks in which *Friends* is located.

However, before we proceed to a close analysis of the humour employed in the series, it is vital to state that the observation of everyday humorous social interaction is different to humour utilised for and within the media. As Giselinde Kuipers claims:

> People increasingly enjoy humor not in face-to-face interaction but through a variety of media: print, television, the internet. This 'mediatisation' of humor has the potential to affect the interpretation of humor, and has resulted in the emergence of new, mediated, humorous forms[.] (2008, 387)

In other words, even though humour infiltrates every area of social life and interaction, 'humour is not synonymous with comedy' (Pickering and Lockyer 2009, 6), an important distinction to make as we are trying to explore the difference between why *Friends* makes viewers laugh (as a sitcom) and how the individual characters employ humour (as part of the narrative).

Indeed, it seems to us that industry and audience expectations influence the mechanisms of comedy quite significantly and, at first sight, seem to be dichotomous to the more intimate and psychological theorisations of how humour works between people (Freud 1990 [1905]; Morreal 1983; Raskin 2008). Furthermore, as we are continually reminded, comedy is also a business, indeed an industry, which—certainly in the context of a network show such as *Friends*—has to appeal to as wide an audience as possible and has to perceive of the 'audience' first and foremost as 'customers'. Hence, in their attempts to define a global mechanism of humour and comedy, Peter McGraw and Joel Warner rightly ask:

> So, then, what's the secret to making people laugh – especially when your audience numbers in the hundreds of thousands? How does someone come up with material that's novel enough, inoffensive enough, and hilarious enough to tickle funny bones the world over? (2014, 43)

Thus, the humour utilised in sitcom—and in many other forms of television comedy—is influenced by two aspects. First, there are the mechanisms of the processes of mediating humour into actual comedy. 'Humour made for television' has to be conceived, written, rewritten, rehearsed, filmed, edited, distributed and marketed, with each step depending on very distinct practices and rules. Second, televisual humour is frequently commercial, and as such depends on the political and economic framework of the entertainment industry from which it stems. This is important to keep in mind when we analyse a distinct type, as well as certain aspects of sitcom humour, and attempt socio-cultural analyses of it.

However, by looking at the historical and cultural development of sitcom we can identify general categories of humour (omni)present in the various programmes across the decades. In his exploration of American sitcoms Paul Wells suggests:

> Television comedy largely divided into two significant strands which absorbed the dominant radio models. First, the Vaudevillian strand, which recovered the visual and physical comedy (so prevalent on the variety stage, but unviable on radio), and combined it with wisecrack humour. […] Second, the Situation Comedy strand, which established the character-led, family centred mode of behavioural humour. This was not the comedy of 'gags', but the comedy determined by a recognition of, and the identification with, human traits and foibles. (1998, 187)

If we accept the concept of behavioural humour as a fundamental characteristic of sitcom, we can theorise its humour as a volatile and ever-changing notion reflecting the debates revolving around a variety of society's most controversial topics, including (and especially) sex, gender and race.

For instance, the clowning of physical comedian Lucille Ball, who became the star of what is argued to be the first sitcom on American television, *I Love Lucy* (1951–1957), worked on two levels. On the one hand, it presented an enjoyable variety-show-style type of comedy, which set out to entertain its audience and keep it receptive to the commercials which accompany programmes broadcast in commercial television landscapes. On the other hand, it introduced a more subversive strand of humour, which rendered Ball as a woman striving for a bigger career in showbiz and, more importantly, showed her behaving in a way which was not acceptable for a proper housewife in 1950s America: as an 'unruly woman' (Rowe Karlyn 1995). As such, Ball's physical comedy is 'essentially a symbolic mode of empowerment in which she controls and reconstructs her body in terms which give her complete physical freedoms and/or parody patriarchal codes' (Wells 1998, 189).

We can trace this ambiguity pertaining to the deployment of humour within the genre through the decades, for instance with series like *M*A*S*H* (1972–1983), which, though set during the Korean War, offered a subtle and subversive commentary on the social unease associated with the Vietnam War dominating the political and cultural discourse at the time of the programme's first broadcast. And despite the often-lamented conservatism endorsed by the 'harmless comedy' in one of sitcom's main topoi, the family home, in series like *Family Ties* (1982–1989) and *The Cosby Show* (1984–1992), alternative concepts of family were offered, endorsed and discussed in sitcoms such as *The Mary Tyler Moore Show* (1970–1977), *The Simpsons* (1989–present) or *Roseanne* (1988–1997). For example, Alessandra Senzani explores the latter's critique of gender and class in the United States:

> In the case of *Roseanne*, the domestication of the unruly woman was not carried out through humor, but rather at the level of the narrative structure and of the metatexts, where Barr's political laughter was, and still is, systematically turned into the hysterical laughter of a naughty wanna-be diva. (2010, 246)

In contrast, one could argue that despite all these (re)presentations of subversiveness, sitcom has played a vital part in maintaining the dominant social order by precisely confirming stereotypes of sex, race and gender and rendering all deviations from the established norm as funny, as in 'not to be taken seriously'. It's fine if women act like clowns (*I Love Lucy*) or challenge the values of a patriarchal middle-class (*Roseanne*), as long as they do so in the course of a half-hour sitcom. When the programme is over, the dominant order is re-established. (We will discuss issues relating to representation in more depth in Chapter 5.)

However, there is no denying that sitcom, both in America and elsewhere, has reflected socio-cultural changes. Moreover, by introducing ideas and behaviours formerly perceived as threats to the dominant norm in a generally accepted comedic discourse, sitcom has played a vital part in offering alternative and subversive notions of sexual orientation and questions of gender and race. A prime example in *Friends* would be the representation of Ross's former wife Carol and her partner Susan who collectively agree to raise Ross's and Carol's son Ben. The young boy being co-parented by a (mostly) single heterosexual father and a lesbian couple is presented as simply one of the many available life designs, both in the series and in the reality of its imagined audience. Their social constellation is not made fun of but is used as a source for comedy, just as any other love and relationship issue in the programme's narrative. Here, the recent backlash against *Friends*—which we have mapped in the introduction to this book and explore further in Chapter 5—clearly misinterprets the series' comedic sensibility and confuses the thematic subjects of the jokes (a lesbian couple) with the comedy's target; namely, the programme does not make fun of a lesbian couple for being a lesbian couple but creates comedy from how other characters react towards them and how they respond (often rather dryly) to these reactions.

As Kuipers has argued, humour plays a role in the construction of social relationships:

> not only by providing social solidarity in the functionalist sense, but by the sense of ingroup humor, repeat jokes, and specific humorous styles and tastes that literally get to define a group, and be used to demarcate its identity. However, this creation of a group culture also provides a strong outside boundary: humor includes and excludes at the same time. (2008, 374–375)

Before we turn our attention to the group quality and ensemble dynamic of the show's humour and comedy, we are going to introduce the main characters as 'comedic types', which serve not only specific purposes in terms of their characterisations, but also as fundamental storytelling elements of the show's narrative.

The One where They Look from the Pitch to the Pilot: A Comedic Typology

In his discussion of recent American sitcoms, such as *Scrubs* and *The Office—An American Workplace*, Antonio Savorelli struggles with defining how sitcom, as a genre, handles the thematic hybridity of combining comedic and dramatic storylines. He claims that 'during its ten years on the air, *Friends* featured several deaths (grandparents, neighbours, even a psychic), and all of them, no matter how painful, were always sources of immediate euphoric release – for both the characters and the audience in the laugh track' (2010, 29). According to him, classic sitcoms, such as *Friends*, have been avoiding 'dysphoria', and he concludes that newer sitcoms more actively present and engage with dramatic storylines and character developments, thus no longer fitting the (classic) definition of sitcom. In light of our own theorisations of the genre, it strikes us as odd to limit the thematic scope of a situation comedy by rendering 'comedy' and 'drama' as irreconcilable approaches to a programme's narrative and character design. After all, a situation comedy is about people and their major and minor everyday struggles, or in the Bergsonian sense 'situations' and 'words' in the 'theatre of life' (2008 [1911]). The comedic sensibility in *Friends*, embodied by its core group, seems particularly well suited to addressing darker themes and personal struggles. This is because of, as we are going to show, a distinct capability to facilitate intimacy, both among its fictional characters and between those characters and the audience (in the live studio setting and at home).

The way the programme handles this challenge is perhaps best described by the series' co-creator Marta Kauffman, who commented in our interview that, in *Friends*, comedy and drama are intertwined: 'You can't have one without the other', continuing that, for all her work in television, 'the jokes work so much better when it's real.' We want to suggest that, in addition to well-crafted joke writing, this 'realness'—detectible in the form of both a thematic and performance 'authenticity'—forms the basis of the series' comedic sensibility. This has to be viewed in contrast to more farcical, slapstick-oriented or wise-cracking (Wells 1998) types of humour prevalent in many situation comedies from the 1950s onwards. As a consequence, *Friends'* main characters can be categorised into both instantly recognisable 'qualities of humorous behaviour' as well as distinct comedic types (which relate to broader schemes and themes of the mediatisation of humour as outlined earlier).

Given the collaborative nature of any television show, in particular through the creative input of the writers, directors and actors, it strikes us to what degree the creators of *Friends*, David Crane and Marta Kauffman, have managed to maintain their comedic vision as postulated in the initial pitch for the programme. This pitch, written in 1993 and titled *Insomnia Café*, offers a short description of the overall approach of the show: 'After our recent foray into the world of family comedy, we're very excited about getting back to something more sophisticated. Something more grown up' (Kauffman and Crane 1993). It also provides short descriptions of the six main characters. We will follow the original structure of presentation of this pitch in our analysis of the main characters as comedic types and illuminate their initial 'comedic qualities' as envisioned by their creators.

Furthermore, building on the reflection by Kevin S. Bright that 'the most important episode is always the pilot', we find it particularly noteworthy that the very first scene of the pilot episode of *Friends* ('The One where Monica Gets a Roommate')—directed by one of our interviewees, James Burrows—not only sets up the premise of the entire series, but also works to a striking (albeit incomplete) extent as a template for the core group's comedic characterisations. The scene, set in one of the show's central locations, the coffeehouse Central Perk, runs for just over five minutes and introduces the six main characters. Monica, Chandler, Joey and Phoebe are sitting around the couch, discussing Monica's love life. After a while, Ross joins them, depressed about his recent split with Carol who left him for another woman. Finally, Rachel enters the coffeehouse, wearing a bridal gown after having escaped from her own wedding, and is introduced to the others. In what follows, we will offer a categorisation of the main characters' comedic types and personas by referring to specific elements of this first sequence, as well as other relevant moments from the programme.

The One with Rachel Green: 'So here she is, trained for nothing' (Kauffman and Crane 1993)

The comedic framework that encompasses the character of Rachel Green consists of a distinct meta-commentary on—and deconstruction of—a certain type of middle-class femininity. Rachel is introduced as the 'spoiled brat', the 'baby-gets-what-baby-wants' type of girl, who in the course of the programme's broader story arc develops into an emotionally and professionally successful woman and mother. Much of the humour in relation to her character is initially distilled from the fact that she is too spoiled and inexperienced to maintain herself in a grown-up world. In 'The One with the East German Laundry Detergent' (1.5), Ross discovers that she has never done her own laundry when she comments, 'I'm being like a total laundry spaz. I mean, am I supposed to use like one machine for shirts and another machine for pants?' Though not eliciting instant likeability, Rachel's humorous characterisation as 'inexperienced' enables the assumed younger audience to identify with her and is one example of the series' humour not becoming dated because of its use of widely recognisable themes, which might explain the continuous success of *Friends*' comedic agenda. Comedic moments in the same vein include her comment 'I'm gonna go get one of those job things' (1.1) and the caretaker Mr Treeger making her cry after lecturing her about not putting pizza cartons in the trash chute ('The One with the Ballroom Dancing', 4.4).

Utilising an emotionally darker context, her parents' imminent divorce in season two is also used for comic effect. In 'The One with the Two Parties' (2.21) Rachel's parents cannot be in the same room together, which is why her birthday party has to take place in both Monica's and Joey and Chandler's apartments, with Rachel alternating between the two celebrations. Although using a classical farcical set-up, including hiding from other characters, lots of running back and forth and slamming doors, the premise of the comedic situation is, nevertheless, grounded in Rachel's emotional dilemma of being stuck between her parents, trying to please them both. As a consequence, she ends up being stranded in the hallway, having an honest, emotional talk with Chandler about divorced parents with only a few, gentle comedic moments and jokes to break the scene's sad undertones. Here, the narrative establishes an intimacy, both between the characters of Rachel and Chandler, as well as between Rachel and the series' audience, framing the farcical comedic tone and pace of the party scenes with emotional heft and dramatic character development. (The 'hallway meetings' between Rachel and Chandler develop into something of an authorial trope in the course of the series, for example in 'The One with The Fake Party' [4.16], after Rachel's attempt to seduce Joshua [Tate Donovan] with her old cheerleader uniform fails miserably.)

Rachel's comedic persona is often 'involuntary', in the sense that she does not use humour deliberately to make other characters laugh or express a humorous mind set in the way that, for instance, Chandler does so frequently. This approach is established in the show's first scene when she enters Central Perk with wet hair wearing a wedding dress. She has just escaped her own wedding with Barry, the orthodontist, and run to the city to find shelter with her old friend, Monica. Her first appearance is a performative, well-timed entrance familiar from especially farcical sitcoms and hints at both *Friends*' more 'outrageously' comedic moments as well as its specific interconnection of humour and comedic performances. It is followed by a slightly hysterical and rambling introduction:

> *Rachel:* (turning around, relieved) Oh god, Monica! Hi, thank God! (hugging Monica) I went to your building and you weren't there and then this guy with the big hammer said you might be here, and you are … you are! (grabbing both of Monica's hands and shaking them)

In this first scene, Jennifer Aniston is given comparatively more lines and, thus, more opportunities and options to support, enhance and inflect the written dialogue with body language, non-verbal utterances and variations in her voice. Using syncopated cadence and pitch, Aniston links Rachel to the tradition of comedic female performances, in particular those in Hollywood screwball comedies, such as *Bringing Up Baby* or the onscreen comedic persona of Doris Day in films such as *Lover Come Back*.

Following the introduction to the rest of the group, the script and Aniston's performance establish both the comedic sensibility of Rachel as a character, as well as her relationship to Ross. Rachel, self-centred and preoccupied with her personal drama, does not notice how Ross helps her preparing the coffee (which further hints at the fact that Rachel will indeed become a terrible waitress working at Central Perk). Furthermore, the performance is interspersed with small moments of improvisation. For instance, after the waitress hands her the coffee and Rachel asks, 'Sweet and low?', Aniston's timing gets slightly thrown off because of the delayed non-diegetic laughter, which causes her to repeat the words 'I realised' twice. Her comedic timing is then used to full effect in the delivery of the following lines:

> … and that's when it hit me … (looking at Ross) … how much Barry looks like Mr Potato Head (non-diegetic laughter) … you know, I mean, I always knew he looked familiar, but … (non-diegetic laughter)

Here, the writers (David Crane and Marta Kauffman) quote themselves by using lines directly from the initial pitch:

> So she [Rachel] got really freaked out and got high with Mindy, her maid of honour, and while she was getting high she realized that Barry looks an awful lot like Mr. Potato Head. She always knew he looked familiar. So she had to get out of there. (Kauffman and Crane 1993)

This illustrates to what extent the initial conceptualisation of Rachel's comedic character informed the script writing and, consequently, Jennifer Aniston's performance of Rachel: a coherent process from pitch to aired episode.

Rachel's personal development and growing up are used to comic effect in two of the programme's narrative approaches: her relationship with Ross and her interactions with her two sisters Amy (Christina Applegate) and Jill (Reese Witherspoon). In the latter, Rachel is eventually presented as the reasonable and sensible older sister, who has to deal with her younger siblings' irresponsible behaviour. In 'The One with Rachel's Sister' (6.13), Rachel tries to help spoiled Jill 'quit shopping' and find a job, having to deal with her jealousy when Jill asks out Ross. Christina Applegate's Amy is even more anarchic and constantly undermines Rachel's authority with her self-centred ignorance. In 'The One where Rachel's Sister Babysits' (10.5), Amy enthusiastically talks about her new soon-to-be husband, 'Do you remember my old boyfriend Mark? It's his dad!' By the final season of *Friends*, Rachel's comedic persona is so far developed that the jokes related to immaturity are no longer on her, but help to map out how much her character has developed. What this illuminates is how sitcom, a genre often criticised for relying on its repetitive and conservative approach, can indeed accommodate (if not invite) character growth and narrative development without losing its comic appeal. As the characters are growing and developing, so does the show's humour and comedic sensibility.

The One with Monica Geller: 'For all her toughness, she has a real maternal side' (Kauffman and Crane 1993)

In many ways, Monica Geller is the emotional centre of the core group. Her apartment is the series' emotional focal point and, as we will suggest, the main topos for the strategy of intimacy utilised in the aesthetic framework of *Friends* (see Chapter 4). The first line of dialogue of the entire programme is spoken by Monica, 'There is nothing to tell', with the other characters physically and figuratively located around her (see Fig. 2.1), Monica being the one character that connects them all. In the beginning, her comedic persona can be described as a classical 'straight man' in relation to the other comedic characters. In the first part of the sequence, Monica first and foremost provides the set-ups to the actual jokes: 'There's nothing to tell, it's just some guy I work with' is answered by Joey's quip, 'Come on! You're going out with the guy, there's gotta

Fig. 2.1 First episode, first scene: Joey (Matt LeBlanc), Monica (Courteney Cox), Phoebe (Lisa Kudrow) and Chandler (Matthew Perry) in 'The One where Monica Gets a Roommate' (1.1)

be something wrong with him' and provides comedic cues for Chandler and Phoebe. When she interrupts the comical riffing by the others, 'Ok, everybody, relax! This is not even a date. It's just two people going out to dinner and… not having sex', this is utilised as another set up for one of the biggest punchlines in the sequence, namely Chandler's: 'Sounds like a date to me'. In the following scene about Chandler's weird dream, Monica remains completely passive and, after Ross's entrance, is for the most part established as his sister and 'care figure', devoid of any palpable sense of humour: 'Are you ok, sweetie?' and 'Let me get you some coffee!' are her only lines in the middle segment.

The next actual jokes Monica is allowed by the script occur after Rachel has entered and sat on the couch: 'So you wanna tell us now, or are we waiting for four wet bridesmaids?' We suggest that the humorous discourse at work here could be described as a variation of the concept of 'dad humour', a socio-cultural phenomenon which more recently has found its way into zeitgeist commentary and cultural journalism (Kelly 2016; Fetters 2018). This describes a type of joke often characterised by (bad) puns and the predictability of their punchlines, interspersed with a child-like sensibility and goofiness. At the same time, it is a humorous discourse utilised to de-escalate tension in social interactions and employed to signify a non-threatening masculinity; the father figure might be physically strong but is harmless and kind. As such, Monica's 'mom humour' is supposed to address her urge to control the situation and dominate her peers, but still consists of slightly critical remarks commenting on other people's trespassing or incorrect behaviour. Through the character of Monica and her use of humour, the show deconstructs another aspect of femininity, namely that of the 'motherly type'. This is anticipated in the initial pitch by characterising her as follows:

> She tends to take care of people, like taking Rachel in. We talked about an episode where she adopts a young pregnant woman, and the whole group goes through the miracle of birth. [...] And what's surprising is that of all of them, it's Monica who's the most affected. Suddenly she feels like she wants a baby, which gets her really bummed out. (Kauffman and Crane 1993)

In doing so, she takes her cue from a tradition of sitcom mother figures such as Elyse Keaton in *Family Ties*, Clair Huxtable in *The Cosby Show* or Marge Simpson in *The Simpsons*. This is a very different gendered comedic discourse to that of the 'unruly woman' (Rowe Karlyn 1995), whereby humour is found in women exceeding established norms, for instance in the physical clowning of Lucille Ball in *I Love Lucy*. It is successfully developed during the course of the series, by directly addressing and satirising Monica's caring and motherly qualities. For example, in 'The One with Rachel's Crush' (4.13) when, after the apartment switch with Joey and Chandler, she realises that the group prefers to hang out in the bigger apartment, she cleans the new apartment non-stop for two days, desperately screaming 'I'm always the hostess'. However, at the same time, many comedic moments throughout the show address Monica's pronounced obsessiveness and competitiveness; she is definitely not motherly and kind when she is playing for the

Geller Cup in 'The One with the Football' (3.9). As opposed to many sitcom mothers whose sole narrative purpose seems to be to tell off the naughty men, Monica is actually and actively allowed to be funny. In fact, her layered characterisation and the ensuing jokes have become so popular that numerous websites are dedicated to Monica's perfectionism and competitiveness, including a YouTube compilation (see Warner Bros TV 2017).

Monica's compulsive behaviour is her defining humorous discourse for the first four seasons of *Friends*, and despite a long onscreen relationship with Richard (played by Tom Selleck), it is not before her romantic engagement with Chandler that Monica's comedic persona develops further and includes other types of humour and comedic moments. For instance, exploring the comedic potential in her character's sexuality takes more centre stage from the fifth season onward. Her attempt to seduce Chandler despite being sick in 'The One with Rachel's Sister' (6.13) is a striking example of the successful combination of Monica's (the character) more refined comedic trajectory and Courteney Cox's comedic performance capabilities. Playing someone with a cold who is trying to cover up having a cold—with her red robe ostensibly a prop for seduction but in actuality keeping her warm (see Fig. 2.2)—she tries to entice Matthew Perry's Chandler: 'Are you saying that you don't wanna get with this?' Here, the 'motherly type' is distinctively not asexual and actually allowed to be as sexually driven and outrageously ridiculous as any male sitcom characters.

In her analysis of Monica, Hannah Hamad acknowledges the subversive potential of the character's comic depiction, but concludes that:

> However, given her long-term narrative arc that adheres both to the inherent conservativeness of the sitcom genre and the dictates of the postfeminist life script for women in having her couple, marry, have children, and relocate from the city to the suburbs, the potential for this humor to operate to subversive or counter-hegemonic ends is contained. (2018, 696)

As we have been arguing in our typology of Rachel, neither is sitcom characterised by the intrinsic conservatism that Hamad and others

Fig. 2.2 'Are you saying that you don't wanna get with this?': a sick Monica (Courteney Cox) tries to seduce Chandler in 'The One with Rachel's Sister' (6.13)

assume (see also Chapter 5), nor can Monica's development as female character be productively captured in this way. Rather, her character development presents a struggle to negotiate the gendered expectations put on her by society, family, friends and herself. *Friends*' comedic sensibility as well as its strategy of intimacy, here employed on a narrative level, allow Monica to be funny, with all her shortcomings and failures as a rounded sitcom character, laughing both with and at her struggle.

That Monica becomes part of a couple is part of the same struggle, a struggle which only ends with the final episode and which always bears the potential for comedic exploit. Eventually, Monica and Chandler, Ross and Rachel, and to a certain degree Phoebe and Mike (Paul Rudd), represent fundamental and accessible truths about relationships, but the writers extract different types of jokes and comedy from the respective couples. In her psychoanalytic approach to sitcom characters, Deborah Klika explores *Friends*' couple dynamic as follows:

Chandler and Monica, each comic in their own way, are normal compared to the perpetual misunderstandings and confused attempts by Ross and Rachel to get together; Chandler and Monica fulfil the roll of parental truth-tellers, particularly when they begin a committed relationship. (2018, 109)

The coupling of established characters is always considered a risk, and introducing Monica and Chandler as a couple was approached with a certain hesitation (Adalian 2016), but from the initial 'shock' (as audible in the non-diegetic reaction to Monica's head appearing from underneath Chandler's blanket in 'The One with Ross's Wedding', 4.24), the writers realised that there was a lot of original and innovative humour to be found both in their dynamic as a couple as well as in the performance chemistry between Matthew Perry and Courteney Cox.

More specifically, their relationship is scrutinised for humour and comedic moments to be found in the negotiations of power relations, failures of communication and struggles for identity. When Ross walks in on Chandler in full house-cleaning gear, he provokingly refers to him as 'Mondler' suggesting his friend's slow dissolution into a state of self-denying coupledom ('The One where Phoebe Runs', 6.7). Thus, *Friends* presents Monica's coupling with Chandler as a complex and challenging process, the eventual happy endings for the central couples notwithstanding. *Friends* has a 'universal' agenda and approach in the sense that it is a show trying to cover the human psycho-social experience to a considerable extent (see Chapter 6), and as such, it has to be interested in how its central characters negotiate being part of a couple, which does not necessarily represent an ideological closure.

The One with Phoebe Buffay: 'She's sweet, flaky, a waif, a hippie' (Kauffman and Crane 1993)

Phoebe Buffay is often described in relation to a whimsical 'quirkiness', with her jokes characterised by the tropes of absurdist humour, such as can be gleaned in her comment 'I wish I could, but I don't want to' (1.1) or her choice for a new name for herself, Princess Consuela Bananahammock (10.14). Furthermore, Phoebe is frequently either deliberately or non-deliberately refusing 'irony', with specific jokes often found in her taking things at face value. When Rachel's sister Jill criticises Rachel by asking 'Who made her queen of the world?', Phoebe replies enthusiastically 'I would love that job!' (6.13); or, when Rachel apologises to her after a fight about who gets to be Monica's bridesmaid, 'I'm really sorry that I was a baby', Phoebe retorts, 'That's ridiculous, Rachel, we were all babies once' (7.6). However, more significantly, Phoebe finds humour in the reconciliation of her traumatic, petty-crime and homeless past with the more esoteric, urbanite, Manhattan coffeehouse present. (For example, an established running gag is her trying to use her mother's suicide to gain sympathy or advantages.) In the first scene in the pilot, Phoebe's first spoken line—in reference to Monica's failed date—is: 'Wait … does he eat chalk?' Instantly, her first joke establishes her as a character who is a little ditsy, thinks outside the box and exceeds the usual patterns of conversational small talk. Seemingly unaware of how the others (and the audience) react towards her, she continues, 'Just cause I don't want her to go through what I went through with Carl'. Followed by non-diegetic laughter, she then makes an empathic sound which triggers more laughter and a confused look by Chandler.

Instantly, Phoebe's characterisation is synchronised with the comedic performance of Lisa Kudrow, the non-verbal utterance rendering the character as both empathetic but located within her own world, a character operating from within a very particular behavioural space. Phoebe's second characteristic cue occurs after Ross has entered the coffeehouse and, broken and depressed from his recent divorce with Carol, sits down on the sofa. Phoebe gives Ross a concerned look, grabbing invisible objects from above his head, throwing them away with her left hand:

> *Ross:* (annoyed) No no no, don't … stop cleansing my aura! (non-diegetic laughter)
> *Phoebe:* (tries to continue)
> *Ross:* Just leave my aura alone, ok? (more non-diegetic laughter)

In this short exchange, three fundamental narrative tropes are introduced and executed simultaneously. First, Phoebe's esoteric, 'hippie' demeanour and free-spirited nature are established. Second, her well-meaning behaviour related to the esotericism is, for the most part, rejected by the rest of the group, either through direct confrontation (Ross) or more passive comments and looks (Chandler, Monica, Joey). Third, Lisa Kudrow's distinct performance style is established and given room to align itself with the more verbally and dialogue-based punchlines by the other characters. As such, Phoebe's integration into the group works better and, eventually, helps to facilitate the—at the time of the programme's first broadcast rather risqué—narrative arc of showing her as a surrogate to her brother's triplets.

More significantly, whereas Phoebe as character was incidentally written in terms of her Otherness in relation to the rest of the group—the 'stupid hippie' as Rachel calls her in 'The One with Ross's Inappropriate Song' (9.7)—Lisa Kudrow found the character's comedic trajectory and, ultimately, appeal in the total casualness with which Phoebe responds to her earlier traumas: 'I thought this would also be funny if she thought, look, I'm normal like everybody else, I have the same experience like everybody else has, mother commits suicide, dad's in jail, and that it's just all not a big deal' (2014). Consulting the initial pitch, we find it noteworthy that the character of Phoebe is not as fleshed out, with her character presented in terms of her more unconventional (and poorer) life circumstances than the series' narrative eventually allowed her to be:

> She beads barrets and sells them on the street. She doesn't have an apartment of her own. She lives with different guys or she crashes on somebody's couch. Basically, she owns what she can fit in her backpack. (Kauffman and Crane 1993)

This roughness is neither addressed in the narrative of the actual series nor by Kudrow's performance; instead, aspects of it are presented as firmly located within Phoebe's past. For example, she talks about never having had a bike of her own as a child but being dragged around by her step dad in the card-board box for another bike as a substitute ('The One with all the Candy', 7.9). (Interestingly, Lisa Kudrow recalls feeling isolated and struggling to find Phoebe as character in particular in relation to the rest of the group; an improvisation exercise with director James Burrows in preparation for the filming of the pilot episode saw her performing her lines from under a table, not visible to the other actors, leaving her insecure about whether the character would work for the show [Maron 2019].) Partly as a result of Phoebe's different socio-economic background, her humour can, at times, convey a judgemental attitude towards the other characters; for instance when she sarcastically comments, 'Ooh, I have tasted my own medicine and it is bitter!', when Monica starts fictionalising her in revenge for Phoebe's book hobby project (in 'The One where Ross Meets Elizabeth's Dad', 6.21). Not necessarily judgemental but somewhat alienating, Phoebe strikes us as not instantly likeable in the pilot episode; a character who has to grow on its audience as it becomes more familiar with and accustomed to her character's sense of humour and comedic attitude. More significantly, though, *Friends*' comedic sensibility embraces Phoebe's Otherness, making room for her humour to unfold and connect with the other characters, and eventually also with the audience. Through this discourse of intimacy, specifically drawing from each character's diegetic sense of humour, the odd one out eventually becomes the odd one in.

The One with Ross Geller: 'He really really really doesn't want to be single' (Kauffman and Crane 1993)

In his analysis of *Friends*' gender representation, Brett Mills suggests that 'Ross […] who has been married three times and repeatedly suppresses his masculine sexual desires in order to demonstrate an emotional development, is portrayed as feminine and laughably unmasculine' (2005, 113). Even though it is apparent that Ross Geller is clearly struggling with several aspects of traditional masculinity, Mills arguably misinterprets the character's comedic agenda: we are not supposed to laugh at Ross because he is effeminate, but because of his desperate struggle to appear unambiguously heterosexual, traditionally male and, as we discuss in Chapter 3 (and Chapter 5), cool. When in

'The One with the Nap Partners' (7.6) Ross and Joey accidentally discover that the best way to take a nap is cuddled up together on the couch in Joey's apartment, they are shocked and ashamed at first; however, they decide to ignore their anxieties—informed by long-standing discourses concerning appropriate behaviour for heterosexual males—and become 'nap buddies'. Even though they are judged by the rest of the group when they are discovered napping peacefully on the couch together, the comedic approach and laughter is not directed at them for being 'unmanly men', but at their insecurities around their own expectations concerning masculinity (for a discussion of *Friends*' approach to metrosexuality, see Hamad [2018].) In fact, Ross, the only central male character presented as a father almost from the beginning of the series (his son, Ben, is born at the end of season one in 'The One with the Birth', 1.23), is used as an effective source for humour on many occasions specifically *because* of his anxieties around expected values and tropes of masculinity. For instance, in 'The One with the Metaphorical Tunnel' (3.4), Ross tries to force a G.I. Joe action figure toy on his son, who prefers to play with a Barbie doll. The series' comedic narrative framework offers an additional layer of meaning by politicising the violent masculinity represented by the toy through Ross's line of dialogue: 'Look, Ben, it's a toy that protects US oil interests overseas!'

For the most part of the series, Ross fails at a conservative, hegemonic approach to masculinity (see Chapter 3). Rather, he is portrayed in various situations as thoughtful, kind and also more responsible than his peers Joey and Chandler. Furthermore, and in contrast to that, he is presented as a 'nerd' or 'geek'. Be it his love for dinosaurs—or 'dragons', as Phoebe refers to them in 8.14—his avant-garde approach to making music (4.7) or his pedantic way of handling everyday challenges and situations (for instance, manically screaming 'pivot' in 5.16), Ross is made fun of by the other characters for his lack of 'coolness'. For instance, Ross's dorky sense of humour—another variation of 'dad humour'—is subject to (albeit withheld) criticism during his short stay with Joey and Chandler (5.7), when he re-records the answering machine with a variation of the Queen song 'We will rock you' ('We will, we will, call you back'). When they find out, the others try to hide their true feelings about (t)his sense of humour:

> *Joey* (to Chandler): You're fake laughing too, right?
> *Chandler*: Yeah, but the tears are real.

In the show's first scene in Central Perk, two main tropes of Ross's comedic persona are clearly observable. First, his whininess and inherent tendency towards struggles with his mental health, established through his first utterance of the word 'hi' after entering the coffeehouse. The same 'hi', performed in a similar manner, is used again as a verbal running gag in later episodes, as can be gleaned from a YouTube compilation (Формируй Реальность 2015). (Extracting comedic moments and humour from Ross's mental instability comes into particular focus in 'The One with Ross's Sandwich' [5.9], where his issues with anger and rage are treated with medical tranquilisers.) The second decisive aspect of the character's comedic persona is unequivocally connected to the performance capabilities of David Schwimmer—physical and slapstick humour. As Monica is introducing Rachel to the others, Rachel recognises Ross and moves towards him to shake his hand, but just before they meet, his umbrella pops open between them, clumsily pushing them apart (see Fig. 2.3). This is, to be sure, a classical comic moment, part of the generic conventions of sitcom, triggering non-diegetic laughter while functioning as a character-defining moment that renders Ross as clumsy and insecure with women: the sudden umbrella opening symbolises a premature ejaculation, which results in an awkward moment that can only be resolved by a retreat to the couch. David Schwimmer addresses both layers of comedic meaning in his performance, without overplaying or over-accentuating the moment.

Chapter 3 explores Schwimmer's aptitude for physical performance in detail, but it is worth noting here that his physicality informs the comedic persona of Ross and the comedic sensibility of *Friends* as a sitcom. Ross's framework of humour is most prominently cued by physical comedic performance in comparison with the rest of the main cast. Interestingly, this focus on physical humour, or behavioural clumsiness, is not palpable in the initial pitch, where his failure at and inexperience with romantic relationships are the main focus:

Fig. 2.3 Premature umbrella popping: Rachel (Jennifer Aniston) and Ross (David Schwimmer) in 'The One where Monica Gets a Roommate' (1.1)

> However, when we meet him, he's just signed his divorce papers. He can't believe it. He's 24 and divorced. He feels like damaged goods. His wife left him for his best friend Debbie. He had no idea. He was having a good time. […] He hates being single. He doesn't want to date. He doesn't want to have to put together all that IKEA furniture by himself. (Kauffman and Crane 1993)

Interestingly, this inherent 'neediness' is also part of the recent backlash against the series, which has identified Ross's behaviour towards Rachel in particular and women in general as 'problematic' (Woodward 2019) or 'the worst' (Rackham 2017). Here, he is rendered as emotionally manipulating and dominating, reflecting an ethical climate linked to notions of wokeness, yet curiously taking the comedic antics of a fictional character's masculinity in crisis at face value. Still, as both audiences and scholars are recalibrating the evaluations of past comedic discourses, we find it noteworthy that Ross's female love-interests—with the exception of Rachel, Charlie and Julie—are continuously defined by their lack of humour, in particular self-irony and self-deprecation. For example, Ross's second wife Emily (Helen Baxendale) is defined by both her British Otherness and lack of humour compared to the core group. Even though Ross's girlfriend in season 8, Mona (Bonny Sommerville), is presented as more understanding and kinder compared to Emily, she is somewhat bland and lacking distinct comedic features. As we will consider in Chapter 5, few outside love interests in *Friends* are allowed to be genuinely funny in their own right, but it is worth here noting that Schwimmer's pronounced aptitude for physical comedy might make his outside love interests look blander by comparison.

The One with Joey Tribbiani: 'He really thinks he's God's gift to women' (Kauffman and Crane 1993)

Out of the six friends, Joey Tribbiani is arguably the character who has developed the most from the original premise over the course of the entire series. In fact, Kevin S. Bright suggests in our interview that Joey's character development eventually went too far from his initial concept, resulting in the failure of the *Joey* spin-off to connect with audiences (see Chapter 6). Indeed, when examining Joey more closely in the first scene of the first episode, both his physical demeanour and type of humour are, in parts, strikingly different from the Joey of later seasons. Dressed in a black leather jacket and sitting astride a chair (see Fig. 2.1), he delivers the show's third line of dialogue in response to Monica's claim that there is nothing to tell about the guy from work she is seeing: 'Come on! You're going out with the guy, there's gotta be something wrong with him!' In this scene and the entire first episode, Joey is established as a cool-mannered macho, slyly commenting on his female friend's romantic life, speaking with a much stronger New York–Italian cadence compared to later episodes. This is neither a sympathetic nor empathic masculinity on display here, in fact, in this

2 The One with All the Laughing and the Hugging …

first impression of the group, Joey seems a bit of an outsider, a guy the others might occasionally bump into at the coffeehouse.

Only in his response to Chandler's recollection of a bizarre dream, a few moments later, do glimpses of his 'slow mindedness', which later serve as a main source for his character's humour, begin to show:

> *Chandler:* All right, so I'm back in high school, standing in the middle of the cafeteria and I realise I'm totally … naked … then, I look down and I realise, there's a phone … there. (non-diegetic laughter)
> *Joey:* (looking confused, trying to figure it out) Instead of …
> *Chandler:* (fast, interrupting) That's right! (non-diegetic laughter)
> *Joey:* (mumbling) … never had that dream …

Though not established as 'dumb' or 'plain stupid' in comparison to a broader comedic performance and humour tradition (Wells 1998; Mills 2005), the basic dynamic between him and Chandler is laid out from the outset: Chandler's well phrased and articulated anecdote requires clarification by and for Joey. Furthermore, he then elicits one of the biggest non-diegetic laughs in the first scene in reaction to Ross's depressed recollection of his recent break up: 'And you never knew she was a lesbian?!' In this original set-up and characterisation of Joey, the joke is not necessarily motivated by his later established naivety, but rather seems to stem from a more condescending perspective of heteronormative machismo. Indeed, the co-creators had envisioned Joey more strongly as a parody of a certain type of toxic masculinity:

> He really thinks he's God's gift to women. And the only woman he can't get is Monica. Which makes for some really fun sparring. If she's complaining that the guys she meets are intimidated by her because she's a strong woman, he explains it's not because she's a strong woman. It's because she's a bitch. She tells him that he's just saying that because she won't sleep with him. (Kauffman and Crane 1993)

Eventually, it was both the warmer tonality of the series' comedic sensibility as well as the performance of actor Matt LeBlanc, who 'could play dumb really well' (as Kauffman put it to us), that led to a much kinder version of Joey, reflected in his character's use of humour and the comedic performance by the actor. The sexually (over)active young male—a characterisation encapsulated in his catch phrase 'How you doin'?'—is combined with the more archetypical comedic trope of being 'the fool', as well as a character approach based on kindness and empathy as well as an unfiltered hedonism. In 'The One with the Birth Mother' (10.9), an initially successful date at a restaurant goes awry when the woman accidentally takes some of Joey's fries. He might be kind, but as he yells out numerous times during the episode, 'Joey doesn't share food!' The comedic framework of a hedonistic character trapped between two basic primal urges is again used as a source for humour in 'The One where Chandler Gets Caught' (10.10), where Joey is incapable of deciding what is more important, sex or food. Moreover, Joey's foolishness is often tinged with a childlike quality, which is expressed in 'The One where Chandler Doesn't Like Dogs' (7.8) when Joey is trying to give Rachel advice on her love life: 'All right, Rach, the big question is, does he like you? Because if he doesn't like you, this is all a moo point [...]. Yeah, it's like a cow's opinion. It just doesn't matter. It's moo.' This childlike innocence and playfulness have an important role in conveying Joey as likeable and non-threatening, despite his overtly hedonistic agenda and the assumption of toxic masculinity as visible in the pitch and the pilot episode. Furthermore, what adds to Joey's warmth and kindness is his general lack of social plotting and manipulativeness. His incapability of lying is vividly evident in 'The One with Rachel's Other Sister' (9.8) when Phoebe is trying to teach him to lie (instead of using a racoon as his go-to cover-up story) or in his desperate struggle to keep Monica's and Chandler's affair a secret in the fifth season.

Establishing Joey as a source for humour based on less sophisticated comedic themes, innocence, honesty and loyalty makes him particularly likeable and thereby enables the narrative to introduce more controversial topics from which to extract humour. In 'The One with Ross and Monica's Cousin' (7.19), Joey is auditioning for a role as a young Catholic man in World War II Italy, which requires full frontal nudity. As the fictitious character is not circumcised but Joey is, he seeks help from Monica who crafts a variety of artificial foreskins for him to wear at his audition. During the episode's final moments, a shot with the

2 The One with All the Laughing and the Hugging …

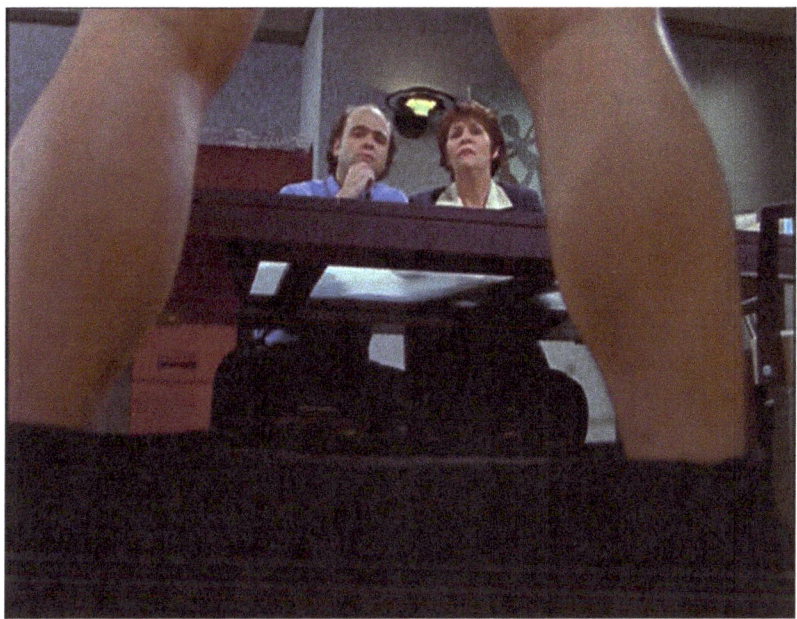

Fig. 2.4 Fake foreskin: Joey's (Matt LeBlanc) legs frame the image as the director (Scott Adsit) and the casting director (Mo Gaffney) get a surprise in 'The One with Ross and Monica's Cousin' (7.19)

camera looking between Joey's naked legs from behind reveals the casting director's and director's surprised faces in the background (see Fig. 2.4), after the fake foreskin has dropped to the floor. We consider this as particularly noteworthy with regards to the industrial context of a (mainstream) sitcom for a national broadcaster, whose Standards and Practices, as we note in the introduction to this book, had deemed mentioning the word 'nipple' problematic only a few years earlier. *Friends*' comedic trajectory, through its thematic pluralism and approach to characterisation, was able to address the show's industrial context and framework, as the particular development and flexibility of Joey, the character, illuminates. As our analysis reflects, in-depth engagement with the show's humour and comedic characterisations challenges some of the existing criticism of the show's politics of representation (e.g., Hamad's [2018] argument concerning postfeminist masculinities).

The One with Chandler Bing: 'He's the droll observer of everybody else's life' (Kauffman and Crane 1993)

In many ways, Chandler Bing is situated at the core of the comedic sensibility of *Friends*. Informed (since the point of casting) by a number of Matthew Perry's personality traits, as Marta Kauffman confirms, Chandler represents the insecurities and incongruities of a distinct urban, white heterosexual masculinity prevalent in the series' imagined target audience during the initial broadcast period from the mid-1990s onwards. Interestingly, he can now also be identified as one of the main targets of the backlash against the series after its 2015 Netflix US acquisition, as evident in, for instance, Ruth Graham's (2015) piece 'Chandler Bing Is the Worst Thing About Watching *Friends* in 2015'.

In general, Chandler utilises sarcasm, irony and self-deprecation, with his humour characterised by a witty and punchline-based verbal style, as well as having a recognisable and surprisingly versatile catchphrase in his 'Could I *be* anymore …' exclamation. In the first scene in Central Perk his comedic persona as the 'ironic witty one' is clearly established by his first line of dialogue, yet another comeback at Monica's date: 'So does he have a hump? A hump and a hairpiece?' It is noteworthy that the scene's blocking establishes Chandler sitting on the armrest of the sofa (see Fig. 2.1), thus potentially implying the superiority of his views and/or humour compared to the rest of the group. It is only when he recounts his weird dream, in which he has a phone for genitals, that he is seen sitting on the couch, next to Monica, at the same level as the other characters, indicating a more self-deprecating humorous approach, which then becomes one of the most decisive characteristic features of his comedic style.

But, more significantly, Chandler is rendered as a character entirely aware of both his sense and use of humour in social interactions. In episode 2.12, 'The One after the Super Bowl', he quips, 'Back then I used humour as a defence mechanism … thank God, I don't do that anymore'. And in a later season, he tells Rachel, 'I'm not great at the advice. Can I interest you in a sarcastic comment?' ('The One with the Tea

Leaves', 8.17). His sense of humour defines his personality and is presented, throughout the series, as a kind of behavioural default position, analogous to, for instance, Monica's obsessiveness, Joey's preoccupation with physical pleasure or Phoebe's absurdist quirkiness. Just how constituting and vital his utilisation of humour is for the characterisation becomes obvious in the (few) instances of enforced withdrawal or sanctioning of his humorous behaviour. For instance, in 'The One with all the Resolutions' (5.11), where Chandler, as a result of a New Year's resolution game, is forced to not utter any sarcastic remarks or make fun in any way of the other main characters' behaviour or life choices, he is portrayed as a suffering, socially crippled and dissatisfied person who is not able to express himself. When he eventually gives up the self-imposed 'ban of mockery' in the episode's closing title sequence, he enters the coffeehouse delivering a round of sarcastic insults to his friends and then slumps down on the sofa with a long sigh of relief; a relief which is likely shared by the series' audience—*Friends* without Chandler's distinct humour would not be the same.

As a final fundamental characterisation related to humour, we argue that Chandler's role in relation to the rest of the series' core group can be described as that of a meta-humorous commentator or narrator, both literally and figuratively observing the others—in the pilot, from the slightly heightened position of the armrest of the couch in Central Perk. In particular, in relation to the narrative's central male friendship between Chandler and Joey, the verbal and punchline humour is most successful: some of Chandler's sarcastic remarks on Joey's 'stupidity' have been identified as particular comedic highlights of the series and are often marked with pronounced non-diegetic laughter, for instance, 'How do you not fall down more?' (2.24) or, 'You have to stop the Q-tip when there is resistance' (2.1). However, not only Joey but everyone is judged by Chandler's sarcasm and dry wit. After Phoebe enjoys a performance of Ross's childish experimental keyboard music in 'The One where Chandler Crosses the Line' (4.7), and claims admiringly, 'It's so different from the stuff you usually hear', Chandler retorts, 'You mean music?'. What is interesting in these moments of sarcastic and cynical humour is to what extent the series' humour can be quite harsh. However, in contrast to a contemporaneous sitcom like

Seinfeld, the crude, mean and tonally 'colder' jokes are framed by a generally 'warmer' narrative and immediate intimacy with a focus on loving friendships, romantic love and group loyalty. In other words, in *Seinfeld*, the humour remains cynical, in *Friends* the laughs are mostly followed by the hugs, as part of a comedic texture where the main characters' comedic types work productively together.

The One with the Group Identity, Comedic Dialogue and the Laugh Track

One of the main achievements of *Friends* is the successful implementation of its ensemble cast as a central part of the series' narrative impetus and comedic sensibility. In fact, we suggest that the show's characterisations are based on the socio-psychological approach to its main characters' comedic personas. Klika characterises *Friends* as a 'group show' (2018, 107) with an ensemble of characters that are trying to define themselves as both individual personalities as well as being part of a distinct social peer group. The group is connected through personal friendship and love for each other as well as their 'shared (narcissistic) view of the world' (ibid., 109).

Throughout the series, we can identify numerous instances where humour is drawn from the characters' self-awareness of being part of a group construction. In 'The One with the Kips' (5.5), when Rachel is afraid of being ostracised by the group after Ross has decided to meet Emily's demands of not seeing her again, she tries to convince Phoebe to choose sides by saying, 'Come on, Phoebe, you and I form a new group, we're the best ones.' However, one of the most prominent examples and a fan favourite is 'The One with all the Embryos' (4.12), an episode almost entirely dedicated to the exploration of the core group and individual identities. The episode's main plot line is based on Monica's initial comment to Joey: 'I just can't believe that you think you and Chandler know me and Rachel better than we know you'. The 'harmless' game then turns into a fierce competition about who knows whom the most, with the consequence that Monica and Rachel lose their apartment to Joey and Chandler (see also Chapter 4). Ross, who administrates the central quiz arrangement, sets up various categories with questions that 'the boys' have to answer about 'the girls' and vice versa. With strong non-diegetic laughter, the hilarious questions and answers are enhanced by the actors' committed, energetic performances, with the characters' eager anticipation evident in their attentive expressions, forward-leaning torsos and clasped hands (see Fig. 2.5). Of particular note here is the well-remembered answer to: 'Every week the *TV Guide* comes to Joey and Chandler's apartment. What name appears on the address label?' (Miss Chanandler Bong). During the 'lightning round' of the game, the questions also reference one of the series' running gags, namely that no-one in the group knows exactly what Chandler's job is ('Transponster is not even a word!'). Here, the humour is almost entirely based on the audience's previous knowledge of the characters, the exaggeration of individual character traits and the interplay of different comedic types.

Fig. 2.5 Group comedic sensibility: Joey (Matt LeBlanc), Chandler (Matthew Perry), Rachel (Jennifer Aniston) and Monica (Courteney Cox) in 'The One with all the Embryos' (4.12)

As in many other sitcoms, in *Friends* the characters' identities are constantly mirrored and regulated by a peer group identity. All the main characters' individual story arcs involve issues of being included or ostracised, of finding comfort or disaffirmation, and/or of feeling embraced or judged by the others, for instance, when Rachel assumes that Phoebe might be the first one to leave the group and snaps at her, 'You're not related, you live far away. You'll lift right out' (5.5). And just as sitcoms negotiate most of their narrative themes through their use of humour, the comedic sensibility of *Friends* is driven by a distinctly prevalent group mentality. (Chapter 5 will pick up on issues linked to representational issues linked to the in-group.) As Klika argues, 'the comicality of *Friends* is driven by the exposition of the characters' lack' (2018, 151), a lack of knowledge of how to successfully conduct and navigate professional and personal commitments. In other words, their lack of aptitude for both romantic relationships and the work-related arena makes them funny. As such, we argue, the ensemble-based comedic sensibility of *Friends* facilitates humour in the visible struggle of growing up, with comedic styles that productively complement and/or clash with one another.

Thematically, the humour of *Friends* has developed from more established or conventional sitcom tropes, utilising farcical set-ups, genre parodies and pop cultural pastiches in the earlier seasons. (Examples here include the over-dramatic recollection of Joey and Chandler urinating on Monica's jellyfish sting to ease her pain in 4.1 or the musical montage of Ross and his monkey Marcel to Barry Manilow's *Looks Like We Made It* in 2.13.) In the course of the series' run, the comedic sensibility shifts towards a more character-based and group-intrinsic approach. To illustrate this distinct approach to group humour as well as outlining the density and proficiency of *Friends*' comedic writing, we will now consider the cold open of 'The One where Chandler Doesn't Like Dogs' (7.8), which has a running time of a little over a minute before the opening credits roll. As Ross enters Monica's apartment, Monica is cooking, and Rachel, Phoebe and Joey are sitting at the kitchen table writing, observed by Chandler. The first line, Ross's (over)enthusiastic 'Hey, everybody. Happy Thanksgiving!', is greeted with a forceful round of shushing from everybody else, which prompts

Ross's startled reply, 'Are we keeping Thanksgiving a secret this year, or?' Here, the script facilitates not only an immediate humorous interaction, including a direct joke based on the incongruity of Ross's reaction to the shushing, it also demonstrates economical storytelling (important in the short form of a sitcom) by introducing the theme of Thanksgiving in the first ten seconds of the episode. Chandler then provides the exposition for the scene: 'No, we're playing this game I learned at work. You have to name all the states in six minutes.' Establishing the context of 'the main characters playing games', in addition to being popular with fans, offers the opportunity to assemble the core cast in one space and, simultaneously, introduces a simple and relatable scenario for the series' imagined target audience.

The following exchange is an intricately woven cluster of dialogue, which showcases *Friends'* efficient comedic writing—the episode was written by Patty Lin—based almost exclusively on the character-based comedic sensibilities of its main protagonists:

> *Ross:* What? That's like insanely easy!
> *Chandler:* Nah, it's a lot harder than it sounds. You always forget at least one … or in some cases … 14!
> *Monica:* It's a stupid game, and I wasn't playing against other people, so, technically, I didn't lose!

Ross displays intellectual hubris and is immediately put in place by Chandler, who then continues to single out Monica by judging her sarcastically. Monica, in turn, justifies herself by directly referencing one of her fundamental character traits, competitiveness. The non-diegetic laughter links to audience familiarity with this trait and acknowledges her inability to admit defeat. Still feeling intellectually superior, Ross finds pleasure in teasing Monica ('You forgot 14 states?'), evoking a sibling rivalry which had been previously established in several episodes, most notably in the aforementioned episode 3.9 when they are fighting over the Geller Cup. Courteney Cox's childishly shrill delivery of the reply 'Nobody cares about the Dakotas!' enhances the written dialogue, which is not necessarily as funny 'on paper'. Chandler, administrating the game, provides the set-up for a joke which is rooted in Phoebe's specific character conceptualisation and comedic sensibility. When asked how many states she could name, Phoebe responds: 'Oh, I got tired of naming states, so I started to list types of celery … I have one. Regular celery.' Evidently, the 'weird' and free-spirited friend prefers an 'absurdist' version of the game, opts for a vegetable that (unlike, e.g., potatoes) is not widely known to have different varieties and presents her results without a detectable sense of (self) irony.

The cold open then concludes with the following exchange:

> *Chandler:* Ok, so Rachel's got 48 and Phoebe is the leader in … vegetables. Joey?
> *Joey:* Say hello to the new champion of Chandler's dumb states-game!
> *Ross:* Wow, how many you got?
> *Joey:* 56! (cut to opening credits)

Chandler is responding to Phoebe's absurdist approach with friendly descriptive sarcasm, before including Joey in the exchange, who has been quiet up to this point. His cocky claim of being the 'new champion' of the game generates genuine suspense, both in his friends and the show's audience. David Schwimmer infuses Ross's punchline set-up with a layer of childlike expectation, before Matt LeBlanc delivers the answer with a self-complacent grin. His answer here works on three levels: first, it is a well thought out punchline as part of the sitcom's narrative structure; second, it stems from one of Joey's constituting character traits, stupidity; and, third, it provides the climactic release to the 'round of results' and concludes the dramaturgy of the cold open sequence by triggering the biggest non-diegetic laugh.

In this short opening sequence, which also establishes one of the episode's plotlines (Ross can't name all the states and is denied Monica's delicious Thanksgiving food), the written dialogue is well adjusted, funny and efficiently smart. Most significantly, it is believable as actual utterances from these familiar characters and delivered by their actors with ease and performances grounded in realism and naturalism (see Chapter 3), creating the impression for fans that they could have overheard this exchange while spending time in the kitchen with the characters, whose comedic types and interplay they have come to know well (albeit not necessarily consciously)—here, an intimate discourse of humour is effectively at play. Obviously, for the comedy in the sequence to work, an audience has to be familiar with the fact that the United States has 50 states, which could complicate the sequence with international audiences. Simultaneously, the programme is ridiculing the fact that many Americans are not able to name all the states of their home country, a satirical approach which is even more enhanced throughout the episode when Ross, frustrated that he is unable to name all the states, exclaims, 'I hate America'. Again, the show's narrative presents a slightly subversive statement, given that this was a popular US network sitcom, which is successfully turned into (mainstream) comedy through *Friends*' inclusive comedic sensibility and warm tonality.

Before we conclude, however, we find it important to note that the experience of the humour of *Friends* is obviously shaped and influenced by the non-diegetic laughter on the soundtrack. The laugh track is a mix of the actual laughter of the studio audience that was present during (most of) the recording and for which the episode was performed, as well as a few elements of 'canned laughter', which were added or edited when scenes had to be restructured or in case certain scenes were filmed without a live audience present. This is a standard practice in multi-camera sitcom production, for instance in scenes which are more difficult to stage or perform, or to prevent spoilers embedded in season finales. Lydia Buckingham comments that:

> While the studio audience reaction is highly influential in terms of timing for the actors and gauging the comedic value of lines for the writers, in terms of performance analysis it is not appropriate to credit the actor with achieving the aural appreciation that we hear on the soundtrack, as the laugh track is manipulated in post-production[.] (2019, 219)

Given that our interviewees confirm that the relationship between the performers and the live studio audience was from *Friends*' first season marked by a pronounced mutual energy exchange, we suggest that it is not inappropriate to give some credit to the actors. Likewise, it seems useful to recognise the laugh track on sitcoms that deployed a live studio audience as (at least potentially) linked to notions of achievement and for its complex textual status, as it converts the (invisible) studio audience into an actual textual element of the show.

As Mills argues, it 'doesn't just suggest that something is funny; it suggests something is obviously, clearly, unarguably, unproblematically funny, and that such responses are collectively defined and experienced' (2005, 81). A remnant of the genre's roots in live entertainment, the laugh track has to assure a target audience of the unambiguous funniness of the performed text, as well as creating a social experience while watching the show, usually in the privacy of individual viewers' domestic spheres. However, various scholars have pointed to the fact that the existence of a laugh track might also trigger contradictory and negative responses in its audience (Smith 2008; Schwind 2014), who may, for example, feel patronised or not agree with the signalling of certain jokes or scenes as 'laugh out loud' funny. Furthermore, the laugh track has also been identified as an indicator for 'less prestigious' comedy shows or lowest common denominator sitcoms as part of the debates of 'quality' television and the legitimisation of television (Newman and Levine 2012). We argue that in the case of *Friends*, the laugh track does not have an alienating effect or actively works against the strategy of intimacy that marks the programme. On the contrary, after repeated viewings, the laugh track becomes part of the series' sonic landscape and fulfils a similar structuring and atmospheric function as the musical cues. Most significantly, perhaps, it supports a communal feeling of inclusion and familiarity, making the audience at home a part of the group experience unfolding on the screen.

Conclusion

In this chapter, we have explored the distinct humour of *Friends* and have identified the 'comedic types' of the main characters. In addition to each character's 'comedic agenda'—which is an amalgam, or palimpsest, of the initial character layout developed by the co-creators, the character-appropriate jokes and humorous lines of dialogue by the series' writers and the individual actors' comedic performance—the humour of *Friends* is characterised by its ensemble approach. In other words, the friends in *Friends* are funny as individuals and they are funny as a group. Moreover, as we have shown through our analysis of the pitch and the first sequence of the pilot episode, most of the core group's comedic personas and the show's approach to character-based humour were already in place from the outset. This speaks to the specificity marking the creation of the series, as noted in the introduction to this book. Furthermore, what is clearly palpable in these first scenes of the pilot episode is a focus on supportive friendships, romantic relationships and friendly competition as part of the series' comedic sensibility and narrative framework, all of which are relevant notions to facilitate *Friends*' strategy of intimacy that has connected and continues to connect the programme with its viewers.

Before we conclude, though, we would like to address the backlash directed towards the show's humour a little further. Most of the criticism in recent years is directed towards the series' representational politics, which receives the critical attention and scrutiny it requires in Chapter 5. However, as the present chapter engages with the programme's distinct comedic sensibility and humorous framework, we have to here consider and critically evaluate to what degree the humour in *Friends* may have become 'dated'. Some of the comedic choices in the show cause a feeling of unease in viewers, leaving an 'aftertaste' that sees even 'die hard' fans of the show having to negotiate notions of nostalgia and intimacy with contemporary sensibilities concerning race relations, body image and gender politics. For example, Monica's past fatness is presented as a physical and emotional deficit she had to overcome to become a successful, attractive and thin woman, within 'particular narratives of fatness that depict it as a form of deviance' (Gullage 2014, 187). More significantly, when 'Fat Monica' (Courteney Cox in a 'fat suit') appears in flashback scenes, the comedy and humour are often on her, with both the jokes and the laugh track repeatedly suggesting that viewers are supposed to laugh *at* her because of her 'funny' look and movements, perhaps most strikingly in the tag for episode 10.11 when she is partying next to a pizza box (see Fig. 2.6), dancing and eating at the same time before collapsing into a bean bag chair.

Fig. 2.6 Fat Monica (Courteney Cox) in 'The One where the Stripper Cries' (10.11)

Whilst there is some representational complexity to be further unpicked here—Mathilda Gregory (2015) has commented that Fat Monica's joy and lack of shame helped to make the character her role model—*Friends*' comedic sensibility stands in contrast to more contemporary sitcoms where the physical appearance of fat women is either treated as normal or not funny in itself, such as Donna Meagle (played by Retta) in *Parks and Recreation*, or where fat shaming is explicitly sanctioned by the narrative's comedic sensibility, for instance in the way the socially inept boss Michael Scott (Steve Carell) treats his overweight employee Phyllis Vance (played by Phyllis Smith) in *The Office—An American Workplace*, who enjoys a healthy sexual relationship with her partner Bob in which she is clearly marked as attractive. The joke in this dynamic is on Michael Scott for being inappropriate and insensitive, not on Phyllis.

Moreover, *Friends* has been subject to strong criticism for being homophobic, or more specifically, for relying on homophobic jokes. Here, it is the character and behaviour of Chandler Bing in particular that have caused most offence and critique. In her opinion piece for *Slate*, Ruth Graham calls Chandler 'the most agonizingly obsolete' (2015) character, 'endlessly paranoid about being perceived as insufficiently masculine' (ibid.). Unpicking this argument (aided by our analysis of Chandler's comedic type), we are struck by the lack of acknowledgement and understanding of the narrative and comedic context of *Friends* as sitcom in general and his character in particular. No doubt, when Ross wonders if his ex-partner Susan is still a lesbian because 'You never know' (1.2) or when Monica jokingly assumes that Chandler might be gay because he knows and likes the musical *Oklahoma!* (9.2), the show's humour relating to LGBTQ+issues seems dated and uninformed. Interestingly, the series' co-creator David Crane, who is openly gay, has addressed the criticism of Chandler's attitude towards homosexuality, commenting that: 'He has his own anxieties and issues, but I don't think the character was homophobic in the least' (in Butler 2016). What we want to suggest is that, as part of the show's general comedic sensibility, the treatment of and the humour derived from LGBTQ+ issues are more nuanced and inclusive than the backlash has recognised. Most of Chandler's unease and problematic attitude towards homosexuality is based on his own insecurity of living up to and negotiating internalised expectations concerning heteronormative masculinity, which he shares with Ross (see Chapter 3) and (to a lesser extent) Joey. Throughout the seasons, his struggle becomes part of *Friends*' comedic sensibility with his insecurity and lack of insight being ridiculed much more so than homosexuality as such. In Chapter 5, we propose that John Ellis's notion of 'working through' (2002) may be particularly productive for critical engagement with sitcom as a genre, and here it strikes us that such 'working through' is highly significant to *Friends*' comedic sensibility.

The backlash against the programme's humour strikes us as particularly unfair and unbalanced when this links the show with the ethical issues relating to the work of, for instance, Louis C.K. and

Woody Allen, and the question of whether we are still allowed to laugh at the jokes and enjoy the work of such individuals. To be clear, it is neither our mandate nor our interest to propagate a singular way of how to read the humour in *Friends*; rather, we wish to encourage more thorough, reflective and robust critical engagement with the show's framework of humour, its comedic tonality and sensibility. This is why our detailed analysis of the humour and comedy of *Friends* is located in this chapter, framing the discussion in the subsequent chapters. What we have shown with our theoretical conceptions of humour as a psycho-social phenomenon is that humour in general and in its mediatised form as television comedy in particular fulfils a vital function in the discourses of media and society. It offers an appraisal and a taking stock as to where a society stands, where its discomforts are located and how individuals negotiate socio-cultural issues. By extracting humour from the struggles of the fictional characters on screen, sitcoms offer both relief from and points for engagement with viewers' own struggles.

When once asked what is required to write a successful sitcom such as *Friends*, Marta Kauffman suggested 'pretty words' (in Blacker 2015), and, indeed, as this chapter has hopefully illustrated, there is much to appreciate about the writing of the show. However, it is not just 'pretty words': in *Friends*, the main characters with their distinct comedic personas and sensibilities enable a carefully balanced mix of comedic approaches and comic themes. Moreover, the humour is quietly smart, as Monica's line that 'they don't know that we know that they know' (5.14) reflects. In her analysis of the inclusive humour in *Cheers*, Michele Hilmes suggests that 'the appeal to an upscale audience had to be made without alienating television's mass audience. High culture viewers had to be entertained, but not at the expense of low-culture fans' (1990, 218). The issues with some of its comedy having not aged well in terms of representational politics notwithstanding, the humour in *Friends* is similarly inclusive: always accessible, never elitist. As we have noted in the introduction to this book, explicit intertextuality was reduced early on to help give the show a timeless feel, and this also facilitates a feeling of inclusiveness, as viewers are invited in. The laughs are indeed followed by the hugs.

Bibliography

Формируй Реальность. 2015. Ross Hi from 'Friends'. YouTube. https://www.youtube.com/watch?v=-zvUuGuwM94. Accessed 30 May 2019.

Adalian, Josef. 2016. How Friends Decided to Pair Up Chandler and Monica. *Vulture.* https://www.vulture.com/2013/11/friends-monica-chandler-how-writers-paired-them-off.html. Accessed 3 February 2019.

Aristotle. 2016. *Poetics—Translated, with Introduction and Notes by Joe Sachs.* Newburyport: Focus Publishing.

Bergson, Henri. 2008 [1911]. *Laughter: An Essay on the Meaning of the Comic.* Maryland: ArcManor.

Blacker, Ben. 2015. Marta Kauffman. *The Writer's Panel with Ben Blacker* podcast. 21 July.

Booker, Christopher. 2004. *The Seven Basic Plots: Why We Tell Stories.* London: Bloomsbury.

Buckingham, Lydia. 2019. Analysing Aniston: Tonal Complexity and Non-comedic Approaches to Sitcom Performance. In *Lucy Fife Donaldson and James Walters*, ed. Television Performance, 209–223. London: Palgrave Macmillan.

Butler, Bethonie. 2016. Should We Forgive 'Friends' for Feeling a Little Offensive in 2016? *The Washington Post.* https://www.washingtonpost.com/lifestyle/style/should-we-forgive-friends-for-feeling-a-little-offensive-in-2016/2016/02/18/e8d47280-d0d3-11e5-b2bc-988409ee911b_story.html?noredirect=on&utm_term=.a1e17020e9c4. Accessed 30 January 2019.

Coser, Rose. 1959. Some Social Functions of Laughter: A Study of Humor in a Hospital Setting. *Human Relations* 12 (2): 181–199.

Critchley, Simon. 2002. *On Humour.* London: Routledge.

Ellis, John. 2002. *Seeing Things: Television in the Age of Uncertainty.* London and New York: I.B. Tauris.

Fetters, Ashley. 2018. The Dad-Joke Doctrine. *The Atlantic.* https://www.theatlantic.com/family/archive/2018/09/deconstructing-the-dad-joke/571174/. Accessed 26 May 2019.

Freud, Sigmund. 1990 [1905]. *Jokes and Their Relation to the Unconscious, Penguin Freud Library*, vol. 6. Harmondsworth: Penguin.

Graham, Ruth. 2015. Chandler Bing Is the Worst Thing About Watching *Friends* in 2015. *Slate.* https://slate.com/culture/2015/01/friends-chandler-bing-and-his-homophobia-are-the-worst-thing-about-watching-the-nbc-sitcom-in-2015.html. Accessed 30 January 2019.

Gregory, Mathilda. 2015. Fat Monica Was the TV Role Model I Never Expected. *Buzzfeed*. https://www.buzzfeed.com/mathildia/why-i-loved-fat-monica. Accessed 30 January 2019.

Gullage, Amy. 2014. Fat Monica, Fat Suits, and *Friends*. *Feminist Media Studies* 14 (2): 178–189. https://doi.org/10.1080/14680777.2012.724026.

Hamad, Hannah. 2018. The One with the Feminist Critique: Revisiting Millennial Postfeminism with *Friends*. *Television & New Media* 19 (8): 692–707. https://doi.org/10.1177/1527476418779624.

Hilmes, Michele. 1990. 'Where Everybody Knows Your Name': *Cheers* and the Mediation of Culture. In *Critiquing the Sitcom, a Reader*, ed. Joanne Morreale, 213–223. Syracuse: Syracuse University Press.

Jenner, Mareike. 2016. Is This TVIV? On Netflix, TVIII and Binge-Watching. *New Media & Society* 18 (2): 257–273. https://doi.org/10.1177/1461444815415523.

Kant, Immanuel. 2012 [1790]. *Critique of Judgement*. New York: Star Publishing LLC.

Kauffman, Marta, and David Crane. 1993. *Insomnia Café* Pitch. 7 December.

Kelly, John. 2016. The Dad-ification of Language Shows That Masculinity Is Still Evolving. *Slate*. https://slate.com/human-interest/2016/12/dads-are-changing-the-way-we-talk-and-how-we-think-about-masculinity.html. Accessed 26 May 2019.

Klika, Deborah. 2018. *Situation Comedy, Character and Psychoanalysis: On the Couch with Lucy, Basil and Kimmie*. New York: Bloomsbury Academic.

Kudrow, Lisa. 2014. Interviewed by Karen Herman for the Archive of American Television, Television Academy Foundation. https://www.youtube.com/watch?v=uW0G6UDI-mE. Accessed 5 February 2019.

Kuipers, Giselinde. 2006. *Good Humor, Bad Taste: A Sociology of the Joke*. Berlin and New York: Mouton de Gruyter.

Kuipers, Giselinde. 2008. The Sociology of Humor. In *The Primer of Humor Research*, ed. Victor Raskin, 361–398. Berlin: Mouton de Gruyter.

Lacey, Nick. 2000. *Narrative and Genre: Key Concepts in Media Studies*. New York: Palgrave Macmillan.

Lippitt, John. 1992. Nietzsche, Zarathustra and the Status of Laughter. *The British Journal of Aesthetics* 32 (1): 39–49. https://doi.org/10.1093/bjaesthetics/32.1.39.

Maron, Marc. 2019. Lisa Kudrow. *WTF with Marc Maron* Podcast. Episode 1020. 20 May.

McGraw, Peter, and Joel Warner. 2014. *The Humor Code: A Global Search for What Makes Things Funny*. New York: Simon & Schuster.

Mills, Brett. 2005. *Television Sitcom*. London: Palgrave Macmillan.
Mills, Brett. 2009. *The Sitcom*. Edinburgh: Edinburgh University Press.
Morreal, John. 1983. *Taking Laughter Seriously*. Albany: State University of New York Press.
Newman, Michael Z., and Elana Levine. 2012. *Legitimating Television: Media Convergence and Cultural Status*. New York and London: Routledge.
Pickering, Michael, and Sharon Lockyer. 2009. Introduction: The Ethics and Aesthetics of Humour and Comedy. In *Beyond a Joke: The Limits of Humour*, ed. Michael Pickering and Sharon Lockyer, 1–24. London: Palgrave Macmillan.
Rackham, Casey. 2017. 30 'Friends' Moments That Prove Ross Geller Is Literally the Worst. *Buzzfeed*. https://www.buzzfeed.com/caseyrackham/moments-that-prove-ross-geller-is-literally-the-worst. Accessed 30 May 2019.
Raskin, Victor. 2008. *The Primer of Humor Research*. Berlin: Mouton de Gruyter.
Rowe Karlyn, Kathleen. 1995. *The Unruly Woman: Gender and the Genres of Laughter*. Austin, TX: University of Texas Press.
Rustad, Gry C., and Kai Hanno Schwind. 2017. The Joke That Wasn't Funny Anymore: Empathy in Contemporary Sitcoms. In *Metamodernism: Historicity, Affect and Depth After Postmodernism*, ed. Robin Van den Aker, Alison Gibbons, and Timotheus Vermeulen, 131–146. London: Rowman & Littlefield.
Savorelli, Antonio. 2010. *Beyond Sitcom: New Directions in American Television Comedy*. Jefferson: McFarland.
Schopenhauer, Arthur. 2014 [1818]. *The World as Will and Representation*. Cambridge: Cambridge University Press.
Schwind, Kai Hanno. 2014. 'Chilled-Out Entertainer'—Multi-Layered Sitcom Performances in the British and American Version of *The Office*. *Comedy Studies* 5 (1): 20–32. https://doi.org/10.1080/2040610X.2014.905094.
Senzani, Alessandra. 2010. Class and Gender as a Laughing Matter? The Case of *Roseanne*. *Humor: International Journal of Humor Research* 23 (2): 229–253. https://doi.org/10.1515/humr.2010.011.
Smilauerová, Anna. 2012. TV Sitcom Friends: Analysis of Character Humor Strategies Based on the Violation of Grice's Conversational Maxims. Master's dissertation, Charles University in Prague.
Smith, Jacob. 2008. *Vocal Tracks: Performance and Sound Media*. Sacramento: University of California Press.
Spencer, Herbert. 1860. The Physiology of Laughter. *Macmillan's Magazine* 1: 395–402.

Warner Bros TV. 2017. Monica the Perfectionist. YouTube. https://www.youtube.com/watch?v=8mQea59u5hA. Accessed 30 May 2019.

Wells, Paul. 1998. 'Where Everybody Knows Your Name': Open Convictions and Closed Contexts in the American Situation Comedy. In *Because I Tell a Joke or Two: Comedy, Politics and Social Difference*, ed. Stephen Wagg, 180–201. London: Routledge.

Woodward, Ellie. 2019. 21 Really Problematic Things Ross Did in 'Friends'. *Buzzfeed*. https://www.buzzfeed.com/elliewoodward/problematic-things-ross-from-friends-did. Accessed 30 May 2019.

Television

Cheers (1982–1993), USA: NBC.
Family Ties (1982–1989), USA: NBC.
Friends (1994–2004), USA: NBC.
I Love Lucy (1951–1957), USA: CBS.
Joey (2004–2006), USA: NBC.
*M*A*S*H* (1972–1983), USA: CBS.
Parks and Recreation (2009–2015), USA: NBC.
Roseanne (1988–1997, 2018), USA: ABC.
Scrubs (2001–2008, 2009–2010), USA: NBC, ABC.
Seinfeld (1989–1998), USA: NBC.
The Cosby Show (1984–1992), USA: NBC.
The Mary Tyler Moore Show (1970–1977), USA: CBS.
The Office—An American Workplace (2005–2013), USA: NBC.
The Simpsons (1989–present), USA: Fox.

Film

Hawks, H. 1938. *Bringing Up Baby*. USA: RKO Radio Pictures.
Mann, D. 1961. *Lover Come Back*. USA: Universal Pictures.

3

The One where They Tame the Three-Headed Monster: Foregrounding Holistic Performance

In recent years, matters of casting and performance have received increasing attention within the scholarship on television. This attention has encompassed both television comedy more broadly and sitcom specifically (e.g. Mills 2005, 2010; Becker 2008; Cantrell and Hogg 2017), but overall, performances located within dramatic and/or single-camera contexts continue to be much more on the receiving end of scholarly engagement. Simultaneously, as Tom Cantrell and Christopher Hogg (2017, 146) note, the growing literature on television comedy rarely examines performance or the actor's work. This relative shortage of attentiveness to the history, developments and practices of comedic acting and performance is surprising, especially when considering how significant casting and performance are to sitcom, which 'tends to highlight and foreground performance in ways that other genres do not' (Hight 2010, 178).

Multi-camera sitcom in particular foregrounds the presence and work of actors through its shooting methods, which are sometimes referred to in terms of 'the three-headed monster'. Here, the cameras and editing work to capture the performance by the actors, for whom space and time are kept much more intact than is the case with single-camera production. As Christine Becker notes, actors must 'modulate their performance [...] for both a continuous acting style and a piecemeal method' (2008, 2), often drawing on a range of skills, including those concerning physical comedy. Moreover, while actors can benefit from the laughter and applause of the studio audience that may be present, they also—regardless of whether the laughter originates from a studio audience or not—have to negotiate the 'pauses' necessitated by the laugh track. Clearly, the three-headed monster presents a number of particular opportunities and challenges for the creative practitioners in front of the cameras.

Given the overall scholarly neglect of *Friends*, it is not surprising that correspondingly little has been said about how casting and performance inform the show's meanings, with welcome exceptions to be found in the work by Brett Mills (2005), Gary Cassidy and Simone Knox (2015) and Lydia Buckingham (2019). Yet, much remains still to be said about how performance and acting choices function within *Friends*, not least because, as John Mundy and Glyn White rightly point out, '*Friends*' great strength is its brilliant ensemble, with six characters given nearly equal weight. [...] The ensemble playing allowed the audience to feel they were part of the group, rather like being a patron of *Cheers*, only more select and intimate' (2012, 119). Indeed, the six main actors and their work are not only crucial to *Friends*' considerable popularity, but also at the core of much paratextual discussion, the programme's official and unofficial histories (e.g. Wild 2004; Littlefield 2012), as well as the reflections by Marta Kauffman, Kevin S. Bright and James Burrows in our interviews with them.

The strong paratextual engagement with the series already noted in the introduction to this book abounds with rumours and reports concerning the actors who either unsuccessfully auditioned for the core cast in *Friends*, which includes *Will & Grace*'s Eric McCormack (Ross) or Vince Vaughn (Joey), or were cast but turned it down, such as Craig Bierko (Chandler). Deeply ingrained in fan lore are such facts as the part of Rachel having been initially offered to Courteney Cox, who had the biggest profile in a relatively unknown cast (following an appearance in Bruce Springsteen's *Dancing in the Dark* video); David Schwimmer being cast first and that the role of Ross was written with him in mind; and the close off-screen friendship between the six main actors.

Moreover, the key creative personnel have commented numerous times that the show started to write to the particular qualities and strengths of the specific performers. As Kevin S. Bright confirmed in our interview with him, 'Joey became dumber because Matt [LeBlanc] plays dumb really well'. Marta Kauffman agrees with this, further noting that the 'tough, defensive, cynical, sarcastic' characterisation of Monica as it appears in her and Crane's (1993) original pitch was redeveloped once Courteney Cox, who 'has a real sweetness to her', secured the part. Moreover, the strength of the performers also affected the storytelling more broadly, as Kauffman reflects:

> One lesson from the show was that everything was better with the six of them together. Sometimes it was better to hear them talk about something that happened, rather than see it dramatically. What the audience wanted, we found out, was the six of them in the room.

That the actors and their work affected the scriptwriting is not uncommon, especially in long-running shows. However, what is less common is the pronounced ensemble quality of the core cast, who—supported by the showrunners and James Burrows, and informed by David Schwimmer's background as co-founder of the Lookingglass Theatre Company—became a tight-knit group. Winning a Screen Actors Guild Award for Outstanding Performance by an Ensemble in a Comedy Series in 1996, the group of six suspended the usual rules of the social culture of acting by agreeing, at Courteney Cox's suggestion (see Wild 2004), to give each other notes on their acting, to help improve their performances. They also began to collectively negotiate for salaries, resolving deadlocks with NBC to eventually receive $1 million each per episode as well as a percentage of the syndication income. So, the very existence and production history of the show became closely intertwined with the actors and their shared sensibility and approach.

As one of the few scholars to have paid in-depth attention to performance in sitcom and *Friends* specifically, Brett Mills (2005) has rightly identified an approach to acting in sitcom that displays its own artificiality and performativity. He has furthermore argued that the multi-camera shooting style with its tendency towards wider framing and the physical distance between camera and actor can be understood as signalling that a show is 'not particularly interested in the psychology of its characters, or in them as realistic, believable, fully-formed human beings' (2005, 85). Building on the critical ground laid by Gary Cassidy and Simone Knox (2015), we will argue that *Friends*' considerable success is closely informed by its core cast's approach to performance, which does not follow the performative sitcom style of acting conventionally associated with multi-camera sitcom, but instead locates itself within a realist/naturalist approach within the heightened context of the proscenium arch proxemics. (For a discussion of the notoriously flexible terms 'realism' and 'naturalism', see Gordon [2006].) Through detailed analysis of several scenes, we will scrutinise Jennifer Aniston's portrayal of Rachel and David Schwimmer's of Ross, as well as Matt LeBlanc's of Joey. Furthermore, we will demonstrate the particularities of multi-camera performance by considering the struggles experienced by some of the guest actors of the show, particularly Brad Pitt, which reflexively point to the comprehensive skills set and qualities needed when dealing with the 'three-headed monster'.

As the above indicates, our discussion will be engaging with notions of 'good acting' and 'bad acting', which are highly loaded and subjective terms. As Jean Benedetti points out, 'what is recognised as good or bad acting change[s] from period to period, as society and taste change' (2005, 3). With our analysis located within a broadly Stanislavskian context (Stanislavski 2013 [1937]) concerned with realism and notions of truthfulness, we agree with Cassidy and Knox that 'notions and judgments of what is good and bad acting feature significantly in industry and audience discourses, and if scholarship wants to meaningfully engage with acting, then this must include a reflexive consideration of achievement *and* failure' (2016, emphasis in original). Just as we will engage with sitcom performance in a holistic manner by exploring both success and struggle, so we will foreground in our discussion the distinctly holistic approach to performance to be found within the core cast in *Friends*. While Mills sees that 'in *Friends* […] much of the comedy is presented as performance but the serious emotional moments are instead acted' (2010, 144), our analysis will emphasise that the more emotional as well as the slapstick-driven moments within the programme are underpinned by nuanced acting choices concerned with character-based realism.

In her analysis of Jennifer Aniston's work in *Friends*, Lydia Buckingham has sought to reveal 'a more complex relationship between comedic sitcom performance and naturalism that is neither entirely oppositional nor entirely compatible' (2019, 212). Her argument is hinged around the 'covert […] acknowledgment of the audience' (ibid., 215), focusing on how Aniston places her body so that it is angled towards (and visible for) the studio audience and can invite the audience to contribute laughter, which, she understands to be 'in direct tension with naturalism's fourth wall that separates and ignores the meta-theatrical realm' (ibid., 216). However, Buckingham here conflates different types of naturalism and displays insufficient awareness of the actor's process, which regularly contends with production frameworks and prescriptive parameters. In multi- and single-camera productions, actors engage with their material in such a way that they incorporate marks, cameras, lighting and so on (and may draw energy from a studio audience, if present) into their performance; thus, realist and naturalistic approaches to acting may indeed underpin and facilitate comedic performance. It is this distinctly holistic approach to performance informing and enriching the series' overall strategy of intimacy that we identify as crucial to *Friends*' significant and continuing popularity.

The One with David Schwimmer and Jennifer Aniston: Performing Ross and Rachel

While scholarly attention on Jennifer Aniston has been shifting from her (pre- and post-Brangelina) stardom (Johnson 2012) to the details of her acting (Cassidy and Knox 2015; Buckingham 2019), David Schwimmer's performance on *Friends* has not been critically assessed in any great detail (Mills [2005] and Buckingham [2019] pay only passing attention to it). Given that *Friends*' success, especially in its early seasons, was hinged around the Ross-and-Rachel storyline, it is worth exploring how Aniston's and Schwimmer's acting choices inform that storyline. We will now demonstrate in detail how the core cast in *Friends* facilitates a distinctly holistic performance style which fuses 'dramatic' (e.g. portraying serious emotions) and 'comedic' (e.g. the delivery of punchlines) forms of acting and which, despite the supposed artificiality of multi-camera production, remains rooted in realism/naturalism and thus successfully conveys psychologically plausible behaviours and truthful emotions.

Cassidy and Knox (2015) offer a useful approach in their close analysis of Aniston's performance in a scene from 'The One with the Kips' (5.5), in which Ross tells Rachel, who has just received the news that her family's dog Le Poo has died, that his new wife Emily demands that he stops spending time with Rachel. Their work draws on terminology associated with Constantine Stanislavski, one of the most influential theorists on acting and actor training, concerned with being able to channel actors' unconscious processes and convey a 'grammar' of acting (Stanislavski 2013 [1937]). In their Stanislavskian-influenced analysis, Cassidy and Knox break down the scene into 'units' (segments of the script defined by a character's single action or goal), 'objectives' (the specific goals a character wants to achieve or execute) and 'verbs' (the specific choices, actions and means a character chooses to reach their objective). By doing so, they map out Aniston's route through the scene.

For example, when Aniston's Rachel realises that Ross has agreed to Emily's demand, Cassidy and Knox explore how:

> Aniston is physicalising the verb '*to realise*' by moving her hands to her chest after a beat, letting the news to her body. The slight delay in this suggests that her character needs a moment to take in the enormity of the information, and the quality of her hand movement (which is quite firm, producing an audible 'smack') reflects that the weight and pain entailed within this news is now approaching her. (2015, emphasis in original)

It is worth noting that Jennifer Aniston's route through this scene simultaneously touches on dramatic and comedic beats, eliciting laughs in the audience but without sacrificing what is the scene's dramatic core (i.e. that Rachel feels betrayed by Ross's decision). Very shortly after Rachel realises what has happened and Ross's scant consolation that they can spend time together until Emily joins them, Aniston's character responds:

by erupting into applause; the enjoyable spontaneity of this is rendered via the swift, hard movement of her arms and hands, which, with her eyes fixed on Schwimmer's Ross, seem to be acting almost independently of her. This combines with Aniston's use of her voice, who varies her pitch to bring it above and below her usual register [...] to modulate her *mocking*, deliberately unconvincingly performed comment that this is the best news she has heard 'since Le Poo died!' (Cassidy and Knox 2015, emphasis in original)

If anything, the comedic beats make the dramatic moment more 'realistic' because, as we have argued in Chapter 2, humour is frequently utilised in social interactions to provide relief from negative tension. Thus, we would expand Mills's claim that 'sitcom, then, must forever unite narrative conventions and comedic requirements, displaying the complexity of the former while actually relying on the latter for its effectivity' (2005, 35), by suggesting that, in *Friends*, the narrative framework is comprised of both dramatic and comedic requirements and not only negotiates possible tensions between them, but facilitates their productive coexistence, not least through the performance capabilities of the core cast.

David Schwimmer's and Jennifer Aniston's performance is particularly noteworthy given the subtleties and nuances required in interpreting the emotionally turbulent relationship of Ross and Rachel, which simultaneously drives the dramatic narrative and serves as a regular source for humour as part of the series' comedic sensibility. For example, in the episode 'The One where Ross Finds Out' (2.7), Aniston, at first, is given the opportunity to deliver an explicit 'drunk' performance, when Rachel in an attempt to get over Ross (who at this point is dating Julie) is going on a date with another man, Michael (Arye Gross). During the date she gets drunk, obsesses about Ross and, when finally realising that she 'needs closure', leaves an ill-advised drunk message on Ross's answering machine. Here, Aniston employs a looser physicality that suggests inebriation, as do her facial expressions and verbal performance. However, the inebriation is suggested in a restrained, subtle manner based in naturalistic behaviour and body language. For example, her elbow slips off the

90　S. Knox and K. H. Schwind

Fig. 3.1 'Drunk' performance: Rachel (Jennifer Aniston) tries to get over Ross in 'The One where Ross Finds Out' (2.7)

back of her chair and her eyes are not focusing on her date when she is talking to him; and as Fig. 3.1 shows, her gestures become somewhat erratic, and she is too tipsy and distracted to brush back her hair when it is hanging into her face.

In the climax of the scene, when Aniston reaches her character's 'objective', namely that Rachel convinces herself that she is over Ross (by declaring it to him), Aniston adds the slightly exaggerated element of throwing the mobile phone into the ice bucket after delivering the line: 'And that, my friend, is what they call closure.' This infuses the message with a self-satisfied attitude by adding an emphasis to the first syllable of the word 'closure', which creates a strong comedic moment (marked by non-diegetic laughter and applause), while simultaneously keeping it based in her character's heartbroken reality (in which she may be feeling as disposable to Ross as the phone she so carelessly discarded).

Thus, when later in the episode, a now sober Rachel tries to prevent Ross from checking his messages on the answering machine, the viewers are invited to laugh at her desperate attempts to do so (jumping on his back trying to get hold of the phone), but can still sympathise with her pain and embarrassment.

While we explore in detail how Schwimmer and Aniston work through the rest of this scene in relation to the use of space and set in Chapter 4, it is worth drawing out further here that, when Ross manages to hear her message, Schwimmer signals his character's stunned surprise when finding out about Rachel's feelings for Ross through a slow and muted response. The tension is relieved with Ross's (punch)line: 'You're over me? When, when were you … under me?' Here, again, the comedic dialogue is enhanced by Schwimmer's acting choices, with a hesitant pattern of speech that shows that Ross is struggling to process the moment and articulate a reply, which he combines with a stunned face, conveying the puppy-like innocence of a character who truly has no idea about what is going on. Here, Schwimmer is channelling a particular way of 'straight man' acting in comedic contexts, namely the innocent (and clueless) person. (This dynamic can, for instance, be observed in Ryan O'Neal's performance opposite Barbra Streisand's outrageous 'unruly woman' [Rowe Karlyn 1995] in the screwball comedy *What's Up, Doc?* [1972].) The disjuncture between the sexual subtext (i.e. Rachel being 'under' Ross) and Ross's innocence only heightens the comedic potential, just as Schwimmer's comedic skills concerning timing and vocal delivery (his pause before and vocal twinge during 'under me') support and speak to his character's emotional turmoil. (He is trying to come to terms with longed-for news at a difficult point in time, seeing as he has recently started a new romantic relationship with Julie [Lauren Tom].)

The above is one of numerous fights and much emotional turbulence marking the 'Ross and Rachel' storyline, in which internal power relations are constantly renegotiated, epitomised in one of the series' many catchphrases: 'We were on a break!' As we have already noted, Schwimmer's and Aniston's performances are significant to the show's strategy of intimacy, especially in the early seasons, before Courteney Cox's and Matthew Perry's performances of 'Mondler' came into focus.

What is important to acknowledge here is that the performances foster intimacy not so much through the individual actors' work, but through the ways in which the actors listen and react to each other, which in actor discourse is called 'acting off the line' (Cassidy and Knox 2015). While Chapter 4 will explore how Aniston and Schwimmer engage with each other's acting choices in 2.7 like players in a tennis match, delivering volleys and parries, and Buckingham's (2019) work also attests to this interplay, another illuminating example can be found in Rachel's hurt response after discovering Ross's list of all her negative characteristics in 'The One with the List' (2.8).

When Ross hurries in from the balcony to Rachel's closed bedroom door, asking her to give him another chance, Aniston responds to Schwimmer's entreating tone by delivering Rachel's 'No' with an elongation and vocal tremble. Schwimmer takes a beat and physically deflates slightly to register Rachel's stance and her audible pain. He asks 'No?' in a tone of slight disbelief, and Rachel's confirmation materialises via a rather calm and unemotional voice, as Aniston works to suggest that Rachel is trying to shut down the difficult moment and stay on top of her painful feelings. When Chandler suggests that he and the other friends should leave, Aniston accompanies her line that she and Ross are 'done talking' with a swiping hand gesture against his torso that indicates a distance between them (but the fact that her hand ends up close to his heart subtly suggests that her emotional connection will persist). Ross's protest that he knows 'how you must [feel]' is marked by Schwimmer picking up on Aniston's gesture and turning his hand towards his chest (his heart, again) and then towards her, as well as a tone of frustration. Aniston cuts off his last word with Rachel's insistence that he does not, with her two-handed 'stop' gesture (which visually rejects his connecting hand gesture) and forceful vocal delivery conveying that Rachel's anger is emerging at Ross's exasperation. This is met with a slight shrug and blink of disbelief by Schwimmer, indicating that he is feeling at a loss. Rachel then explains her feelings as follows:

> Imagine the worst things you think about yourself. Now, how would you feel if the one person that you trusted the most in the world, not only thinks them too, but actually uses them as reasons not to be with you?!

Here, Aniston conveys her character's feelings through such acting choices as forcefully exhaling after the word 'imagine', to signal that Rachel is gearing herself up for articulating her pain, while moving her hands downwards towards him, which continues their interplay of gestures. As she says the words 'thinks them too', Schwimmer briefly drops his head and gaze, reflecting that Ross is feeling some shame about what he has done. Aniston's voice quavers on the word 'reasons', as Rachel is struggling to keep control of her emotions, and after her dialogue, Schwimmer's facial expression has softened through the understanding Ross has gained about the pain he has caused her. Then, when Rachel responds with sarcasm to Ross's explanation that he would want to be with her 'despite' reasons not to and snaps at the other four 'I said, don't go!', Aniston brings a meticulously delivered comedic beat into this emotional scene through changing her volume and pitch very abruptly and hardening her facial movements to the point where it looks like she is almost barking. She then shifts back into a softer and tender tone as she retreats with the comment that she would 'never make a list' and shuts the door on him. What this scene, filmed in a shot/reverse shot pattern with medium framing, attests to is how *Friends*' strategy of intimacy is engendered through holistic performances in which dramatically intense moments are synthesised with beats of comedic performance, as well as through finely attuned and synergised 'acting off the line'.

The One with the Leather Pants: David Schwimmer and Physical Comedy

As we have noted earlier, David Schwimmer's performance as Ross Geller has not received in-depth scholarly analysis thus far. This is perhaps because Schwimmer's performance frequently draws on slapstick, which, as Mundy and White ascertain, has often been regarded 'as rather a crude and basic form of humour, unlikely to appeal to those who prefer a more "intellectual" or "clever" kind of comedy' (2012, 210). To consider physical comedy and slapstick as the lowest form of 'superiority humour' (see Chapter 2), however, does not suffice to explain their widespread appeal. Rather, as Pierre Bourdieu (2010 [1984]) and others have argued, judgements of 'low brow humour' are interconnected with complex discourses of taste, class and gender, as well as socio-cultural legitimation processes of television (Newman and Levine 2012). More significantly, the dismissal of slapstick comedy—be that by audiences, critics or scholars—neglects to explore and assess the challenges and intricacies of a successful physical comedic performance and the particular skills and craft involved, which are prevalent in numerous scenes in *Friends*, especially those involving David Schwimmer.

As Marta Kauffman recalled for us, David Schwimmer's talent for physical performance was known to her and David Crane before production began, as he had auditioned for them previously, and they wrote the part of Ross with him in mind. Out of the ensemble cast, Schwimmer, who has a background in the Chicago theatre scene, was perhaps most aware of the full range of performance opportunities and challenges presented by multi-camera filming before going into production and, more significantly, how to engage with them in front of a live audience. This is particularly visible in Ross's many slapstick moments in which Schwimmer's strength of physicality, vocal delivery and comic timing are used particularly well. As we have outlined in Chapter 2, his comedic persona is already established as 'physical' in the first scene of the pilot episode with the 'umbrella popping' incident, but there are numerous other moments related to slapstick throughout the entire series in which his physical comedic performance dominates the narrative approach.

For example, in episode 5.11. 'The One with All the Resolutions' Ross goes on a date with Elizabeth (Sarah Peterson) and ends up watching a movie at her place. The date turns into a disaster because of a pair of tight leather pants that Ross decided to wear in one of his many misguided attempts to be 'cool' (see Chapters 2 and 5). Ross's 'objective' is articulated in a voiceover, a device occasionally used in *Friends*, especially to set up slapstick-based comedic moments for Ross that often result in his total embarrassment. (For instance, in 'The One with Ross and Monica's Cousin' [7.19], Ross's inner monologue leads him to make an inappropriate move on his cousin Cassie [Denise Williams].) Ross's 'super objective' (which is a deeper objective) is established: he wants to avoid embarrassment and retain the cool persona he has constructed in front of his date. The 'cool' leather pants are actually too hot, making him sweat, and so they must come off; and Ross retreats to the bathroom. The following sequence, which runs for a total of just over three minutes, is entirely based on and constructed around Schwimmer's physical slapstick performance, with Schwimmer deploying distinct performance strategies to achieve the super objective.

First, Schwimmer's Ross's objective is to try to get relief: Ross pulls down the pants with swift and desperate movements, takes a seat on the bathtub and fans some air on his exposed legs with a magazine. Here, the costume designers have opted for an oversized long-sleeve shirt which, when removed from the trousers, covers the actor's underpants and genital area, in keeping with the 'family friendly' nature of the series and restrictions of nudity by NBC's Standards and Practices at the time. He then moves to the sink and splashes some cold water on his legs. The action is filmed in a long shot and almost in one take, with one intercut when Ross sits down on the bathtub, for a tighter framing on him while he is fanning his thighs. Once he gets up and moves towards the sink, the editing cuts back to the wider framing to be able to capture his movement across the space. The splashing of the water on his legs is concluded with a long, exaggerated sigh of relief and pleasure.

Then, Schwimmer's Ross moves to playing the verb 'to realise': after Elisabeth calls him back to the living room and Ross answers with a forced fake-casual ''kay', he has to try to get fully dressed in order to not over-step social boundaries. However, the leather pants are not coming higher than his knees, despite forceful, scrabbling pulling, all filmed in one static shot. Schwimmer delivers an utterance of panic: 'Oh my god!' The vocal twinge on the word 'god' emphasises his epiphany that he will be cool in neither the physical nor the social meaning of that word, and the resemblance in pitch to the earlier sigh of relief and pleasure traces Ross's rise and fall within the sequence. Interestingly, Schwimmer gives a little shrug just before he makes the utterance, which implies that, after all the forceful pulling, Ross's body is shrugging off that upward energy, because his body takes in the information before his brain does, as part of the process of the news sinking in.

When the storyline (this episode's B-plot) picks up again, Schwimmer's Ross takes bad advice from Joey, playing the verb 'to plead' twice, despite the evidently unsound nature of Joey's suggestions: when Joey takes a phone call from an increasingly desperate Ross, the editing cuts back to the latter, who is shown sitting on the toilet, with his knees together, which implies vulnerability and emasculation. In the following, even though the dialogue—a rendition of what has happened to him—refers to the heightened comedic situation, Schwimmer's performance is directed towards the phone (see Fig. 3.2), addressing the secrecy of the situation, which restricts his physical movement (as do the leather pants around his knees). Ross's (deliberately barely) suppressed panic, expressed through the use of a shrieky voice, is contrasted with Joey's casual and relaxed manner on the other end of the line—to him, this is just an interesting and amusing situation, while Ross is in a state of panic.

Fig. 3.2 Ross struggles with his leather pants: David Schwimmer in 'The One with All the Resolutions' (5.11)

Joey suggests using powder: 'sprinkle some of that on your legs, it will absorb some of the moisture and then you can get your pants back on'. Ross's reaction is characterised by an almost child-like quality, pitched between relief and euphoria, with Schwimmer clutching the powder bottle in relief as his character is clutching at straws. There are no cuts in the editing when he powders his legs, which helps to draw attention to the fact that he applies the powder quite sloppily, giving prominence to how Schwimmer shows that his character's panic is affecting his control over his physical movements. Ross then realises, horrified, that the pants still cannot be pulled up. Almost crying, he bends his entire upper body down to speak into the phone: 'They're not coming on, man!' As he does so, his hands are still pulling the pants, with his arms visibly shaking—a tension vocally mirrored in the quaver in his voice—which subtly implies that Ross is not ready to give up and face embarrassment just yet. Invoking a sense of male solidarity through the use of the word 'man', the written dialogue contrasts with the ridiculing of Ross's masculinity: an adult man, trapped in a bathroom with powder on his legs and his trousers around his knees; all because he wanted to be cool in his leather pants. Could Ross *be* any further removed from the 'strong, successful, capable and authoritative' (Feasey 2008, 2–3) hegemonic male? Indeed, he could, as he is about to take more of Joey's bad advice, as Schwimmer's earlier demonstration of Ross's unwillingness to give up subtly indicated.

The sequence is taken to its comedic peak—and Ross's nadir—when Joey suggests putting on lotion on top of the powder to lube Ross's legs to make the pants move up. The absence of cuts again draws attention to Schwimmer's performance, who finds interesting nuances in the slapstick moment of applying the lotion in order to locate his comedic performance in character-based realism: he utters a muffled vocal exhaling sound when the lotion touches his legs, to indicate a feeling of discomfort at the experience of the lotion's stickiness on his skin (and the mess he is making). Then, when he applies the lotion to the back of his upper thighs, he gives a surprised facial expression, with a glimpse of a smile and upwards tilt of the head (see Fig. 3.3), suggesting that the lotion has been squirted onto sensitive areas where it was not intended

Fig. 3.3 Ross continues to struggle with his leather pants: David Schwimmer in 'The One with All the Resolutions' (5.11)

to go (but is not unwelcome), which is marked by strong non-diegetic laughter. As a final touch of the comedy grounded in realism, while trying to pull the pants back on, Schwimmer lets his lotion drenched right-hand slip from the pants and hits himself in the head with an audible smack. After Joey asks if he is OK, Ross replies, 'They're still … they're still not coming on, man. And the powder and the lotion have made a paste!' His shriek on the word 'paste' and his messy look (with his legs, shirt and the leather pants smeared with lotion) contrast sharply with his desire to handle the situation authoritatively and effectively, anticipating his imminent total defeat.

Finally, after having been abandoned by Joey on the phone and called out by Elisabeth from the living room, Schwimmer plays the action of capitulation as Ross finally has to come clean and face his judgement. Exiting the bathroom, he slowly appears in the door frame,

Fig. 3.4 Ross struggles with his leather pants no more: David Schwimmer in 'The One with All the Resolutions' (5.11)

his legs covered in white splotches from the powder and lotion, holding the pants in a wrapped bundle in front of his crotch (see Fig. 3.4). Again, there is a comedically productive tension between innocence—with his posture and body language invoking the image of a naughty school boy (one who has had a toilet-related 'accident')—and a sexual undertone, as the trousers are covered in white splotches and bundled and held somewhat phallically. In the final moments of the storyline, Elisabeth's shocked reaction is answered with Schwimmer's slow delivery of the line 'I had a problem', speaking in a subdued and slightly child-like voice: Ross is not only semi-dressed, but stripped of his masculine pride and dignity. If the hegemonic definition of manhood is 'a man in power, a man *with* power, and a man of power' (Kimmel 2004, 184), then Ross has here failed on all accounts. Schwimmer 'underplays' this particular moment, by which we mean that he remains physically and vocally passive, which connotes vulnerability. Following the exuberance of Schwimmer's physical movements in the earlier shots, his Ross here is a defeated man, asking for the viewers' empathy, while Schwimmer, as actor, offers them enjoyment and delight in his performance. Finally, it is worth noting that this sequence works both as a standalone comedic scene—which is circulated frequently on social media—but in the context of the narrative and character development, also serves Ross's broader story arc of turning his life around after his recent divorce from Emily, trying to achieve something positive by everyday doing 'one thing that I haven't done before'. (Unfortunately, he seems off to a bad start.)

In the course of the series, David Schwimmer gets several opportunities for these types of performances, often negotiating the embarrassment and social ridicule of his character Ross with the desire to evoke empathy and understanding. *Friends* as a sitcom is interested in the processes of growing up and coming-of-age, and thus frequently dissects the numerous ways its core group performs as participants in all kinds of social interactions. Here, the programme has resonance with the notion of the performativity of everyday life, whereby people's identity is constituted through the daily performance of different roles, as Erving Goffman's (1990 [1959]) seminal work established. Goffman (1967) has a particular interest in how the performance of daily life links to embarrassment, which he identified as a fundamental component in human interaction. We argue that the failure of conducting social interactions and situations successfully and appropriately is located at the centre of *Friends'* comedic and performance sensibility, and most noticeably performed by David Schwimmer, whose Ross should be, in many ways, the most mature of the core group. (He is, after all, a scientist whose life entails high educational achievement, professional success and co-parenting.)

Goffman describes the individual's desire to 'maintain face' as a central force in almost any kind of social interaction, and this clearly informs many of the storylines in *Friends* (as well as, to be sure, other sitcoms), but Schwimmer's pronounced physical skills and his strong modulation of his voice—very evident when he insists that he is 'fine!' (in 10.2)—strikingly animate notions of embarrassment (and the desire to avoid it) in moments that include the ill-advised leather pants, his fake English accent (in 6.4), his over-whitened teeth (in 6.8), his mismanaged tan (in 10.3), and many more incidents in which expectations of certain social encounters and interactions are not fulfilled, and the established codes are violated (Goffman 1967, 105). Indeed, his physical and vocal acting choices at times convey a strong sense that Ross is 'losing it', which strongly speaks to Goffman's suggestion that embarrassment may lead to the experience of the dissolution of the coherent self. Of course, this sense of lack of coherence and control can only be effectively conveyed through an actor as much in control of his craft and material as David Schwimmer is; just as a character's complex relationship with embarrassment is effectively articulated and animated by an actor without self-consciousness. In Ross's struggles with the leather pants and his other experiences of embarrassment, Schwimmer is 'in the moment', a state of unselfconscious, relaxed concentration: in Stanislavskian terms, a state of 'public solitude' in which 'actors tune out anything external' (Carnicke 2010, 9).

In his discussion of multi-camera sitcom performance, Mills argues that 'the actor [is presented] as a skilled performer demonstrating their skills in moments of comic business which […] often rely on excess, usually physical though sometimes emotional or linguistic' (2005, 88). This is clearly the case when David Schwimmer engages with Ross's struggles with leather pants and other social dilemmas. However, the distinction between performance and acting that Mills takes from Josette Féral (1997), namely that the former 'places the performer's body as the subject of the audience's attention' (Mills 2005, 86), does not productively capture Schwimmer's portrayal of Ross Geller. David Schwimmer realises the slapstick and heightened physical comedy through not only strong physical skills—embarrassment is often explicitly hinged around Ross's physicality and the materiality of his being—but also nuanced acting choices grounded in realism and naturalism, asking his audience to relate to Ross's only too human dilemmas, which works to support the programme's strategy of intimacy. We want to suggest that *Friends* offers audiences a dual bond, with both the characters (into whose experiences viewers can emotionally invest) and, crucially, simultaneously also the actors (whose skilled performances they can appreciate). Just as Schwimmer and his colleagues work holistically, so audiences may have holistic, complex relationships with performance in programmes such as *Friends*.

The One with the Hollywood Guest Stars: Wrestling with the Three-Headed Monster

After the success of *Friends* during the early years of its broadcast run, in particular from season 2 onwards, the appearance of celebrity guests, both as one-off cameos or in longer-running supporting roles, became part of the series' approach to casting. Whereas famous actors and personalities in the first season (e.g. *Mad About You*'s Helen Hunt, *ER*'s George Clooney and Noah Wyle or the model Jill Goodacre) were included to boost the series' profile and ratings, provide pop-cultural legitimation and facilitate cross-over promotion for NBC's other prime-time programmes, later guest stars were included for reasons of novelty and originality and often at the request of the guests themselves. (*Friends*' impressive roster includes Chrissie Hynde [2.6], Isabella Rossellini [3.5], Robin Williams and Billy Crystal [3.24], Susan Sarandon [7.15], Gary Oldman [7.23 and 7.24], Alec Baldwin [8.18] and Sean Penn [8.6 and 8.7].)

What is interesting for our argument is to what extent these guests, often renowned dramatic Hollywood actors, succeed or fail in adapting to multi-camera sitcom's particular performance context. For example, the action/reaction performance rhythm, the comedic interaction with the rest of the ensemble and the requirement of staying in character in the prolonged, 'unnatural' pauses during non-diegetic laughter pose a particular and visible challenge for actor Brad Pitt who appears in 'The One with the Rumour' (8.9) as Will, Rachel's old high school nemesis and co-founder of the 'I hate Rachel' club. Pitt's considerable A-list celebrity status, including his (then) high-profile marriage to Jennifer Aniston, provides most of the energy marking his character's first appearance at the door of Monica's apartment to join the others for Thanksgiving dinner. The audience erupts in a loud cheer when he enters, a reaction which was edited down and shortened in the final edit of the show, as Marta Kauffman points out. This response attests to the fact that high-profile guest stars in particular are endowed with an intertextual presence on screen, evoking both their previous body of work and broader star image (Dyer 1998), partly fostered through discourses such as their extra-textual interviews and press coverage, in a process which Marion Jordan (1981, 197) calls 'background resonance', offering a layered cluster of associations for viewers.

The episode's dialogue provides Pitt with a plausible storyline and solid joke material, with a few of them finding (meta) humour in his own stardom and good looks:

> *Ross*: So what are you up to?
> *Will*: I'm a commodities broker.
> *Ross*: Really? Yeah, yeah … that sounds interesting.
> *Will*: Yeah … it's not. But I'm rich and thin.

His character's scripted enmity towards Rachel draws additional humour from his then high-profile relationship with Aniston, who, together with Schwimmer, has the most interactions with him within the show. Interestingly, Pitt noticeably struggles with various aspects of his performance, which has to negotiate both the comedic moments and the character's naturalistic behaviour. For example, his character's joke commenting on the healthy food he brought to the dinner seems staged: 'It's no fat, it's no sugar, it's no dairy … it's no good, throw it out!' The through-line of his thought is not clear as he rushes the last part, which means that the scene reads not in terms of it occurring to his character that the dish is likely to taste bland, but that he (the actor) knows the line. Thus, what is compromised here is the 'illusion of the first time', a challenge for actors working within realism which William Hooker Gillette articulated as follows:

> Now it is a very difficult thing [...] for an actor who knows exactly what he is going to say to behave exactly as though he didn't; to let his thought (apparently) occur to him as he goes along, even though they are there in his mind already; and (apparently) to search for and find words by which to express those thoughts, even though these words are at his tongue's very end. (in Cole and Chinoy 1974, 565)

Pitt's Will should not have his words here at his tongue's very end, but evidently does, which makes his words appear as the line from the script that they are (and are supposed to be only) on an extra-textual level. This differs quite noticeably from, for example, David Schwimmer's approach to dealing with Ross's leather pants, discussed earlier, which Schwimmer clearly rehearsed, but invests with acting choices (e.g. the muffled vocal exhaling sound when the lotion touches his skin, the upwards tilt of the head when the lotion has been squirted onto sensitive areas) that make it seem that his character is experiencing these moments for the first time.

Later in the episode, after Rachel has entered the room and triggered Will's high school trauma, his performance of 'smouldering', repressed aggression through mouthing 'I hate you' to her, is also rushed; and slightly longer beats in between the mouthed words would have attested to the sentiment his character is supposed to be feeling more strongly. He also rushes his advice to Joey about the relationship between food and emotions: 'I actually know what you're talking about, and I'm here to tell you something, friend: you can eat and eat and eat, but nothing will ever fill that void.' As delivered by Pitt with a lack of engagement with punctuation, a more accurate representation of these lines would be: 'I actually know what you're talking about and I'm here to tell you something friend, you can eat and eat and eat but nothing will ever fill that void.' Moments before he mouths to Rachel, when talking to Ross, Will angrily grabs a piece of Thanksgiving decoration, but Pitt readjusts his grip, which makes this physical movement come across as inorganic. His vocal and physical acting choices show Pitt to not be 'in the moment'.

Once Rachel moves over to talk to him, asking if they 'fooled around' at a party during high school, Pitt is again very quick to reply, and could have taken another beat to let Aniston's line land, which would have conveyed a stronger sense of his character listening to her. As already noted, Aniston is very skilled when it comes to 'acting off the line', but the same cannot be said for Pitt here. He not only does not listen well, but moreover through the aggression of his response, 'You are unbelievable', via a forceful vocal tone and a set look on his face, also does not help to set up Aniston's response as necessitated by the script: Aniston's Rachel happily mistakes his comment as a compliment, which does not work, and more ambiguity from Pitt would have seen them play off each other much more effectively.

Once everyone is seated at the dinner table, Pitt's struggles with his performance continue. When, following more aggression from Will (this time intended by the script), Rachel asks him if he has a problem with her, Will replies: 'I don't know – do I?! Do I?!' Pitt then noticeably waits for Lisa Kudrow's Phoebe's line: 'I think you do!' He holds his facial expression, without conveying any kind of further thought or emotional process. Moments later, when he tells Rachel about the 'I hate Rachel' club and that Ross was a member, pointing at him, Ross exclaims: 'No need to point, she knows who Ross is!' Pitt waits before Schwimmer's line and during the non-diegetic laughter, and then when Ross explains that his participation in the club stemmed from his romantic feelings for her, Pitt is visible in the background, seemingly a little unsure where to look before his next line (suggesting that he is uncertain about how the framing and editing of the scene may work). Just before Ross confesses that the club spread a rumour concerning Rachel's gender identity, Pitt corpses a little before his character laughs gleefully. These issues reinforce the fact that Pitt is not 'in the moment'; indeed, they indicate a level of self-consciousness. As Cassidy and Knox note, 'self-consciousness (which is to be distinguished from self-awareness) has long been identified as a hindrance to (good) acting, if not a signifier of bad acting, in both actor and actor training discourses' (2016).

Overall, Pitt's performance in the episode is marked by a weak through-line, by which we mean that he does not shape Will's emotional arc sufficiently: he is a character whose high school 'trauma', thought to be dealt with and in the past, slowly re-emerges to comic effect in front of everybody. This lack of shaping links to weaknesses in his vocal performance: of course, vocal performance is complexly intertwined with sound technology (Robertson Wojcik 2006), but it is evident that Pitt rushes some of his dialogue, slurs the line about Rachel living 'in her little Rachel-land' and delivers his confrontations to Rachel without enough modulation. From the coughed 'typical' to his screaming for 'yams', the similar cadence and rhythm of speech render Will as somewhat static, with important gearshifts in emotion and/or thought missed both within and across his lines. This reflects the importance of vocal acting for multi-camera sitcom, contrasting with the modulation of pitch, register and texture to be found in the vocal performances of the core cast (especially Schwimmer and LeBlanc). Moreover, it contributes to an absence of layering and insufficient building of the performance, which could and should have mapped out more convincingly how this character gets to the point he ultimately arrives at, by for example seeding his future 'meltdown' more earlier.

Having presented our analysis of his struggles, we do not intend to suggest that Brad Pitt is a mediocre or unskilled actor. Quite the opposite; his acting work from around the same time period as his *Friends* appearance (e.g. *Seven* [1995], *12 Monkeys* [1995], for which he won a Golden Globe, *Fight Club* [1999]) already demonstrates his ability as an engaging and versatile actor who utilises a naturalist approach to portray complex characters. His performance in the infamous final scene of *Seven*, when his character realises the horrifying content of the cardboard box, particularly deserves recognition; and even though Pitt's acting is arguably 'always intertwined with his celebrity' (Schaberg and Bennett 2014, 7), as Linda Ruth Williams (2011) has noted, he has over the course of his career managed to secure respect for his body of work rather than just his good looks. What we wish to articulate with our analysis of his performance in *Friends* is how even an actor with his level of experience and success may struggle with not only the actual experience of performing in front of a live studio audience and a multi-camera set up—Aniston has commented that Pitt was 'so nervous' (in Wild 2004, 156)—but also in comparison with the distinctly holistic performance style marking the *Friends* ensemble cast. For example, Pitt's wait during the non-diegetic laughter after Ross tells Will that there is 'no need to point' is located right next to Schwimmer wordlessly offering Aniston's Rachel a dish in supplication (see Fig. 3.5). (In addition to successfully acting off the line, the strengths of the *Friends* core cast further include not 'waiting out' the pauses for the audience laughter, filling them instead with acting choices that do 'not [...] signal comic intentions' [Roof 2018, 96].)

Fig. 3.5 Brad Pitt watches as David Schwimmer fills the pause in 'The One with the Rumour' (8.6)

Brad Pitt is not the only Hollywood A-lister who struggles in their guest appearance on the show (and far from the only one who experienced nervousness, as the interviews in Wild [2004] show). Though more successful in portraying Chandler's revenge-driven childhood friend Susie in 'The One after the Superbowl' (2.13), the performance of Julia Roberts in *Friends* also bears out some difficulties. She is convincing in her scenes with Matthew Perry, believably seducing Chandler, but her climactic outbreak—part victory dance, part nervous breakdown—feels out of character and reads as generalised, too big and repetitive (especially through her hand flapping). In contrast, the performance of Tom Selleck—well-known from *Magnum, P.I.*—as Monica's periodical boyfriend Richard is more successful, convincing and integrated into the ensemble cast's performance style. For instance, in 'The One where Ross and Rachel … You Know' (2.15), Richard, a friend of Monica's parents, meets her again after many years while she works as a caterer for a party. In a short conversation about the different ways that friends and family have expressed empathy towards him following his recent divorce, Selleck's Richard subtly demonstrates the 'sympathetic head tilt' he has been receiving and his 'I'm OK head bop', illustrating both his character's competence in social performance and the actor's ability to convey that trait convincingly.

In the course of the series, Richard interacts well with the other characters, just as Selleck successfully plays off the other actors. This is partly due to his character construction as an older father figure, with a recurring narrative emphasis put on his age difference and suave masculinity, which is productively contrasted with Chandler and Joey. (In 'The One where Old Yeller Dies' [2.19], they are impressed by how Richard tips people. The smooth gesture of 'slipping a waiter money' signals Richard's mature adulthood and experience, both of which Joey and Chandler lack and, crucially, attempt and fail to perform. This failure of performance is still present many episodes later, when Chandler clumsily fails to slip a waiter money when trying to secure a restaurant table in 7.10.) Moreover, Selleck utilises a restrained performance style, centred around his facial features and (calm) physical presence, not reliant on exuberant body language or elements of 'clowning'. Unlike Roberts, he is not concerned about filling the space of the multi-camera studio with his performance, adopting a restrained performance style which requires one of the most important qualities an actor can possess, namely confidence (Cassidy and Knox 2019).

Confidence—to be restrained or not—also marks the guest appearance by Bruce Willis, who plays Paul Stevens, the intimidating father of Ross's girlfriend Elisabeth (Alexandra Holden) in a number of episodes in the sixth season. Winning an Emmy for Outstanding Guest Actor in a Comedy Series, Willis's presence within the show demonstrates how *Friends*' approach to casting guest stars takes a keen interest in playing with and against the guests' star image, in ways that interestingly intersect with character-based realism. Willis's performance as Paul successfully parodies his own taciturn, Hollywood 'hard man' persona, developed in the *Die Hard* film franchise. In 'The One with the Ring' (6.23), Paul breaks down about his childhood trauma, crying in

Rachel's lap, and moments later screams 'Chicken Boy', the nickname given to him by his childhood bullies, in a somewhat chicken-like manner. Here, his sobbing is not an embodied act, with a slight disjuncture between the distressed sounds he makes and his face; and the few tears visible on his face have been produced by a tear stick. However, this reads not as a performance that fails to be grounded in realism, but as Bruce Willis having fun and enjoying playing against his 'hard man' persona, drawing the comedic acting abilities that he developed during his time as the lead in the successful 1980s series *Moonlighting*. For viewers, the scene offers the pleasures of watching *Die Hard*'s John McClane screech 'Chicken Boy', and of seeing that Willis enjoys it; which is detectible through the hint of a smile. Alex Clayton refers to this as the 'comic twinkle': 'Difficult to pinpoint but impossible to ignore, the "twinkle" is that oblique bodily disclosure of comic intent – call it irony, cheekiness or a certain sense of "I-know-you-know-I-know"' (Clayton 2012, 51). Not dissimilar pleasures are presented in 'The One where Paul's the Man' (6.22), when Willis's Paul gives himself a pep talk in front of a mirror, singing a snippet from The Miracles' *Love Machine*. So, as far as Willis's presence within *Friends* is concerned, a performance grounded in character-based realism is not as much the focus as the relationship between performance and star image, and the viewing pleasures it may offer, are. (This also applies to other star guest appearances in the show, such as Gary Oldman's spitting actor.) It is worth adding that Willis fully commits to this interplay, screeching 'Chicken Boy' in a chicken-like manner and growling a deep roar after his *Love Machine* dance.

Brad Pitt's and Bruce Willis's guest appearances give a useful indication of the complex ways in which performance can function within multi-camera sitcom. Mills has paid some attention to unsuccessful sitcom acting, commenting: 'Trying to make sense of, and define, "bad" acting is virtually impossible and certainly comes down to the individual' (2005, 92). As our analysis above has sought to demonstrate, this is not necessarily the case: attentive engagement to material detail that is informed by established, Stanislavskian-based discourses on acting can uncover such important issues as (not) being 'in the moment', (not) acting off the line, (not) preserving the illusion of the first time, (not) developing characterisation diachronically and (not) texturising performance sufficiently. Through these issues, Brad Pitt's guest presence contrasts with the performance dexterity of *Friends*' core cast and other guest stars. What these issues point to, individually and accumulatively, is the notion of truthfulness (or lack thereof). 'Another problematic and contested term, "truth" is a key concept within Stanislavskian approaches to acting and frequently (especially within actor and actor training discourses) considered as a key component of good acting' (Cassidy and Knox 2016). As Trevor Rawlins (2012, 40) has noted, good acting contains, and bad acting lacks, a leap of the imagination, whereby the good actor experiences something as if it were for real. Such truthfulness is absent for Pitt in *Friends*, but, as we will next explore, present in Matt LeBlanc's performance of Joey.

The One with Rachel and Joey: Matt LeBlanc and Emotionally Truthful Performance

Friends puts performance as a discourse both in terms of psycho-social as well as more artificial and mediated contexts at the centre of its narrative sensibility. In other words, just as *Friends* is a show about humour, as we noted in Chapter 2, so it is also a show about performance. This is most obviously noticeable in one of the central characters' profession, as Joey Tribbiani is an actor with experience across film, theatre and television, which the programme's narrative repeatedly explores. Joey is a character partly defined by and through a playful deconstruction of performance, from 'smell the fart acting' (2.11) and parodying the soap opera genre—he stars as Doctor Drake Ramoray on the fictionalised version of the soap opera *Days of Our Lives*—to the effects of the precarious working conditions of a freelance actor by showing him going to unsuccessful auditions and revealing in 'The One where Rachel Is Late' (8.22) that Chandler paid for his living expenses over several years.

Joey is mostly shown to be a bad actor, partly because of a limited understanding of the complexity of the craft of acting, but also because of a lack of intelligence and awareness (both of himself as an adult in a complex world and of the psycho-social group dynamics surrounding him). It would be fascinating to explore, to draw on Martin Esslin's words: 'How, in fact, does a good actor act a bad actor?' (1987, 72). However, our focus here lies not with those moments when LeBlanc plays Joey while he is acting, but with how LeBlanc approaches his performance when this is not marked by such self-referentiality. Mills has addressed how the particular characterisation of Joey impacts on LeBlanc's approach to performance by arguing that:

> Joey […] is performed differently, for his funniness rests on an unintelligence of which he's not fully aware, and which therefore hasn't required Matt LeBlanc to demonstrate a duality of character in his performance; at least, not a duality which his character is aware of. (2005, 86)

This, of course, does not mean that the role of Joey is easy or easier to perform; and LeBlanc regularly demonstrates such skills as comedic timing and modulated vocal inflections.

LeBlanc also gets some opportunities to portray Joey's deeper feelings, including in ways that serve to evoke audience empathy. For example, in 'The One where Ross Hugs Rachel' (6.2), viewers can observe a number of nuanced acting choices when Chandler tells Joey that he is moving out of his shared apartment and in with Monica. Both Matthew Perry's delivery of the line 'I'm gonna be moving out, man!'—delivered with diminishing volume, signalling that this is difficult to say—and LeBlanc's stunned, but subdued reaction are based in naturalism. This markedly non-comedic moment elicits an audible reaction within the soundtrack, namely, a non-diegetic, muffled sigh of empathy for Joey. More significantly, several stylistic elements complement and enhance the acting choices. Through blocking and editing, Chandler is presented in a two-shot with Monica when Perry utters the revelatory line, employing a body language that emphasises Chandler's uncomfortableness (with much gesturing and hand rubbing).

Here, Monica and Chandler are presented as the adult couple about to move in together, taking the relationship to the next step—without Joey, whose eyes briefly widen, bringing a child-like quality to his face. The contrast between the child-like Joey and Monica's and Chandler's position as adults is further emphasised by the costumes and props:

Fig. 3.6 'I'm gonna be moving out, man!': Joey (Matt LeBlanc) gets hurt in 'The One where Ross Hugs Rachel' (6.2)

Monica is wearing a loose purple blouse alluding to maternity wear (which is used as a running gag throughout the episode), and Chandler is 'presentably' dressed for work in his shirt and tie (with two purple stripes, which connect him visually with Monica's 'motherly' blouse and her apartment), whereas Joey is dressed in a casual grey sweater, holding a water bottle like a school boy.

The camera then cuts to Joey's reaction, framing him alone at the table, positioned, as Fig. 3.6 shows, behind a bowl containing several large pineapples, with the green tops evoking the image of a bush which he hides behind as a barrier (reinforced through the back of the opposite chair and a water bottle). That this barrier offers insufficient protection for his feelings is confirmed when Joey moves to exit the apartment: LeBlanc delivers the lines 'Wow; well, uh, hey, really happy for you guys, congratulations! See you later!' The quaver in LeBlanc's voice in 'See you later!' indicates that Joey's initial stunned feelings are rapidly giving away to upset, and he tries to run away in order to not put a damper on his friends' happiness. This reflects an effective gearshift within the lines, which Brad Pitt struggled with, helping to make this an emotionally affective scene, which is reflected in the audible reactions on the episode's soundtrack as well as paratextually, as a clip of this scene on YouTube has been tagged with the description 'Friends—The End of an Era, Part 1—Where Everybody Finds Out' (Favorite Videos 2016).

As Joey, Matt LeBlanc has comparatively fewer emotionally 'serious' storylines to tackle than the rest of the core cast, but he is presented with a very particular acting challenge from the eighth season, namely Joey's romantic feelings for Rachel. This storyline proved controversial with many fans and critics, to whom it felt somewhat 'incestuous' and unconvincing. (Certainly, their developing feelings could have been seeded in earlier seasons beyond their attraction in the alternative storyline in the two-parter 'The One that Could Have Been' [6.15 and 6.16], which is abruptly ended by a drunk Rachel's need to throw up when they kiss, ending on a note of friendship.) Moreover, Kevin S. Bright commented in our interview with him that Matt LeBlanc was initially 'really against' this storyline, because he felt that it contradicted Joey's characterisation as a loyal friend (in this case, to Ross). His initial reservations notwithstanding, LeBlanc successfully engages with this difficult acting challenge in ways that are not only truthful but also draw on emotional truth. Noting that it is an unstable term frequently found in Stanislavskian-informed acting contexts, Knox and Cassidy usefully define emotional truth as 'acting that imaginatively utilizes an actor's personal experiences to produce a performance that is read as believable by an audience' (2019, 198–199, note 4). It is most appropriately applied for dramatically/emotionally difficult performance material, which can be found when Joey finally finds the courage to reveal his love to Rachel in 'The One where Joey Tells Rachel' (8.16); with LeBlanc not only engaging with his character's struggle for words non-comedically, but also showing his character's deep concern about the impact on his friend.

When Joey gears himself up to tell Rachel, a broken off smile flashes across LeBlanc's face, he exhales audibly and moves his lips like his character is trying out the words that, as he knows, are likely to sound strange and unexpected to Rachel, and may feel physically unfamiliar in his mouth, given that Joey is a serial womaniser. LeBlanc very briefly shakes his head with a quick smile just before Joey utters the actual words, indicating that his character not only cannot believe that he is about to trigger a paradigm shift in his friendship with Rachel, but also that he is slightly amused that he—Joey 'How you doin'?!' Tribbiani—is so nervous and tongue-tied with a woman. These acting choices indicate a subtlety of performance by LeBlanc and a level of self-awareness on the level of the character. When Rachel slowly realises that Joey is not, in fact, joking, LeBlanc continues with his non-comedic, naturalistic approach to illustrating his character's upset: there is a stiffness around his mouth that indicates a tension within Joey between the urge to cry and trying not to, which is finally broken with his announcement that he will leave. The following exchange, in which Rachel's tears finally make Joey cry, is played briefly for comedic effect, but LeBlanc grounds these emotions immediately by showing that Joey is deeply affected by Rachel's fear of losing him as a friend. What is most noteworthy here is that his exclamation 'There we go' as her crying is setting him off and he moves to hug her, uses a comedic cadence associated with Joey. However, this familiarity only serves to highlight how much this character has emotionally matured over the seasons (and that the actor is fully capable of handling this development), as he reassures her that their friendship will survive this difficulty. When Joey does so, his face has a look of intensity and emotional depth (see Fig. 3.7) that viewers may not readily associate with the character, but which emerges organically from LeBlanc's acting choices and reads as fully believable on the level of characterisation.

As contested as the 'Joey and Rachel' storyline across *Friends*' final three seasons was, it served the purpose of providing Joey with a character arc of maturity and emotional depth, and Matt LeBlanc with the opportunity to tackle this development through a holistic approach to performance. This results in an emotionally truthful performance of

Fig. 3.7 Emotionally truthful performance: Rachel (Jennifer Aniston) and Joey (Matt LeBlanc) in 'The One where Joey Tells Rachel' (8.16)

Joey's feelings of hope, bewilderment, pain, concern and love, which elicits audience engagement and empathy, in ways that speak to and support the programme's overall strategy of intimacy.

Conclusion

As this chapter has demonstrated, performance is a core component of *Friends*' strategy of intimacy and enduring success. We will now move towards a conclusion by reflecting on the particular production practices that enabled and supported the achievements of the core cast. One of these practices concerns collaboration, as David Schwimmer's following reflections show:

> I would give so much credit to David and Marta and the other writers, because they *really* invited our ideas. They created an atmosphere in which we could play *and fail* and pitch stuff, and because of that it wasn't about any individual, it was about all of us trying to come up with the funniest and the best and the most emotional material we could. [...] That kind of collaboration with your director, with those writers, and with the other actors – it's a huge high, and it spoils you for life. It does.'
> (in Littlefield 2012, 179, emphases in original)

It is not uncommon that long-running shows begin to cater to actors' specific strengths and skill sets, but what Schwimmer's words point to is a strong level of trust and investment in the actors, who were afforded a much more uncommon degree of creative agency.

This is further detectible in our interview with Kevin S. Bright, who directed more episodes of the show (54) than any other individual. He articulates his approach to directing in the terms of a 'ringmaster making the score work':

> You're being a choreographer, certainly; you're telling the actors where to stand, if you need them to favour a certain camera when they are delivering a line or being more upstage. You're staging around practicalities. [...] And then the actors ultimately are going to have thoughts about it, and conversations will break out about what they think about the script that day, et cetera. It's not a linear path. [....] But you trust them as the authorities on the characters. The consistency of vision was always the consistency of the characters, and the actors inform that so much.

It is possible that this collaborative approach between director and actors was set up by James Burrows, who directed several episodes of the first season, including the pilot, and who influenced Bright's approach to directing. Burrows takes a non-prescriptive approach in that, as he explained to us, he does 'not stage anything in my head until I work with the actors' and that one of his main tasks is to 'make the actors feel comfortable with each other'. (This is, of course, not to suggest that Burrows takes a laissez-faire approach: Christine Becker notes that 'he barely watches the stage action. Instead, [...] he turns his back on the stage and the video monitors completely, paces around behind the crew, and listens to the comedy play out to ensure that the proper rhythms are being maintained' [2008]. However, as Burrows clarified to us, since the advent of video assist, he watches 'four monitors in front of me, which helps me stay ahead and catch mistakes' and 'when an actor messes up a line, I intervene straightaway'.)

So, while television is often described as a 'writer's medium', particularly in light of debates about 'quality television' and legitimation (Newman and Levine 2012), the importance given to the core cast and their creative input speaks to the deeply collaborative nature of television production. Collaboration is one of the determinants of television acting identified by Roberta Pearson (2010), with others including status, time and genre. We have already indicated at the beginning of this chapter that issues of status played out very interestingly during *Friends*' production, with the actors agreeing to give each other notes on their performance and to collectively bargaining (which involved Jennifer Aniston and David Schwimmer taking a pay cut at one point). As far as time—'the most precious resource in television production' (Pearson 2010, 167)—is concerned, Pearson has pointed out that:

> Television actors have minimal rehearsal and need to get the shot right on the first take – retakes waste time. Time constraints exert tremendous pressure on television actors, making their jobs in some respects more difficult than that of their theatre and film counterparts. (ibid.)

Here, it is interesting to observe that, while formal rehearsal has generally become increasingly scarce in film and television production, and that performance in multi-camera contexts is not as 'pieced together in post-production' (Hewett 2015, 79) as it is with single-camera production, the *Friends* core cast took a particular stance towards rehearsal time: they asked for this to be considerably reduced.

As Kevin S. Bright recalled for us with an illuminating level of detail:

> In the beginning, we shot more takes; I would say the maximum that we would shoot on a given scene was four takes. And if it wasn't working in four, then we would wait until the audience went away and maybe rethink things after the show and then re-shoot a little piece. In the first

year and a half, we would go pretty late. We would start at 7 o'clock and we might go until 2 o'clock in the morning, or 3 o'clock. [...] A lot of it had to do with the perfectionism qualities by Marta and David and myself; when scenes weren't good enough, they had to be re-written on the stage; when scenes didn't look right, they needed to be re-shot or re-staged, or we would do pick-ups. [...] Basically, I think we were wearing the actors out [...] and there was a little bit of friction on the set and we made a commitment to make a greater effort to get the show done in a more expeditious way. So, we were able to do that and basically scale down the entire process. [...] All the rehearsal time was trimmed way down. We would start at 10 o'clock on Tuesday, for example, getting that newly revamped table script that we're seeing for the first time, and we had to show the writers a run through by 3 o'clock that same day. Then a new script on Wednesday, and you had the same thing again; the cast basically had to be out of there by 4 o'clock. And then on Thursdays the agreement was that they needed to be out by 6 o'clock. For the whole camera blocking for the entire episode, we had from 9 o'clock in the morning until 6 o'clock at night, plus lunches and everything. So really, speed is a tremendous asset in sitcom directing.

Picking up on the *Friends*' production 'mantra' by Kauffman, Crane and Bright, that 'Good isn't good enough' (as Kauffman summed it up for us), Bright's memory here attests to the production's investment in and concessions given to the actors, which put more pressure on other production staff. The decision was made to accommodate the actors' process, which in this case was informed by the core cast's understanding that too much rehearsal time can make a performance 'lock down', lose freshness and energy (which are vital to the illusion of the first time). This attests to the fact that the core cast was becoming increasingly familiar with their characters; 'over the course of a long-running series [television actors] spend far more time with a character than they would in the theatre or the cinema' (Pearson 2010, 168). Thus, Aniston, Cox, Kudrow, LeBlanc, Perry and Schwimmer could do their weekly preparation, working out beats, movements and nuances, in a time-efficient manner, which reflects their (and other team members') effective collaboration, professionalism, creative skills and confidence.

3 The One where They Tame the Three-Headed Monster … 119

To conclude, as our analysis in this chapter has shown, *Friends* as a sitcom strongly relies on and foregrounds performance. Indeed, it provides a meta-commentary on performance (especially through Joey's work as an actor), which unfortunately exceeds the scope of this chapter. Much more deserves to be said about *Friends* and performance, such as the ways in which the main actors' training and/or prior professional experience informs their acting choices (e.g. how Lisa Kudrow's background in improvisation shows itself in her portrayal of Phoebe), or how the main cast constructs and develops their performances and characterisations diachronically. (For example, their signature catchphrases, such as Joey's 'How you doin'?', Chandler's 'Could I *be* anymore …' and Monica's 'I know!' are not schematically repeated throughout the series, but successfully utilised as comedic cues because of their variations in delivery, as a fan compilation of Courteney Cox's various renditions of Monica's 'I know!' vividly illustrates [Pantano 2014].) There is also more to be said about how the performances and their readings by audiences work in layered, complex ways. (Just as 'audiences know that comic performers know that they are being comic even as these performers pretend not to know while the audience always know they know' [Roof 2018, 96], so additionally, over the course of its ten seasons, the programme's core actors become more confident, which adds a certain layer of performativity for viewers, but still grounds their acting in character-based realism as they inhabit their roles more fully.)

What we have been concerned to demonstrate in this chapter is that nuanced performance in *Friends* is not, as might be commonly assumed (given the critical bias detailed in Chapter 4), limited or impeded by the multi-camera set-up, with genre being another determinant of television acting (Pearson 2010). Rather, the multi-camera production style facilitates and quite often makes space—both figuratively and literally—for a distinctly holistic performance which finds complex comedic moments without sacrificing its characters' emotional and psycho-social truths. In emphasising performance as distinctly holistic, we join Knox and Cassidy (2019), who highlight that the binary views that often inform (if not overshadow) discussions of acting, do little to help our understanding of acting and what actors do. As such, we conclude that *Friends* has offered a 'blue print' for the multi-camera situation comedies developed and conceived in its trail, some of which, such as *How I Met Your Mother*, have taken up *Friends'* invitation to engage with a distinctly holistic approach to performance which can help to generate an intimate bond between the actors, the characters and the viewers.

Bibliography

Becker, Christine. 2008. Acting for the Cameras: Performance in the Multi-Camera Sitcom. *Mediascape*. http://www.tft.ucla.edu/mediascape/Spring08_ActingForTheCameras.html. Accessed 1 June 2019.

Benedetti, Jean. 2005. *The Art of the Actor: The Essential History of Acting, from Classical Times to the Present Day*. London: Methuen.

Bourdieu, Pierre. 2010 [1984]. *Distinction: A Social Critique of the Judgement of Taste*. London and New York: Routledge.

Buckingham, Lydia. 2019. Analysing Aniston: Tonal Complexity and Non-comedic Approaches to Sitcom Performance. In *Television Performance*, ed. Lucy Fife Donaldson and James Walters, 209–223. London: Palgrave Macmillan.

Cantrell, Tom, and Christopher Hogg. 2017. *Acting in British Television*. London: Palgrave Macmillan.

Carnicke, Sharon Marie. 2010. Stanislavsky's System: Pathways for the Actor. In *Actor Training*, 2nd ed, ed. Alison Hodge, 1–25. London and New York: Routledge.

Cassidy, Gary, and Simone Knox. 2015. What Actors Do: Jennifer Aniston in *Friends*. *CST Online*. https://cstonline.net/what-actors-do-jennifer-aniston-in-friends-by-gary-cassidy-and-simone-knox/#_ftn1. Accessed 1 June 2019.

Cassidy, Gary, and Simone Knox. 2016. What Actors Do: Alec Baldwin in *30 Rock* (Part 1). *CST Online*. https://cstonline.net/what-actors-do-alec-baldwin-in-30-rock-part-i-by-gary-cassidy-and-simone-knox/. Accessed 1 June 2019.

Cassidy, Gary, and Simone Knox. 2019. An Actor Diversifies: A Diachronic Examination of the Work and Career of Tony Curran. In *Television Performance*, ed. Lucy Fife Donaldson and James Walters, 168–187. London: Palgrave Macmillan.

Clayton, Alex. 2012. Play-Acting: A Theory of Comedic Performance. In *Theorizing Film Acting*, ed. Aaron Taylor, 47–61. London: Routledge.

Cole, Toby, and Helen Krich Chinoy (eds.). 1974. *Actors on Acting*. New York: Crown Publishers.
Dyer, Richard. 1998. *Stars*, 2nd ed. London: BFI.
Esslin, Martin. 1987. Actors Acting Actors. *Modern Drama* 30 (1): 72–79. https://doi.org/10.1353/mdr.1987.0044.
Favorite Videos. 2016. Friends—The End of an Era, Part 1—Where Everybody Finds Out. https://www.youtube.com/watch?v=dr5lilVmgb8. Accessed 1 June 2019.
Feasey, Rebecca. 2008. *Masculinity and Popular Television*. Edinburgh: Edinburgh University Press.
Féral, Josette. 1997. Performance and Theatricality: The Subject Demystified. In *Mimesis, Masochism, and Mime: The Politics of Theatricality in Contemporary French Thought*, ed. Timothy Murray, 289–300. Ann Arbor: University of Michigan Press.
Goffman, Erving. 1967. *Interaction Ritual*. New York: Pantheon Books.
Goffman, Erving. 1990 [1959]. *The Presentation of Self in Everyday Life*. London: Penguin.
Gordon, Robert. 2006. *The Purpose of Playing: Modern Acting Theories in Perspective*. Ann Arbor: University of Michigan Press.
Hewett, Richard. 2015. The Changing Determinants of UK Television Acting. *Critical Studies in Television* 10 (1): 73–90. https://doi.org/10.7227/CST.10.1.6.
Hight, Craig. 2010. *Television Mockumentary: Reflexivity, Satire and a Call to Play*. Manchester: Manchester University Press.
Johnson, Victoria E. 2012. Jennifer Aniston and Tina Fey: Girls with Glasses. In *Shining in Shadows: Movie Stars of the 2000s*, ed. Murray Pomerance, 50–69. New Brunswick and London: Rutgers University Press.
Jordan, Marion. 1981. A Study of the Relationship Between the Novel and the Film (for Cinema and Television), with Special Reference to the Novels of Henry James. Master's dissertation, University of Warwick.
Kauffman, Marta, and David Crane. 1993. *Insomnia Café* Pitch. 7 December.
Kimmel, Michael. 2004. Masculinity as Homophobia: Fear, Shame, and Silence in the Construction of Gender Identity. In *Feminism and Masculinities*, ed. Peter Murphy, 182–199. Oxford: Oxford University Press.
Knox, Simone, and Gary Cassidy. 2019. *Game of Thrones*: Investigating British Acting. In *Transatlantic Television Drama: Industries, Programs, & Fans*, ed. Matt Hills, Michele Hilmes, and Roberta Pearson, 181–200. Oxford: Oxford University Press.

Littlefield, Warren. 2012. *Top of the Rock: Inside the Rise and Fall of Must See TV*. New York: Anchor Books.

Mills, Brett. 2005. *Television Sitcom*. London: Palgrave Macmillan.

Mills, Brett. 2010. Contemporary Comedy Performance in British Sitcom. In *Genre and Performance: Film and Television*, ed. Christine Cornea, 130–147. Manchester: Manchester University Press.

Mundy, John, and Glyn White. 2012. *Laughing Matters: Understanding Film, Television and Radio Comedy*. Manchester: Manchester University Press.

Newman, Michael Z., and Elana Levine. 2012. *Legitimating Television: Media Convergence and Cultural Status*. New York and London: Routledge.

Pantano, Angelo. 2014. Friends Monica Geller 'I Know' Compilation. https://www.youtube.com/watch?v=ztXU-X0-Vkc. Accessed 1 June 2019.

Pearson, Roberta. 2010. The Multiple Determinants of Television Acting. In *Genre and Performance: Film and Television*, ed. Christine Cornea, 166–183. Manchester: Manchester University Press.

Rawlins, Trevor. 2012. Studying Acting: An Investigation into Contemporary Approaches to Professional Actor Training in the UK. Unpublished PhD thesis, University of Reading.

Robertson Wojcik, Pamela. 2006. The Sound of Film Acting. *Journal of Film and Video* 58 (1–2): 71–83.

Roof, Judith. 2018. *The Comic Event: Comedic Performance from the 1950s to the Present*. New York: Bloomsbury.

Rowe Karlyn, Kathleen. 1995. *The Unruly Woman: Gender and the Genres of Laughter*. Austin: University of Texas Press.

Schaberg, Christopher, and Robert Bennett. 2014. Introduction. In *Deconstructing Brad Pitt*, ed. Christopher Schaberg and Robert Bennett, 1–8. London: Bloomsbury.

Stanislavski, Constantine. 2013 [1937]. *An Actor Prepares*. London and New York: Bloomsbury.

Wild, David. 2004. *Friends …'Til the End: The One with All Ten Years*. London: Headline.

Williams, Linda Ruth. 2011. Brangelina: Celebrity, Credibility, and the Composite Überstar. In *Shining in Shadows: Movie Stars of the 2000s*, ed. Murray Pomerance, 200–219. New Brunswick and London: Rutgers University Press.

Television

Cheers (1982–1993), USA: NBC.
Days of Our Lives (1965–present), USA: NBC.
ER (1994–2009), USA: NBC.
Friends (1994–2004), USA: NBC.
How I Met Your Mother (2005–2014), USA: CBS.
Mad About You (1992–1999), USA: NBC.
Magnum, P.I. (1980–1988), USA: CBS.
Moonlighting (1985–1989), USA: ABC.
Will & Grace (1998–2006, 2018–present), USA: NBC.

Film

Bogdanovich, P. 1972. *What's Up, Doc?* USA: Warner Bros.
Fincher, D. 1995. *Seven*. USA: New Line Cinema.
Fincher, D. 1999. *Fight Club*. USA: 20th Century Fox.
Gilliam, T. 1995. *12 Monkeys*. USA: Universal Pictures.
McTiernan, J. 1988. *Die Hard*. USA: 20th Century Fox.

4

The One where They Look at Monica's Apartment: Style, Space, Set Design

As the introduction to this book has noted, the early 2000s saw much interest and critical acclaim within industry, press/critic and academic discourses bestowed onto the single-camera sitcom. A natural (if not inevitable) point of comparison for single-camera sitcom (which of course rarely relies literally on only one camera) has proven to be the multi-camera sitcom. Its production methods are broadly marked by the use of a proscenium arch/fourth wall spatial arrangement for the soundstage or studio space, shooting and editing under close-to-live conditions, and audible presence of the live audience and/or laugh track. Pointing to the genre's theatrical origins in music hall and Vaudeville performance, this long-standing approach to sitcom production has come under much criticism in the acclaim bestowed upon single-camera shows, as though praise for the latter inevitably necessitated dismissal of the former. Indeed, the 'three-headed monster' has been constructed and serving as something of a 'bad object' in discourses on single-camera sitcoms.

Probably the most sustained critique of multi-camera sitcom style can be found in Jeremy Butler's (2010) work, in which he refers to multi-camera sitcom as having a 'zero-degree style'. Butler here draws on John T. Caldwell's earlier discussion that had identified that 'television entered an *ascetic* period during the first half of the 1970s' (1995, 56, emphasis in original). He argued that sitcoms such as those produced by Norman Lear and MTM as well as primetime dramas such as *Columbo* were 'remarkably conservative in terms of style' (ibid., 56), reflecting their mass-production contexts (including limited time and budgets). Caldwell further noted that in the case of sitcoms, 'this abhorrence of style was a throwback to the golden age of early live anthology drama' (ibid.), thus providing useful links to notions of authorship and prestige to such 'relevant' shows as *Maude* and *Rhoda*.

Butler continues Caldwell's understanding of multi-camera style as 'antistyle', taking issue with the 'approximate, imprecise framing – as cameras struggle to follow the action' (2010, 193). He finds sitcoms such as *The Honeymooners* (1955–1956) or *The New Adventures of Old Christine* (2006–2010) wanting in comparison to the stylistic flourishes to be found in *Citizen Kane* and the films by 'meticulous visual stylist' (ibid.) Alfred Hitchcock, utilising the particular auteurial prestige afforded such film-making to further his argument. In terms of multi-camera sitcom style, Butler also identifies, amongst other issues, a very restricted use of the cameras that work to capture performance in eye-level medium, medium close-up and long shots, within mostly shallow sets lit blandly by high-key lighting.

According to the view shared by Caldwell and Butler, multi-camera sitcom style is, at best, efficient, functional and cost-effective. But more to the point, it is considered to be determined by restrictions and limitations, 'empty and meagre' (Caldwell 1995, 372, note 95). In their eyes, multi-camera sitcom has no style—or no style they deem worthy of recognition—and is marked by flatness and, above all, lack. As Butler puts it in no uncertain terms:

> The proscenium sitcom, with its visual poverty, warrants little more than a distracted glance at the screen. In the televisual sitcom, as Caldwell contends regarding televisuality in general, are 'images that spectacularize, dazzle, and elicit gazelike viewing'. (2010, 215)

The 'televisual sitcom' Butler here refers to is, unsurprisingly, the single-camera sitcom; and not only do Butler and Caldwell view multi-camera sitcom as not offering aesthetic pleasures, but also as not being truly televisual. In contradistinction to the single-camera sitcom's frequent engagement with 'television's stylistic capabilities' (Caldwell 1995, 57), which draws 'attention to the televisual apparatus or to televisual stylishness' (ibid., 58), they see multi-camera sitcom's 'effaced style' (ibid., 59) as aligned with theatre and older conceptions of television as a medium of relay. Butler articulates this broader distinction as 'not between single-camera and multiple-camera modes of production, but between a schema organized to capture live performance and one organized to allow the medium itself to perform' (2010, 197).

There are a number of issues worth reflecting on here, some of which have already been articulated by Michael Z. Newman and Elana Levine in their work on how certain types of television may (or may not) become legitimated. They point out that Caldwell and Butler adopt 'a film-centered conception of television style, one that emphasizes features such as camerawork and editing' (Newman and Levine 2012, 164), and which 'fails to recognize the style of a theatrical genre like the traditional, multi-cam sitcom in a positive sense' (ibid., 165). Building on their work, it is our view that that the approach exemplified by Caldwell and Butler displays a limited understanding of television style, in its privileging of notions of the cinematic—a term which has been usefully problematised by Deborah L. Jaramillo (2013)—and neglect of other notable aspects of *mise-en-scène*. Moreover, it also does not quite grasp what the aesthetic achievements of the use of camera and editing for multi-camera sitcom may indeed be.

Caldwell and Butler have valued single-camera sitcom as televisual in a cinematised sense; and Newman and Levine have (not wrongly) referred to multi-camera sitcom in terms of the theatrical, insisting that this style should not be considered 'deficient in its difference' (2012, 165). We, however, want to argue that a multi-camera sitcom like *Friends* is very *televisual*. Here, we use this term not via the prism of Caldwell's earlier use of televisuality. We wish to suggest that it will be useful for television scholarship to not feel restricted by Caldwell's very particular, historically bounded use of that term, but to move forward with a broader definition that concerns qualities, practices and attributes that relate to the (constantly evolving) medium. Through its televisuality, *Friends* offers particular aesthetic pleasures that invite and reward more than a 'distracted glance', hinged around the notion of intimacy.

As we noted in the introduction to this book, the significance of intimacy for television was first raised by Horace Newcomb in his seminal *TV: The Most Popular Art*, in which he argued that television should be understood 'as something more than a transmission device for other forms' (1974, 245). Newcomb's analysis made repeated references to the use of close-ups as one major way to achieve intimacy, able to offer to viewers 'faces, reactions, explorations of emotions' (ibid., 245–246), which he saw as television 'at its best' (ibid., 245). This could seem to raise problems for understanding multi-camera sitcoms as (at least potentially) marked by intimacy, given the relative absence of close-ups, certainly extreme close-ups. For example, in episode 3.16 ('The One with the Morning After'), in the emotional moments when Ross and Rachel break up following his one-night stand while they 'were on a break', the camera frames Rachel standing in front of the door to her bedroom in Monica's apartment in nothing tighter than a medium close-up, well below her shoulders. Across the shot-reverse shot pattern, Ross's desperate clinging to her middle is captured in a shot with roughly half of the screen taken up with background space. In addition to the 'distinct distance' (Barker 1985, 236) of the camera to the action, this scene also displays multi-camera sitcom's general absence of point-of-view shots or voice-over narration (though *Friends* uses the latter on other occasions), through which shows such as *Scrubs* achieve access to character interiority.

However, Newcomb himself argued for intimacy being achieved in multi-camera sitcoms such as *Maude* through the emphasis on character relationships and the viewers' familiarity with the characters over time. He further paid attention to how the use of camera movement, composition, editing and the iconography of rooms, especially the home, can convey a concern with intimacy. In *Friends*, a strong sense of intimacy is achieved through the familiarity with the characters, who are afforded memory and development within the serialised storytelling, as well as through particular approaches to the use of humour (see Chapter 2) and performance (see Chapter 3). It is also achieved—the relative absence of (extreme) close-ups notwithstanding—through the use of style. This chapter will explore the aesthetic significance of the use of camera and editing in multi-camera production, exploring how the style in *Friends* not so much denies the televisual apparatus, but instead constructs an intimate viewing experience. However, the chapter will begin by focusing on one aspect of television style that has been receiving long over-due scholarly attention in recent years (e.g. Savorelli 2010; Shabazz 2016; Thompson 2018; D'Arcy 2019), yet still deserves a much more prominent place in scholarly debates on style, namely set design. We will argue that the set design in *Friends* is an integral part of the use of style and achievement of intimacy in the show, thereby making a significant contribution to its popularity.

The One with the Iconic Space: Set Design and Texture

While *Friends* features a number of recurring sets that warrant attention, such as the Central Perk coffeeshop, our focus will lie primarily with the set bearing the fictional address Apartment 20, 495 Grove Street; or as it is commonly known, Monica's apartment. On a narrative level, it is the space in which most of the on-screen time is spent within the show; and it is revealed in the final episode that all six main characters have lived there. Indeed, the final moments of *Friends* confirm the significance of this set—Jillian Sandell calls it 'the affective center and shared familial space of the group' (1998, 144)—with the camera looking through the empty apartment. The 'clip show' episode 10.10 ('The One where Chandler Gets Caught') is also devoted to this space. However, the significance of Monica's apartment far exceeds the storytelling and fictional world of the show: it has become one of the most iconic and attended to sets in the history of sitcom and television more broadly. In her popular publication on sitcom set design, design writer Diana Friedman (2005, 104) notes that the apartment set an influential trend for urban interiors, which links to Pamela Robertson Wojcik's argument that screen representations of apartments offer a 'fantasy of urban living' (2010, xi) to viewers, who may imagine their identities as shaped by such urban spaces. A quarter century after it was first broadcast, the fantasy of urban living offered by *Friends* still finds ready takers, with interest in Monica's apartment continuing to feature strongly in online and other discourses.

For example, lifestyle websites as well as numerous Pinterest pages offer readers advice on how to 'get the look' of Monica's apartment (e.g. Ward 2016), with a British furniture company calling it 'one of the most iconic living rooms in the world' (Furniture Choice 2015). One such website even offers readers a speculative vision of Monica's apartment redecorated for 2018 interior design trends (Savoie 2018). Strong interest in this particular set is also detectible in countless social media articles that periodically circulate, click-baiting readers with promises of 'shocking revelations' about Monica's apartment (which concern mostly inconsistencies and spatial impossibilities, such as the apartment number or kitchen window). Comedy Central (2016), which is currently showing *Friends* repeats in the UK and sponsors the Friendfest, offers online advice about where to buy replicas of props from Monica's apartment. This includes such prominent items as the yellow peephole frame and Jouets poster—both available on Etsy and Amazon, where they can also be found via searching 'as seen on Friends'—as well as more obscure objects, such as Monica's Porto Ramos Pinto poster and (surprisingly expensive) Cookie Time jar (which featured in the 2018 Friendsfest set tour). The Friendfest had at its core a tour of replica key sets, with (at least in the 2018 iteration) Monica's apartment spatially and temporally arranged to be the centre of the tour.

With such strong public interest in the set, academic attention has been noticeably sparse. Lauren Jade Thompson is a welcome exception, and has explored how Monica's and Joey and Chandler's apartments 'act both as a canvas for the expression of gendered identities and behavior, and as a way of limiting and channeling gender transgressions to ensure that, ultimately, its characters follow appropriately gendered postfeminist life scripts' (2018, 772). With her analysis driven by her interest in the function of the two sets as gendered spaces that play out a postfeminist cultural sensibility, Thompson notes that Monica's apartment is 'pleasantly decorated and furnished in line with ideals of feminine

4 The One where They Look at Monica's Apartment …

domesticity, including soft furnishings, chintz patterns, and lamps' (ibid., 761–762). We want to suggest, however, that the meanings and significance of this set are not fully captured by understanding it is a feminine domestic space as per Thompson's argument and the prism of postfeminism.

In doing so, we take due note of the set's standing within industry discourses. For example, the ten-year anniversary issue of the Set Decorators Society of America's magazine *SET DECOR* was devoted to set decoration for television, and featured Monica's apartment on the cover, which it called the 'signature set for the television series' (SDSA 2002/2003, 36). Set decorator Greg Grande, who was nominated for four Emmy awards for his work on the show—as was production designer John Shaffner—has called this set 'the standard by which all sitcoms [are] compared' (in Friedman 2005, 104). Moreover, creative online fan efforts have produced several three-dimensional renderings of Monica's apartment, ranging from miniature models and software programmes to computer games such as *Sims* (see, for example, Romano 2014; Anne-Sophie 2014; Comedy Central 2018). This reflects a desire to explore and grasp the textuality and spatiality of this set, which is especially noteworthy given that multi-camera sitcom has long been linked to notions of flatness. This industry acclaim and fan interest are indicative of the fact that the 'pleasantness' of Monica's apartment rightly recognized by Thompson (2018) needs to be unpicked in much more depth. What *specifically* makes Monica's apartment so pleasant, iconic and acclaimed as a set?

The basic spatial blueprint of Monica's apartment is very much in line with established multi-camera sitcom conventions. It is a large, three-walled set, with several exit and entry points for the performers and purposes of storytelling. It makes use of 'wild walls' that can be adjusted and removed according to the needs of the cameras. However, the set design far exceeds this functionality, with a striking amount of detail invested in the use of decoration and props that draw in some detail on the lived experience of the core creative team as Kevin S. Bright confirmed to us, as well as the New York apartment in which John Shaffner had lived. The well-stocked blue cabinets in the kitchen are free of doors, thus enabling easy visual access to a multitude of food cans and packets, as well as an assortment of kitchenware and multi-coloured crockery, framed by copper pans hanging from the exposed brick ware; all befitting a chef who enjoys hosting guests. The living room features in the foreground a light-coloured sofa, armchair and pouffe, with various cushions and blankets/throws, arranged around a patterned rug. Magazines, knick-knacks, potted plants and frequently also fresh flowers are located on several coffee tables and other furniture, such as the vintage chest of drawers below the Jouets poster (the latter one of several framed prints). The raised platform in the background features more furniture and the back-window/balcony, framed by long curtains with a botanical theme.

As this brief description hopefully conveys, there is certainly no 'visual poverty' (Butler 2010, 215) to be found in the central space of Monica's apartment. Indeed, the considerable size of the space attests to the characters' socio-economic privilege, and John David Rhodes's argument concerning the house in US film can be cross-applied here to suggest that one of the pleasures offered by *Friends* is the temporary access—Rhodes calls it a 'short-term tenancy' (2017, 13)—viewers receive to the spectacle of property. Interestingly, the issue of whether this large apartment would be affordable for the characters, which is so frequently raised as a blind spot in criticism of the show, is something that John Shaffner did consider. As he explained in our interview, he took note of not only the narrative set-up (i.e. Monica is subletting from her grandmother), but also the fact that walk-up apartments tend to be less expensive—'with every flight of stairs, it gets cheaper'—and his own experience of living in the city, further commenting that 'this type of apartment was still affordable when we were renting in the late 1970s'.

More importantly for our argument here, there is a careful attention to detail, especially the small, ornamental and everyday, which John Caughie in his discussion of the classic serial has identified as 'part of a poetics which is specific to television' (2000, 213). This detail that is present in Monica's apartment is informed, as Shaffner told us in our interview with him, by the 'high quality of the detail of the finish: plastering, painting, and so on […] in terms of craftsmanship, *Friends* is as good as it gets'. It is furthermore framed by a visual openness, an invitation to look at the various props put on display, which convey a sense of plenty. (This is reinforced by the fact that the many items visible in the well-stocked kitchen relate to food, and that these items frequently feature in the backdrop of shots filmed with the camera positioned behind the Jouets poster; thus, the kitchen's sense of plenty is present even in scenes that do not involve the kitchen as such.) Grande has spoken of the intention to 'fill' the space, to make it look and feel less like a (blank) set. This desire to achieve a lived-in look and feel (to which we will return later in this chapter) is realised not only through this presence of detail, but also through a bohemian-eclectic style, in which different designs and (albeit stylishly) mismatched furniture are mixed together. Agreed between John Shaffner and Greg Grande, and implemented by Grande—who, Shaffner comments, has a 'real knack for putting things together that are different; so it still talks to each other, but it isn't so studied and selected and *painfully chosen*'—this eclecticism has helped the design of this space to not become visually dated. It is also informed by Shaffner and Grande's attention to characterization, given that Monica, despite her level of privilege, would have been unable to afford full furniture sets in the early seasons.

Through filling (though without cluttering) Monica's apartment with a detailed, eclectic mix of objects and items, what Grande achieves is a rich texture to the set design: there is the rough hardness of exposed brick ware, the warm shine of copper, the soft shimmer of the beads and embroidery on the sofa cushions, the matt smoothness of the purple walls, the soft, fluffy weave of various fabrics (including curtains and several throws), the freshness of green foliage, and the gleam of candle sticks and polished wood, to name but a few. This collection of different textures not only helps to achieve Grande's intended spatial realism—which was also a detectible quality at the 2018 Friendfest apartment tour, even though these were not-to-full-scale set replicas—but also provides a specificity and dimensionality, if not a sensory materiality, to the storyworld, which we see as informing the online fan efforts to recreate the space in three dimensions. In her discussion of production design which draws on Raymond Williams's (1977) seminal work, Jane Barnwell has noted that texture refers to the qualities of the 'surfaces of objects, structures and landscapes and the way these are combined results in a new texture. These have a surface appearance and a structure of feeling' (2004, 81). In *Friends*, the set design for Monica's apartment, through its detail, visual openness, lived-in quality and rich texture, achieves an intimate structure of feeling, as part of the programme's overall strategy of intimacy.

Reflecting Boym's suggestion that the 'notion of intimacy is connected to home' (1998, 499), the importance of these detailed choices in terms of set design become vividly articulated through comparison with other relevant sets. For example, in the episodes when Monica and Rachel are forced to swap apartments with Joey and Chandler following the loss of a game in 4.12, notions of intimacy become much less pronounced in Apartment 20 (which features a barer look, with fewer decorative items), and much more evident in Apartment 19. Monica and Rachel's new home—formerly 'the antithesis of colour', as Shaffner puts it—is noticeably transformed through Monica's copper pans, orange mugs hanging above the cooker, plants, trinket boxes and a red patterned throw over the kitchen cupboard. This transformation would be temporary, and by 4.19, the set for Apartment 19 would feature again a more functional look, which it shares with contemporaneous sitcom *Seinfeld*, in which the set for Jerry's apartment too featured neutral colours, assembled furniture and fewer, barer textures, befitting a character with little interest in hosting guests and homeliness. This 'bachelor pad aesthetic' (Thompson 2015, 29) saw an inflection in Frasier Crane's apartment in *Frasier* via the upper-middle-class taste codes of its older inhabitant, with richer tones off-set by an elegant minimalism.

More recent sitcoms have engaged with such set design conventions in interesting ways: *The Big Bang Theory*, for example, varies this look in that Sheldon and Leonard's apartment features the bland, functional furniture and limited presence of fabrics familiar from Apartment 19 and *Seinfeld*, but features a multitude of props (such as books, CDs and merchandise toys) articulating the inhabitants' 'nerdy' fandom. *How I Met Your Mother* takes the bachelor pad aesthetic to the point of excessive, performative parody with the set for Barney Stinson's apartment. As Thompson has insightfully argued, this set draws on a hyper-masculine design scheme (replete with spring-loaded toilet seat) recalling mid-twentieth century *Playboy* apartments and the domestic spaces associated with 'hyper-masculine womanising figures such as James Bond' (2015, 29), articulating 'the fragile ground upon which heterosexual masculinity now stands' (ibid., 30). As the above reflects, multi-camera set design has long been highly expressive and complemented narrative storytelling; and so the relative absence of warmth, rich textures and sensory materiality in these sitcoms' sets speak to the issues of masculinity marking the inhabiting characters.

Contrasting such bachelor pad sets, the intimate feel of Monica's apartment is crucially furthered through the use of colour and lighting. The colour on the main walls – despite Joey's apparent ignorance as expressed in the final moments of the show: 'Has it always been purple?' (10.18, 'The Last One: Part 2')—has proven 'one of the identifying marks of the show', as Shaffner notes. The colour choice emerged as a response to Kevin S. Bright's interest in using colour 'to make a statement: this is something you haven't seen before'. Having designed the basic set with collaborator Joe Stewart and been invited by Bright to the latter's new home which featured purple and green walls, Shaffner changed the colour from white on the original sketch model to purple, keen to achieve an instantly recognisable look that would stand out in an increasingly crowded television landscape and to avoid a colour that would read cold. (As Shaffner clarifies, this colour can be difficult to capture for the screen, as blue or violent undertones can 'not come out right', but this was helped by the fact that, at Bright's insistence, *Friends* was shot on film, which helps to achieve a warmer look.) Figure 4.1 is a photograph of Shaffner's original model box for the set, and it shows that, while purple is used for the main walls, it is not the only colour; and that there was indeed an early intention to have the purple accompanied with blue for the kitchen. Through the use of this pair of complementary colours in close proximity in the red-yellow-blue (RYB) colour model, Shaffner achieves a harmonious visual look. He explained to us that the strong colour on the walls required a 'careful colour scheme for the décor', whereby the furnishings had to be 'stepped back' and rendered in neutral colours as 'everything had to rest in the purple environment, not compete with it'.

This harmonious look is further accentuated through the approach to lighting. Multi-camera production is generally negatively noted for

Fig. 4.1 Model box for Monica's apartment by John Shaffner

having flat, indiscriminate, overly bright high-key lighting, which is (somewhat unfairly) mocked in the *Scrubs* episode 'My Life in Four Cameras' (4.17). However, as Shaffner observes, 'we started to see more nuance in lighting come in during the 1980s', and Monica's apartment features a modulated use of high-key lighting whereby, as Shaffner explained to us, there was a sustained effort to 'light people a little bit separately from the walls, so there's more depth and reality to the image'. This was of importance to Kevin S. Bright, who points out that the large balcony window allows 'a lot of light to come through, so the texture of the space changes, which gives it that extra feeling of reality'. Bright further comments that he was very keen for 'a more natural look', but that 'things went a little too far and the first season is a little bit too dark in places', crediting Nick McLean, who became *Friends*' director of photography after the first season, for improving the lighting scheme. The modulated approach to lighting is combined with the presence of a number of practicals, both lamps and wall sconces, which as Shaffner puts it, 'help to motivate the way the light falls'. These together produce a softer, warmer, more diffuse lighting state, thereby helping to engender a look and feel of intimacy—as Shaffner sees it, the 'warmth and layers of affection put into that set radiated out of it'.

Again, comparative attention to other sitcom sets helps to bring out the significance of the creative choices at stake. In episode 'The One where Heckles Dies' (2.3), the late Mr. Heckles's apartment shares a somewhat similar (though much smaller) floor plan with Monica's apartment immediately above it, but crucially lacks similar furnishings, colour and lighting. The absence of the purple is especially striking once Heckles's hoarded belongings are boxed up, making this grey space look like a shell, in stark comparison to Monica's warm, intimate space. Other multi-camera sitcoms featuring couples or (blended) families also show the significance of the use of the unusual colour purple in *Friends*. Contemporaneous shows such as *The Fresh Prince of Bel-Air*, *Mad About You*, *Ellen* and *Everybody Loves Raymond*, as well as precursor *The Mary Tyler Moore Show*, all feature some decorative items and props that aid characterisation and help to provide a degree of a lived-in quality. For example, the lighting sconce in Ellen Morgan's apartment doubles as an umbrella hook (see, e.g., the show's famous coming-out episode 'The Puppy Episode') and Mary Richards's nook kitchen features cat-themed tea towels (detectible in the episode 'The Dinner Party'). But these sets do not feature the level of detail and already noted visual invitation to look evident in Monica's apartment, and crucially, through their neutral colour schemes dominated by creams, beiges and browns, they lack warmth and intimacy.

The significance of colour is most strikingly evidenced by *Mad About You*, which *Friends* followed in NBC's Thursday night schedule for its first season: the design of the main living room set shares several qualities with Monica's apartment, including texture via wicker furniture and fabrics, as well as a couch arranged perpendicularly to the fourth wall (an aspect of set design we will examine shortly). However, the neutral cream colours for the walls and curtains, plus some assembled furniture at the centre of the set, make this a much less warm, intimate space. This much more muted approach to colour frequently found in multi-camera sitcoms is often further accentuated by a less diffuse lighting scheme involving fewer practicals. This is perhaps most noticeable in *Everybody Loves Raymond*, where the combination of the brown-cream colour palette of the living room set with a noticeably top-down lighting scheme undercuts the spatial realism intended through the use of pattern across the walls, sofa and fabrics. As these examples attest, the use of colour and lighting makes the set for Monica's apartment much more than a backdrop to the action, endowing this space with a presence. As John Shaffner put it when we asked him about the early design plans, the intention was to create 'a real sense of place there'. (This noticeably differs from David Barker's [1985, 243] analysis of *All in the Family*, who argued that its 'drab and nondescript' set design focused viewers' attention on the narrative.)

The set design for Monica's apartment in *Friends* finds strongest resonance with, if not proved influential for, contemporaneous shows *Dharma & Greg* and *Will & Grace*; and a clear influence is detectible in its flat-sharing successors *How I Met Your Mother* and single-camera show *New Girl*. The main living room sets for all of these shows contain a mix of furniture styles and displayed decorative elements, such as Will Truman's framed art prints and vases, and Ted Mosby's vintage stills cameras. Each also features an interest in the noticeable use of colour, with neutral walls accompanied by regular splashes of bolder colours, such as red fabrics in *How I Met Your Mother*, a contrasting blue sofa and orange scatter cushions in *Will & Grace*, or purple armchairs and a terracotta accent wall in *Dharma & Greg*. Practicals are also frequently deployed, with sconce lighting in *Will & Grace*, *Dharma & Greg* (which also features fairy lights) and *How I Met Your Mother*; and *New Girl*'s loft aesthetic is complemented by pendant lights and vintage lamps. Texture also features strongly, with exposed brick present in all but *Will & Grace* (which has wooden floor boards), a host of fabrics in the form of rugs, cushions, throws and curtains, and notable patterns (such as *Dharma & Greg*'s decorative plates and curtains).

These set design choices each speak to the creative personnel's engagement with characterisation—for example, Dharma Finkelstein is the free-spirited offspring of hippie parents, architects Ted Mosby and Will Truman have much cultural capital—and endow these shows with a recognisable look that has garnered some acclaim and interest. As these comparative reflections underline, the strategy of intimacy marking Monica's apartment is engendered through the combination of a number of careful set design choices. However, further comparison also reveals that there is an additional aspect that sets *Friends* apart, even from such stylistically closely aligned shows; an aspect which contributes to the spatial realism, presence of space, visual openness and aesthetics of intimacy. This concerns the placement of the couch in Monica's living room, and to this we turn our attention next.

The One with the Couch: Multi-Camera Sitcom and Creative Engagement with Space

Antonio Savorelli has rightly identified the couch as 'one of the most common space-defining elements in American sitcom' (2010, 23), arguing that 'space is not only dominated by the couch, it is also defined and designed by it' (ibid., 24). Indeed, the vast majority of multi-camera sitcoms, including those referenced above, have the couch placed centrally in the space and regular shot composition arrangements, in parallel to the fourth wall (along the x-axis). (Variations of this occur in such sitcoms as *How I Met Your Mother*, *Dharma & Greg* and *The Big Bang Theory*—Shaffner was production designer for the latter two—which have the couch placed slightly more on a diagonal line.) This planimetric staging of space allows the actors to move quickly through the set, thus supporting the storytelling, enables an emphasis on their performances when seated and helps the cameras and editing to capture reactions within and across shots.

In *Friends*, such planimetric staging is already evident in the opening credits, which across all ten seasons feature the orange couch from Central Perk in front of the fountain, placed in parallel to the camera. This echoes the use of space in Central Perk, Phoebe's apartment and Ross's final apartment, with the couch in each case placed in parallel to and fairly downstage, that is, in quite close proximity to the fourth wall. Apartments 19 and 20 at 495 Grove Street, however, are exceptions: Joey and Chandler's apartment initially has the couch very downstage, backing the fourth wall (and thus not entirely visible), and then becomes dominated by the two BarcaLoungers, with the fairly small couch placed upstage and thus not very noticeable. Monica's apartment features a large, off-white couch, but in an unconventional position. Savorelli has noted this as follows:

In *Friends*, the couch in Monica Geller's apartment separates the living room from the kitchen, and the space behind it becomes a passage from the entrance door, on the left of the frontal shot, to the bathroom and on the right. Strangely enough, though, the invisible wall is placed slightly to the left of the couch, which makes the lateral or diagonal shot the privileged one for a total shot of the apartment. This also makes Monica's couch hierarchically secondary to the one at Central Perk[.] (2010, 24)

We want to suggest that the spatial arrangement concerning Monica's couch is not actually that strange. Savorelli understands the use of space in what he calls 'classic sitcoms' as marked by constraint, whereas 'new comedies' (single-camera shows such as *The Office—An American Workplace* or *The Comeback*) are enabled to use space more flexibly and imaginatively. What we want to argue instead is that the perpendicular placement of the couch to the fourth wall in Monica's apartment facilitates a creative engagement with the set and space. (Monica's couch is placed in a more conventionally parallel position in episodes such as 'The One with the Flashback' [3.6] and 'The One that Could Have Been' [6.15/6.16], efficiently signalling that these episodes do not take place within the show's regular timeline.)

This creative engagement takes multiple forms. As Savorelli notes in the above quotation, the placement of the couch provides some definition to the open plan space of Monica's apartment. This helps the performers to make use of these delineated sub-spaces, such as when, in episode 3.9 ('The One with the Football'), Ross and Monica withdraw into the corner of the kitchen to confer whether they should defy their parents' Geller Cup orders and play football, watched with amusement by the others who are grouped against and along the back of the couch. The placement of the couch with its back to the front door also enables visual gags such as in the tag for 7.17 ('The One with the Cheap Wedding Dress'): Monica returns home early to find Ross, Chandler and Joey seated on the couch, watching a basketball game. The cameras and editing are broadly aligned with Monica, only showing the backs of their heads, until after a delay, they finally turn around (at the same time and speed), revealing their face masks.

4 The One where They Look at Monica's Apartment …

More significantly, however, the placement of the couch also enables the actors to use the couch as a border which they can utilise (and transgress) for their performances. One particularly important moment in the show here stems from 2.7 ('The One where Ross Finds Out'), when Ross is listening to Rachel's drunk phone message from the night before. Rachel hurries stage right, steps onto the couch and its back, and then leaps onto Ross's back. They stagger further stage right, and once they physically detach, Jennifer Aniston moves stage left behind the couch and then gets on the couch, at first bodily squirming into the couch cushions before kneeling on the couch, facing David Schwimmer across its back. As they deliver their dialogue, the scene begins to resemble a tennis match, with the back of the couch functioning as the net: fiddling with the cushion tassels to avoid eye contact, Aniston's Rachel volleys the first emotionally significant statement at Schwimmer's Ross (that she has had feelings for him), who in a state of shock can only respond by repeating her statement in the form of a question. Rachel then rises to her feet, defensive-angrily points at Ross for her next volley (that she knows that he has had feelings for her first) and Ross parries by mirroring her arm movement, uttering a verbal exclamation and then again feebly repeating her information in the form of a question. When Rachel mentions Ross's current girlfriend Julie, he articulates the need to lie down, but only briefly perches on the back of the couch—despite Rachel's hurried effort to plump up the cushions for him, a quick look of his towards her suggests his realisation that lying down in her vicinity would not be appropriate (or wise)—and he paces across the kitchen. Rachel moves around the couch to face him, as they get both spatially and emotionally closer, with the framing shifting to a two-shot, just in time for the door-bell (Julie) to interrupt the moment.

Evidently, the couch here is not simply part of the backdrop against which the scene plays out. As Andrew Klevan notes concerning films such as *The Cobweb*:

> performer and place find and reveal each other, so that the discovery of location is inseparable from the investigation of psychology: the performers look to their environment to realise their characters. Discreet and considerate disclosure of personality replaces definite announcement and revelation. (2005, 71)

This scene is certainly replete with explicit, unambiguous announcement and revelation, but Aniston and Schwimmer utilise the set to enrich their characterisation and add nuance to the dramatic and comedic dimensions of the scene; and the spatial placement of the couch within the multi-camera set-up helps make these performance choices possible. Savorelli points out that the 'couch surely represents the comfort of home' (2010, 24), but here this becomes interestingly subverted, with the couch representing the developing conflict between the two characters and becoming the focal point of the irreversible paradigm shift in their relationship. Aniston's physical transgression across the couch parallels Rachel's drunk verbal transgression in her phone message, and the couch as border and indeed as a space of discomfort become (re-)established and made explicit through Aniston's bodily squirming into the couch cushions (which fails to achieve what her character evidently wishes, that the ground would open and swallow her), and then Schwimmer's and Aniston's postures and arm movements. Indeed, it is through the couch that Aniston here articulates her character's emotions, engaging with the physicality of the couch—the cushions large enough to squirm into, the tassels just the right length and thickness for nervous fiddling—in such a way to convey a lived-in quality to this space. So, the sitcom couch can just as much represent the conflicts as the comfort of domestic spaces.

It is also worth recalling that Savorelli argues that multi-camera sitcoms have a constrained use of the space around the couch: 'the area directly in front of the couch is largely static, where actors limit their movements to those needed to reach or leave a certain sitting position; in the area behind it movements can be wider, directly feeding the action and supporting scene changes' (2010, 24). However, the perpendicular arrangement of the couch to the fourth wall in Monica's apartment enables a much more dynamic movement across and around the couch. This is already noticeable in the above example, but also strikingly evident in 3.3 ('The One with the Jam') when Chandler seeks advice from Ross and Rachel (now a couple) on how to sleep undisturbed in bed next to his girlfriend Janice. Perry's Chandler pulls up a kitchen chair to the back of the couch, where Rachel is kneeling facing him, and as Fig. 4.2 shows, Ross is sitting slightly more upstage angled towards them both, agreeing with Rachel's pronouncement that they are 'cuddly

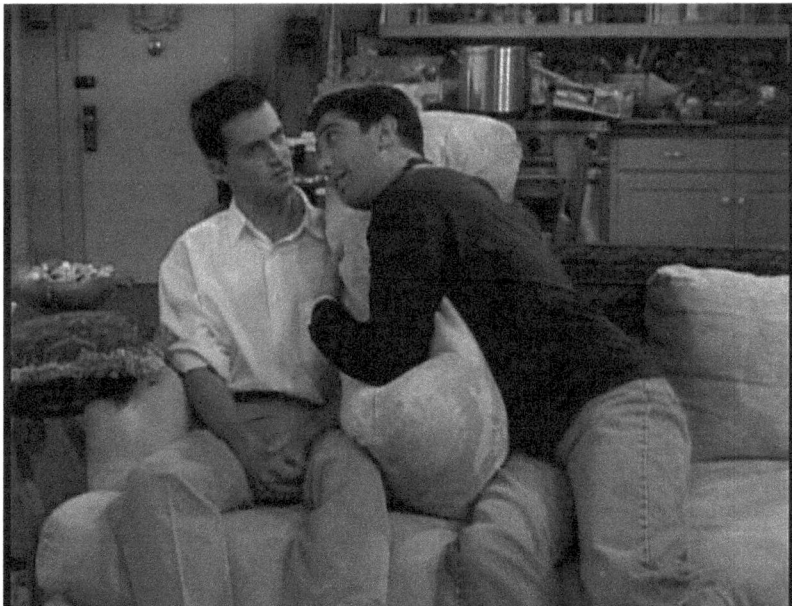

Figs. 4.2 and 4.3 Hug-and-roll: Ross's (David Schwimmer) agreement with Rachel (Jennifer Aniston) is shown to be insincere to Chandler (Matthew Perry) in 'The One with the Jam' (3.3)

sleepers'. Once Rachel exits the apartment, Perry initially sits on the back of the couch with Schwimmer standing in front of him, until both sit on the couch, where Ross proceeds to demonstrate to Chandler his tried-and-tested 'hug-and-roll' technique for undisturbed sleep with one of the large cushions. It is worth noting here that during his 'hug-and-roll' demonstration, Schwimmer's Ross is positioned closely to where he was moments earlier when Rachel happily proclaimed that they were cuddly sleepers: in both cases, Schwimmer is seated more upstage, angled to the person next to him and holds an embrace; but the reversed camera angle for the 'hug-and-roll' demonstration (see Fig. 4.3) underscores the reversal of his happy (and insincere) agreement with Rachel moments before. So, there is dynamic movement here *around* the couch as well as *on* the couch, complementing the narrative beats and humour, with none of the space around the sofa marked by staticity.

Clearly, it is not only single-camera sitcoms that are 'able to use all available space' (Savorelli 2010, 25). The fluid use of space around the couch in Monica's apartment provides a less frontal quality to this space. (This less frontal quality is also supported by the fact that, because the couch is not arranged perpendicularly, we do not see performers arranged in a neat line in parallel to the fourth wall.) Though the staging is planimetric, this is not as obvious or forced as it can appear in other multi-camera spaces, such as the meals taken in the main living room set in *The Big Bang Theory*, a regular occurrence referenced in this show's opening credits, with the performers invariably spread laterally across the space. There is nothing blocking or impeding visual access to the scene with Chandler, Ross and Rachel in 'The One with the Jam', but at the same time, with one person pulling up a chair to seek advice from two friends on a couch (one kneeling and one sitting at an angle), the movement here also reads as embedded within a realistic *mise-en-scène*. This less frontal, less forced and less noticeable approach to planimetric staging that is aided by the placement of the couch runs through *Friends*, present not only in more dramatically focused moments, such as Ross and Rachel confronting their feelings, but also in moments that emphasise physical comedy. For example, in the tag for 5.22 ('The One with Joey's Big Break'), Phoebe, Ross, Monica and Chandler wrestle Rachel onto the ground, physically forcing her to keep still and her eyes open to administer eye drops. Here, the pile-up of bodies in front of the couch allows visual access to the administration of the eye drops, but appears grounded in a realist moment, with the line of the bodies accentuating the couch's diagonal line across the space, which works with the camera angle to minimise frontality and subtly emphasise the depth of the space.

Finally, the perpendicular placement of Monica's couch to the fourth wall not only aids this more realist approach to planimetric staging, but also, crucially, affects the audience's broader viewing experience of the series. This is particularly linked to *Friends*' pronounced intertextual quality: while, as we have noted in the introduction to this book, the show would reduce references to contemporaneous topics and entertainment culture during its early seasons in order to become less dated, intertextual materials in the form of tapes that the main characters watch would continue to feature in the show. Examples here include the (badly) faked *Law & Order* footage Joey shows his grandmother in 5.19 ('The One where Ross Can't Flirt'), Phoebe's twin sister Ursula's 'Buffay the Vampire Layer' porn video in 6.14 ('The One where Chandler Can't Cry') and the home video depicting the events leading up to Monica and Rachel's high school prom in 2.14 ('The One with the Prom Video'). Precipitating a significant development in *Friends*' will-they-won't-they storyline concerning Ross and Rachel, the latter is the final case study for our exploration of the use of the couch.

What the presence of this home video footage within the episode highlights is the significance of the couch arranged perpendicularly and the armchair in parallel to the fourth floor: because of this spatial arrangement, it makes sense that Monica's television set is stage left, in front of the couch. This means that the audience can see the characters watching the television screen, as well as the screen itself when captured in (medium) close-ups. In these (medium) close-ups, the television set here is not absent from the familiar space the way it is in, for example, *Frasier*, where in the episode 'A Tsar Is Born' (7.7), the Cranes watch television together and the television screen is never shown. The television set here is also not disembodied the way it is, for example, in *Seinfeld*, when Jerry and Kramer watch a tape in 'The Little Kicks' (8.4), and the television set, when it fully appears on screen, is framed by the fourth wall, here made visible as a non-descript grey background that underlines the somewhat disruptive disconnectedness of this unusual shot from the familiar space. The effect of the regular presence of the television set within the *mise-en-scène* of Monica's apartment is that this helps to provide a realist lived-in quality to this space and enables the audience to watch with the characters, even to the extent of broadly sharing their eye-lines.

In 'The One with the Prom Video', this plays out as follows: Chandler and Joey are seated on the couch, Phoebe on the armchair, and Rachel and Monica next to the armchair, close to the television set, with Ross retreating over the course of the scene to the front door. As James Burrows explained to us, the shift in Ross's location within the space was not scripted, but emerged during rehearsals, as Burrows developed a 'gut feeling that there's no way that Ross is going to stay next to the others; he had to start to leave'. As they watch the prom video, the moment when Ross scrambles up the stairs to get changed so that he can take Rachel (whose date appears to be standing her up) to the prom is shot in such a way that the fictional television screen fills the entire frame. Immediately following Ross's stumble, a cut shifts the framing so that the television set is visible in its regular position, captured by a camera behind the sofa, with all six actors visible (see Fig. 4.4). The audience is very much watching with the characters here as they uncover something about the past (that Ross intended to help Rachel); something unknown framed by the familiar sight of the vintage dresser and Jouets poster. The familiarity of this framing, through sheer contrast, highlights the newness, and thus significance, of the information being revealed.

Then once the home video shows a (full-screen) shot of a younger Ross looking frame left, distraught to see Rachel leaving with her late date, a cut to present-day Ross looking frame right shows that Ross is looking at his younger self across the shot pattern, connecting to the painful emotions of this past moment. Then Rachel walks across the set to Ross to reconcile with him (following their recent falling-out), which, as Burrows recalls, 'I'm not sure if everyone on the set was a fan of immediately, but it's really dramatic'. This well-remembered moment from the show is made especially interesting by both the length of the walk (which enables the cameras to capture the emotionality played out on Aniston's face) as well as Aniston very briefly dropping her gaze to ensure she can manoeuvre

Fig. 4.4 Watching friends with *Friends*: 'The One with the Prom Video' (2.14)

around the couch. So, both the depth and (especially) the length of the space are being deployed as Rachel symbolically and physically traverses the space between Ross and herself, reflecting Burrows's interest in complex blocking. As Ross and Rachel reconcile accompanied by non-diegetic cheers—which, Kevin S. Bright in the DVD commentary observes, 'really points out an intimacy that the audience has with this show'—and Phoebe's insistence that Ross is Rachel's 'lobster', a reaction shot of the four friends captures them framed next to the fictional television screen, only this time with their emotional engagement visible on their faces. With the prom video stopped, the television screen no longer shows the past emotional pain and separation, but as a black mirror reflects the group in their present unity.

As this close analysis and the previous examples suggest, any argument that the absence of proscenium-style staging is what facilitates a creative use of space in sitcom, is in need of substantial development. Just as 'the room is [...] an actively shaping environment', as Williams

(2011 [1974], 12) argued regarding television space, so the space here is actively and productively shaped. (Phil Chidester [2008] considers the function of the couches in relation to the exercise of white privilege within the programme, which we will consider in Chapter 5.) The placement of the couch in Monica's apartment, while still allowing planimetric visual access for the audience, enables a nuanced use of space that is not reductively determined by the proscenium arch. In 'The One with the Prom Video', the use of space engenders a scene with considerable visual complexity, enhancing the emotional significance of the storytelling because the television set is not a disconnected, disruptive presence but embedded within the familiar space. It thus benefits from the intimacy that marks the space, but it also contributes to it, because the positioning of the couch facilitates a regime of looking where the audience not only watches the characters and their reactions, but also watches *with* them. This particular viewer engagement brings us to the final two sections of this chapter, in which we will consider how multi-camera sitcom engenders a particular viewing experience for the audience that further informs the strategy of intimacy in *Friends*.

The One with the Diachronic Space: Layers and Patterns

So far in this chapter, our discussion has to some extent argued for a certain kind of exceptionalism for *Friends*. We have explored the programme as a multi-camera sitcom with a distinct use of set design marked by an unusual level of detail and rich texture, as well as noticeable presence of space and aesthetics of intimacy. Our analysis has shown how, through its placement of the couch in Monica's apartment, *Friends* is not entirely bound to certain multi-camera sitcom conventions that are typically understood as restrictive. However, its use of style and space is also very representative of multi-camera sitcoms, in ways that inform and contribute to the aesthetic achievements that we have identified thus far. With the presence of the fourth wall across its recurring sets, and the cameras adhering to the 180-degree rule (bar brief exceptions, such as the scenes on Monica's balcony), *Friends* is typical of multi-camera sitcom production in that it establishes a particular regime of looking over time: viewers look at the same spaces from similar positions again and again. This links to notions of intimacy on two levels, as we will consider in this and the next section.

Through repeated exposure, the core sets become intimately familiar to viewers, which in the case of Monica's apartment has informed the considerable, ongoing fan interest that we noted earlier. The core sets in *Friends* develop over the seasons, as is likely to be the case for long-running shows. For example, changes are especially noticeable for Apartment 19 once Rachel moves in with her daughter Emma in the last two seasons. However, changes to Monica's apartment are subtle, usually concerning the soft fabrics or minor decorative items. As Shaffner comments, such minor changes provide the space with 'a life to it' and prevent it from becoming 'locked down'. Grande has noted that there was a clear limit to the changes he could introduce:

> I changed a few things around, but these are iconic sets. People want the comfort level of tuning in and seeing these familiar sets week after week, especially in these uncertain times. For Monica's apartment, I recovered the club chair once. It was a huge deal to get the producers to agree to it, because based on viewer response, the public resists change. (SDSA 2002/2003, 37, 58)

What runs parallel to this level of resistance to bigger change is a more dynamic use of space in relation to the wall art in Central Perk and the Magna Doodle in Joey and Chandler's apartment. Over the ten seasons, the paintings in Central Perk regularly change (becoming more patriotic in the wake of 9/11; see Howie 2008). The message board, which would find its way into the *Joey* spin-off, provides a host of amusing notes, drawings and indeed references to storylines within the show. (One such example is the message 'Thanks for all your stuff!' in 4.2, left by the robber who locks Joey into the oversized entertainment unit.) With very little textual attention being drawn to it within the show, the Magna Doodle provides pleasurable 'Easter eggs' for attentive viewers and adds to the longevity of the show's appeal, as improvements in reception technology have made it easier for viewers to discern the messages and doodles on their high-definition television sets and laptops.

The combination of this insistence on consistency and the more dynamic engagement with the sets together informs the spatial realism of *Friends*, aiding the show's intimacy through the dual pleasure of continuity and carefully managed change. It is interesting here to consider the already mentioned fascination with spatial inconsistencies for Monica's apartment. Numerous 'clickbait' articles promising to reveal to readers the 'weird things going on with Monica's apartment' circulate regularly on social media, with a frequent focus on the 'numerous fenestral realities' (Waring 2016) concerning the kitchen window and the (disappearing) wooden post that separates the kitchen from the living room. We suggest that this fascination is so pronounced precisely because of the spatial realism and strong level of intimacy that mark Monica's apartment, which these inconsistencies highlight through their disruptive difference. These spatial irregularities perhaps also play a part in the show's critical reception, which, as we have explored in the book's introduction, has not ascribed to *Friends* the status of 'auteur television' in the way that has happened with *Seinfeld*. It is here interesting to note that the wooden post was implemented at the suggestion of James Burrows, who directed the pilot and several episodes of the first season. With a strong interest in using space for dramatic and comedic effect, he told us in our interview with him that he seeks 'to add dimension' to what would otherwise be 'big, open, wide expanses'. He likes 'putting things into the space so that it isn't so flat', which is why, just as the post 'helps to break up the space' and offer definition to Monica's kitchen, the main apartment in *Will & Grace* features a step up into the kitchen. John Shaffner comments that Burrows is 'very clever when it comes to using landmarks like that to define space' and that the post worked well as a 'cutting piece of the edge of the frame'. The post was then removed but reinstalled for further episodes directed by Burrows at his request (Bright also liked using it when directing episodes). So, what existing discourses on *Friends* have so far not given enough recognition to is that some of the apparent spatial errors can actually be understood in terms of directorial authorship.

However, more central to our discussion is the thought that, because of the overall consistency and through repeated exposure to the core sets, intimacy in *Friends*—and multi-camera sitcom more broadly—may also be achieved because those core sets become layered spaces that develop particular resonances over time. Our discussion here links to Karen Lury's (2005) analysis of space in soap opera and Lucy Fife Donaldson's (2016) on crime drama, Amy Holdsworth's (2011) work on television and memory, and Sérgio Dias Branco's (2013) engagement with issues of inhabitation and duration in multi-camera sitcom. Driven by an interest in how 'the "stagy" feel of these series [*Cheers* and *Frasier*] is connected with the closeness of the characters and with their delimited, *intimate world*' (2013, 95, emphasis added), Dias Branco considers 'the significance of inhabitation (of living in a space and finding a place in it) and duration (of experiencing time and valuing it)' (ibid., 94). He comments that: 'According to Heidegger, not all buildings are devised for dwelling, but the bar in *Cheers*, which bears the same festive and warm name as the series, certainly *allows* for dwelling' (ibid., 96, emphasis in original). Given what we have argued in this chapter thus far, Monica's apartment certainly also allows for, and indeed strongly invites, dwelling. (Central Perk does so too; other recurring sets, like Ross's final apartment, through their use of colour and space, do so much less, and are not coincidentally narratively marginal.) Such dwelling in *Friends* gives rise to storylines and dramatically and/or comedically significant moments clustering within these spaces. This facilitates what Holdsworth has expressed as follows:

> Central to [the relationship between memory and television] is the idea of the television viewing experience as one of accumulation, where viewing experiences and references are built up over time, and the memory of 'afterimages' and 'moments' is accumulated over a life lived across television. (2011, 34)

Such accumulation abounds in Monica's apartment. The couch, which has already received detailed attention by us, becomes imbued with layers of meanings and memories for long-term viewers: it is not only where the 'hug-and-roll' technique is demonstrated by Ross in 3.3, but also where, in one of the show's most frequently quoted moments, Monica teaches Chandler about erogenous zones in 4.11. It furthermore plays a central role in Ross and Rachel's developing relationship:

in addition to the scenes discussed earlier, the couch is also where Rachel has an erotic dream about Ross in 1.22 and where Chandler inadvertently reveals Ross's feelings for Rachel in 1.24. So, Monica's couch is one of the spaces in *Friends* that have 'become thickened through multiple encounters' (Fife Donaldson 2016, 11). In this, it is joined by other sites in Monica's apartment, such as the space in front of Rachel's room, which is where Ross and Rachel have their emotional break-up in 3.16; where Ross declares his wish to maintain the possibility of a future relationship with Rachel in 6.14; and where Monica awaits Chandler with her marriage proposal in 6.25. With its narrative prominence across ten seasons, Monica's apartment has, to borrow from Lury, 'become extraordinarily familiar […] to regular viewers' (2005, 154), with a '"time-rich" quality' (ibid., 16) that complements and accentuates its rich visual texture.

Such a time-rich thickening and layering of space is not limited to Monica's apartment, but also present in the other spaces within the show. For example, the centre of the living room next to the kitchen counter in Apartment 19 is where Phoebe and Joey hold the race between the chick and the duck in 5.12; where a helmeted Joey celebrates getting his health insurance back by inviting the others to beat him up in 6.4; and where the race of children's toys is held as part of baby Emma's birthday celebrations in 10.4. The step in the hallway between the two apartments is where Chandler comforts Rachel about her divorced parents in 2.22, and where Rachel comforts Ross about Emily's impending departure in 4.16. The couch in Central Perk is where Chandler is twice exposed to Phoebe's date 'showing brain' in 3.13; where Phoebe spots that Monica has been secretly wearing a garter in 4.20; and where Joey reveals to Phoebe that he is wearing women's underwear in 7.22. There are interesting patterns detectable here (which exceed the scope of this chapter), with a noticeable specificity to the layering (e.g. Rachel and Ross occupy the same spot on the step in 2.22 and 4.16). Even if this specificity is not necessarily deliberate, it adds an echoing effect across the seasons, enriching the accumulation of meaning. The patterns also become more discernible, because the spaces in the show have become extended: while *Friends* with its 236 episodes does not have as much textual mass as the soap operas that Lury discusses, its spaces have been 'revisited frequently and on a long-term basis' (2005, 16) through the show's innumerable repeats and continuing availability over the last quarter century.

This continuing availability and presence of these spaces on television and laptop screens not only extends them and thus makes patterns more noticeable, but also links to notions of emotion and affect (see also the conclusion to this book). As Lury has argued in relation to a different genre: 'the repetition of key images and the revisiting of particular locations is also important to the development of sentiment and empathy by the viewer of the series' (2005, 16). For long-term viewers of *Friends*, the core sets become thickened, layered spaces, onto which the character relationships are mapped over the seasons. In this way, in *Friends* and other multi-camera shows (including those with a lesser degree of spatial realism), the core sets may become 'lived spaces' inscribed with emotional investment by fans. (The latter's articulation on social media and at the Friendsfest supports the idea that the dramatic moments noted above become more, not less, affective through repetition.) This is why the final moments of *Friends* show Monica's apartment stripped bare, which invites viewers to imaginatively fill it with their memories of not only the furniture and decoration, but also what has happened within this space across time and the emotional ties viewers may have formed with it. Holdsworth has identified 'endings and beginnings as privileged spaces for reflection and remembering, where patterns are initiated and revealed' (2011, 36), and the ending of *Friends* both reflects and reflects on the affective quality this intimate space has accumulated over ten seasons (and potentially many more years of viewing).

The One with Multi-Camera Sitcom's Regime of Looking In and Rupture

Before we conclude this chapter, we wish to return to the argument that opened the previous section, namely that *Friends* is typical of multi-camera sitcom production in that it establishes a particular regime of looking over time. It is now time to address the significance of the fact that when viewers look at the same spaces, they do so from similar positions, and how this links to notions of intimacy. We are of course by no means the first to become aware of multi-camera production's use of set camera positions. Dias Branco notes such habitual placement, whereby 'the camera adopts positions that become usual' (2013, 96). Thompson has commented that in:

> the traditional three-camera-setup style of shooting, [...] the same spaces are viewed repeatedly from the same angles on the studio's fourth-wall. Imbued within this set-up is the potential for much richness of meaning to be carried across through design. (2018, 761)

This chapter's analysis supports her point concerning design, but we now wish to extend this and argue that this set-up itself also carries meaning, through the regime of looking it enables, in ways that link to intimacy.

Multi-camera sitcom engenders a consistent, habitual way of looking for viewers: they watch from one side of the fourth wall, via cameras that occupy recurring positions, heights and angles, and that utilise similar compositions and framings (predominantly medium shots and medium close-ups). Barker (1985, 238) has argued that this means that viewers 'only look at a character rather than with them', but we want to propose that this set-up engenders a regime of *looking in*. With the cameras facing into the three-walled set, viewers look in 'sideways' through and across the invisible fourth wall, their eye lines privileged through planimetric staging and the trapezoidal design of the sets. There is no marked border between their viewing space and the fictional space, which open onto one another, with the viewing screen merging with the fourth wall to become a 'shared threshold', to borrow a term from Rhodes (2017, 11). As Kevin S. Bright sees it, multi-camera makes 'the show more intimate, making you feel like you're in the room observing rather than on the outside watching. I think the multi-camera format really lends itself to that, to bringing you in'. This contiguous spatial field is marked by a notion of inclusivity and, through its links to the theatrical, communality; and this looking in has a familiarity in itself (which informs the already noted familiarity of the sets). (This merging of space is further extended for fans who buy replicas of props from Monica's apartment, as Anne Marie Todd argues: 'As viewers appropriate physical objects featured in the show, their living rooms become extensions of the *Friends* set, even when the television is off' [2011, 861].)

Two examples will vividly demonstrate the effectiveness (and affectiveness) of this regime of looking, and the ways in which it helps to engender the programme's strategy of intimacy. The first is Ross and Rachel's break-up in episode 3.16. As we pointed out earlier in this chapter, the framing here remains quite wide, never going beyond a medium close-up, and this could be understood as lessening any notions of intimacy. However, a very different argument is possible and indeed necessary here, in order to be able to understand how this moment is both intimate and affective. The cameras are positioned directly in front of the couch, slightly to its left and in front of the entrance to Rachel's bedroom, capturing Ross's movement to the couch, where Rachel is initially seated, and then, following Rachel, to the space in front of her bedroom door. The cameras are placed at below shoulder height, emphasising together with the medium framing their facial expressions and poignant gestures, such as Aniston covering her eyes, or Schwimmer grasping her hand.

This set-up engenders multi-camera sitcom's typical regime of looking, where any deployment of, for example (extreme) close-ups or point-of-view shots that serve to highlight emotional significance in single-camera filming, would be distracting—indeed, in James Burrows's view, they would be 'really jarring'. They would disrupt the intimacy Newcomb notes concerning the 'sense of becoming a part of the lives and actions of the characters [that viewers] see' (1974, 253), an intimacy which is inextricably bound up with *how* viewers see those characters. But our argument does not rest on habit: the break-up has a strongly affective and intimate quality, because the multi-camera sitcom regime of looking is one of looking in. Viewers watch Ross and Rachel experiencing the break-up through and across the shared threshold, via multiple camera angles that together offer a sense of fullness of access to the dramatic moment. (The intimacy is furthered through the immediate quality of the [ostensibly] continuous action, captured through cutting between different cameras.) This looking in is accentuated through the camera work: when Ross sits down next to Rachel on the couch, the camera pans, tilts and zooms in; when Ross approaches Rachel by the space in front of her bedroom door, the camera zooms in; at the end of the sequence, just before the end credits appear, the camera zooms out. The zooming in subtly conveys a sense of immediacy and urgency, of looking and witnessing; the zooming out communicates a sense of exiting the fictional moment, inviting viewers to process the paradigm shift in the show's storytelling. Interestingly, when Ross approaches Rachel by the door, the camera deployed here is located downstage and stage left to the immediately preceding camera position. This decision by director James Burrows (who also directed 'The One with the Prom Video') to deploy a more distant camera means that more zooming in is required. As much as Burrows insisted in our interview that 'the camera is not a character in this show, it's a way to capture the action', the careful use of camera here enhances the sense of viewers looking in on Ross as he approaches Rachel in his desperate attempt to save their relationship. So, the deliberate use of the film-making apparatus—commonly linked to the 'cinematic'—here works with the 'theatrical' setting to foster a sense of intimacy.

This regime of looking in is marked by 'relatively distant framing' (Butler 2010, 193), but intimacy is supported through two other means. First, pertinent visual detail is observable through choices pertaining to the use of lighting and colour. The break-up takes place at night, and low levels of lighting are present. In the medium close-ups in which Rachel is articulating her feelings of hurt and betrayal, her facial expressions (e.g. her quivering lip and scrunched brow) are accentuated through the surrounding darkness, her black top and the soft key light on her. In the medium close-up when a tearful Ross cradles her hand and arm, his expressive hand movements are very visible against his dark top. So, the affectiveness of the performance is captured through these stylistic choices, the medium framing notwithstanding. Second, the wider framing locates them within the familiar, intimate space which at this point of the third season (even during the initial broadcast run) has

4 The One where They Look at Monica's Apartment …   157

Fig. 4.5 Ross (David Schwimmer) and Rachel (Jennifer Aniston) break up in 'The One with the Morning After' (3.16)

started to thicken with layers of meaning, especially as so much of Ross and Rachel's will-they-won't-they relationship is mapped onto Monica's apartment. As Ross crouches to clasp Rachel's middle (see Fig. 4.5), they are framed by the familiar backdrop that includes the purple walls, the balcony window, the Jouets poster and decorative items such as two warmly glowing lamps. By virtue of its familiarity, warmth and intimacy (increased by the low levels of lighting and prominence of the practicals), the framing through sheer contrast (not dissimilar to 'The One with the Prom Video') emphasises the significance and rawness of the break-up, adding a poignant layer to the show's diachronic accumulation of meanings and memories.

The second example to vividly demonstrate the effectiveness (and affectiveness) of this regime of looking is dramatically much less significant, but nevertheless striking. It occurs in the episode 'The One with

Fig. 4.6 Moment of rupture: Chandler (Matthew Perry) in 'The One with the Secret Closet' (8.14)

the Secret Closet' (8.14), when Chandler discovers that Monica has a messy closet, at the same time as the camera crosses the 180-degree line and presents the viewers with a rare sight: the fourth wall (see Fig. 4.6). This moment links to other instances within the programme that disrupt the show's habitual engagement with spatiality, such as the occasional switch away from in-studio exterior shots to actual location shooting (most prominently in London), or shots such as of Phoebe upside down in an armchair in 4.12. With the latter, Thompson argues, the unusual angle 'presents itself as a disruption to audience expectations, asking us to "look closer" by offering a view of the apartment that we cannot usually access' (2018, 763–764). However, the moment with the messy closet exceeds not only such disruptions but also other scenes that show the fourth wall, such as storylines taking place on the balcony, where the fourth wall can only be glimpsed in the background through the balcony window. As years of teaching have confirmed to us, the shot from within the closet needs to be understood as a moment of rupture that creates a somewhat unsettling viewing experience and undercuts intimacy.

Savorelli's argument concerning the centrality of space to sitcom will help establish how this rupture functions. He notes:

> While the use of three or four cameras creates a *dynamic effect of openness*, in reality the scenes are confined to enclosed, repetitive places, with *a strong sense of orientation*. In every represented space, one wall is never shown, and for obvious reasons: it is the proverbial fourth wall that separates the scene from the audience, and which can never be shot because it is not physically present. (Savorelli 2010, 23, emphases added)

In 8.14, the seven-second long shot ruptures the effect of openness and the strong sense of orientation, both of which inform the regime of looking in. As Fig. 4.6 shows, the space is suddenly closed, which is reinforced through the corridor and the panelling on the walls. The imaginary fourth wall has momentarily taken form, and is accompanied by items of furniture and decoration that for the viewers have not existed until this point, such as a framed painting, wooden cabinet and bookcase. (This is why this episode is of great interest to fans when producing three-dimensional renderings of Monica's apartment, as *Sims*-player Elliandra's [2018] commentary confirms.) The contiguous spatial field is unsettled, with the shared threshold that connects the fictional world and space of the audience highlighted as a border that demarcates and separates the two spaces. The orientation is disturbed, both in the sense of the direction with which viewers look in and in terms of their positioning within the space. The viewers' regular space, which is so familiar and usually presented as stable, is cut off and cut out, highlighting it as a construct marked by non-fixity and a non-space that here cannot merge with the on-screen space. The regime of looking in creates a particular viewing experience marked by intimacy and immersion, but the latter becomes here somewhat unsettled, albeit briefly.

This links to texture, which as Fife Donaldson has explored 'is not limited to the sense of touch, but encompasses broader expressions of quality and nature' (2014, 1). Her work has perceptively demonstrated that television needs to be understood as:

> a strongly textured medium, one created and perpetuated through a process of layering, where the fine detail of the narrative (the moment) contributes to the pattern of the overall fabric (the series/serial structure). 'Texture' […] concerns the character or quality of something as resulting from its making or composition; an affective connection between detail and structure. Texture is at once the material consistency produced by aspects of *mise-en-scène* within a shot *and* rhythmic progression of editing from shot to shot. (2016, 5–6, emphasis in original)

In 8.14 the moment with the messy closet ruptures (albeit temporarily) the usual texture of multi-camera sitcom. It is worth noting that the closet door is present from the beginning of the programme, and a brief glimpse of what it may conceal is available in 1.6 ('The One with the Butt'). John Shaffner explained to us that he sees it as the responsibility of the production designer to allow for scope for future storytelling: 'We put a door in the hallway, without saying where it went to, and I thought: Let's see where the story will take us.' The revelation of its messy contents and use as a camera position occurs over halfway through the eighth season, so the rupture was already notable during the initial broadcast run, breaking as it does with viewers' habitual spatial experience of and the regime of looking in at Monica's apartment and multi-camera sitcom space more broadly. Just as Chandler finds out something about the apartment, so the viewers can become aware of something much more significant than Monica's hidden mess: through the rupture, the intimacy facilitated by multi-camera sitcom's regime of looking becomes through its absence more noticeable and highlighted as deserving more attention and recognition.

Conclusion

In his engagement with sitcom style, Butler has pointed out that single-camera programmes may 'employ a zero-degree schema despite their single-camera mode of production' (2010, 197). Dias Branco has noted that notions of zero-degree style have not been ascribed 'to single-camera sitcoms such as *Scrubs* [...] because these series do not rely on a fixed system of several cameras and so stylistic choices become *more evident*' (2013, 95, emphasis in original). What this chapter has worked to demonstrate is that, instead of being approached via notions of lack and restriction, it is more productive to understand multi-camera sitcom as having a style. This style, through drawing on notions linked to the 'cinematic' and the 'theatrical', may be understood as a style marked by intermediality (see Uricchio 1999; Pethő 2011). It is style that can be as subtle as it is complex, involving a myriad of creative choices and practical decisions, and operating at a synchronic and diachronic level. It both deserves and requires careful, detailed attention to recognise and indeed appreciate the pleasures of multi-camera sitcoms.

These pleasures differ to those offered by single-camera sitcoms, which frequently link to the markers of intensified continuity (see Butler 2010, 83), especially as concerns speed, mobility and flexibility. A move beyond the long-standing focus on apparatus helps to uncover the pleasures of multi-camera sitcom style as hinged around texture, repetition and intimacy. For this, they are no less televisual—indeed, these pleasures are central to the medium and future engagement with televisuality. These pleasures speak to the importance of craft and the achievements of the multi-camera sitcom production personnel, both above-the-line and (perhaps especially) below-the-line. Set design warrants more attention as an integral part of style and in terms of how choices here influence the deployment of camera and editing in multi-camera sitcom, and vice versa. Certainly, John Shaffner and Greg Grande are the tip of the iceberg, with Shaffner having a long-standing partnership with Joe Stewart and Grande attesting to the importance of his crew as a 'well-oiled machine' (SDSA 2002/2003, 37).

Butler concluded his 2010 book on television style (which mentions *Friends* once) by suspecting that 'the multiple-camera proscenium schema will indeed die off, but that some mutated version of the single-camera televisual sitcom will survive. As with any mutation, the new, hybrid species will be more hearty than its ancestors' (2010, 217). A quarter century after it began, *Friends* continues to be the show most watched by our students, with countless articles, memes and clips shared on social media, and in late 2018, streaming services including Netflix and Hulu battled for the rights to this show, not the many descendants that have sought to emulate it. With its strategy of intimacy continuing to engage new viewers across multiple digital contexts (which will include HBO Max from 2020), *Friends* shows no signs of dying off. Neither does multi-camera sitcom more broadly, with *The Big Bang Theory* finishing the 2017/2018 season as US television's most watched series in terms of total viewership (de Moraes and Hipes 2018), critical and commercial success for shows such as *Mom*, the recent revival of *Will & Grace* and other programmes, as well as Fox shifting towards multi-camera comedy in 2018.

As this chapter has shown, *Friends* is both exceptional and representative of multi-camera sitcom, working with (and not against) the conventions of multi-camera production, without being reduced to them or them being as reductive as is frequently assumed. In doing so, *Friends* highlights that multi-camera sitcom has more possibilities for creative engagement than has been generally acknowledged. Indeed, while Butler's definition of televisuality significantly differs from ours, *Friends* fulfils some of the central achievements of Butler's televisual schema, in which style 'carries meaning. It makes jokes. It might call attention to itself. It can even make familiar things seem strange, creating art as technique' (2010, 197). But, while it can make the familiar seem strange, its strongest artistic achievement is its aesthetics of intimacy, through which *Friends* is marked by and speaks to some of the pleasures and achievements of its medium.

Bibliography

Anne-Sophie. 2014. Friends' Apartment in 3D: Oh My God! HomeByMe. https://home.by.me/blog/friends-apartment-in-3d/. Accessed 14 January 2019.

Barker, David. 1985. Television Production Techniques as Communication. *Critical Studies in Mass Communication* 2: 234–246.

Barnwell, Jane. 2004. *Production Design: Architects of the Screen*. London and New York: Wallflower.

Boym, Svetlana. 1998. On Diasporic Intimacy: Ilya Kabakov's Installations and Immigrant Homes. *Critical Inquiry* 24 (2): 498–524.

Butler, Jeremy G. 2010. *Television Style*. New York and London: Routledge.

Caldwell, John T. 1995. *Televisuality: Style, Crisis, and Authority in American Television*. New Brunswick, NJ: Rutgers University Press.

Caughie, John. 2000. *Television Drama: Realism, Modernism, and British Culture*. Oxford: Oxford University Press.

Chidester, Phil. 2008. May the Circle Stay Unbroken: *Friends*, the Presence of Absence, and the Rhetorical Reinforcement of Whiteness. *Critical Studies in Mass Communication* 25 (2): 157–174. https://doi.org/10.1080/15295030802031772.

Comedy Central. 2016. What to Buy to Turn Your Home Into a Friends Apartment. http://www.comedycentral.co.uk/friends/articles/heres-where-to-buy-all-the-iconic-props-from-the-friends-apartments. Accessed 14 January 2019.

Comedy Central. 2018. Artist Makes Amazing 3D Miniatures of the Coolest TV & Movie Sets. http://www.comedycentral.co.uk/friends/articles/artist-makes-amazing-3d-miniatures-of-the-coolest-tv-movie-sets. Accessed 14 January 2019.

D'Arcy, Geraint. 2019. *Critical Approaches to TV and Film Set Design*. London and New York: Routledge.

De Moraes, Lisa, and Patrick Hipes. 2018. 2017–18 TV Series Ratings Rankings: NFL Football, 'Big Bang' Top Charts. Deadline. https://deadline.com/2018/05/2017-2018-tv-series-ratings-rankings-full-list-of-shows-1202395851/. Accessed 14 January 2019.

Dias Branco, Sérgio. 2013. Situating Comedy: Inhabitation and Duration in Classical American Sitcoms. In *Television Aesthetics and Style*, ed. Jason Jacobs and Steven Peacock, 93–102. London: Bloomsbury.

Elliandra. 2018. FRIENDS APARTMENT | Sims 4 Speed Build (No CC). YouTube. https://www.youtube.com/watch?v=iRh3jQufzCk&fbclid=IwAR-3JfsijgdVRZdqQLtep1Mc-pwgja6lebXN0srMwyLM15-n4FsxYdD8W21c. Accessed 14 January 2019.

Fife Donaldson, Lucy. 2014. *Texture in Film*. London: Palgrave Macmillan.

Fife Donaldson, Lucy. 2016. Series Spaces: Revisiting and Re-evaluating Inspector Morse. *Journal of Popular Television* 4 (1): 3–28. https://doi.org/10.1386/jptv.4.1.3_1.

Friedman, Diana. 2005. *Sitcom Style: Inside America's Favorite TV Homes*. New York: Clarkson Potter.

Furniture Choice. 2015. 17 Awesome Ways to Recreate Monica's Apartment. https://www.furniturechoice.co.uk/blog/inspiration/17-awesome-ways-to-recreate-monicas-apartment/. Accessed 14 January 2019.

Holdsworth, Amy. 2011. *Television, Memory and Nostalgia*. Basingstoke: Palgrave Macmillan.

Howie, Luke. 2008. I'll Be There for You—The Meanings and Consequences of 9/11 in *Friends*. The Annual Conference of the Australian Sociological Association 2008. Re-imagining Sociology: Conference Publication Proceedings, 1–21.

Jaramillo, Deborah L. 2013. Rescuing Television from 'the Cinematic': The Perils of Dismissing Television Style. In *Television Aesthetics and Style*, ed. Jason Jacobs and Steven Peacock, 67–75. London: Bloomsbury.

Klevan, Andrew. 2005. *Film Performance: From Achievement to Appreciation*. London and New York: Wallflower.

Lury, Karen. 2005. *Interpreting Television*. London: Hodder Education.

Newcomb, Horace. 1974. *TV: The Most Popular Art*. Garden City, NY: Anchor Books.

Newman, Michael Z., and Elana Levine. 2012. *Legitimating Television: Media Convergence and Cultural Status*. New York and London: Routledge.

Pethő, Ágnes. 2011. *Cinema and Intermediality: The Passion for the In-Between*. Cambridge: Cambridge Scholars Publishing.

Rhodes, John David. 2017. *Spectacle of Property: The House in American Film*. Minneapolis: University of Minnesota Press.

Robertson Wojcik, Pamela. 2010. *The Apartment Plot: Urban Living in American Film and Popular Culture, 1945 to 1975*. Durham and London: Duke University Press.

Romano, Andrea. 2014. Superfan Perfectly Recreates 'Friends' for 'The Sims 4'. Mashable UK. https://mashable.com/2014/09/08/friends-in-sims/?europe=true. Accessed 14 January 2019.

Sandell, Jillian. 1998. I'll Be There For You: *Friends* and the Fantasy of Alternative Families. *American Studies* 39 (2): 141–155.

Savoie, Gabrielle. 2018. We Redecorated the "Friends" Apartments for 2018. My Domaine. http://www.mydomaine.com/friends-apartment/. Accessed 14 January 2019.

Savorelli, Antonio. 2010. *Beyond Sitcom: New Directions in American Television Comedy*. Jefferson, NC: McFarland.

Sepinwall, Alan, and Matt Zoller Seitz. 2016. *TV (The Book): Two Experts Pick the Greatest American Shows of All Time*. New York, NY: Grand Central Publishing.

Set Decorators Society of America (SDSA). 2002/2003. *SET DÉCOR* Winter 2002/2003. Hollywood, CA.

Shabazz, Demetria R. 2016. Negotiated Boundaries: Production Practices and the Making of Representation in *Julia*. In *The Sitcom Reader: America Re-viewed, Still Skewed*, ed. Mary M. Dalton and Laura R. Linder, 91–104. Albany: State University of New York Press.

Thompson, Lauren Jade. 2015. Nothing Suits Me Like a Suit: Performing Masculinity in *How I Met Your Mother*. *Critical Studies in Television* 10 (2): 21–36. https://doi.org/10.7227/CST.10.2.3.

Thompson, Lauren Jade. 2018. 'It's Like a Guy Never Lived Here!': Reading the Gendered Domestic Spaces of *Friends*. *Television & New Media* 19 (8): 758–774. https://doi.org/10.1177/1527476418778414.

Todd, Anne Marie. 2011. Saying Goodbye to *Friends*: Fan Culture as Lived Experience. *The Journal of Popular Culture* 44 (4): 854–871. https://doi.org/10.1111/j.1540-5931.2011.00866.x.

Uricchio, William. 1999. Intermedial Challenges to Television's Definition. In *Intertextuality & Visual Media: Sekvens 99*, ed. Ib Bondebjerg and Helle Haastrup, 171–183. Copenhagen: Institute for Film.

Ward, Maria. 2016. The Cast of *Friends* Is Reuniting! 40 Must-Haves from Monica Geller's Apartment. *Vogue*. https://www.vogue.com/article/friends-apartment-how-to-get-the-look-monica-geller-cast-reunion. Accessed 14 January 2019.

Waring, Olivia. 2016. There Was Something Really Weird Going on with Monica's Apartment in Friends—But Did You Spot It? *Metro*. http://metro.co.uk/2016/03/04/there-was-something-really-weird-going-on-with-monicas-apartment-in-friends-but-did-you-spot-it-5731671/. Accessed 14 January 2019.

Williams, Raymond. 1977. *Marxism and Literature*. Oxford: Oxford University Press.
Williams, Raymond. 2011 [1974]. Drama in a Dramatised Society. In *Raymond Williams on Television: Selected Writings*, ed. Alan O'Connor, 3–13. London and New York: Routledge.

Television

All in the Family (1971–1979), USA: CBS.
Cheers (1982–1993), USA: NBC.
Columbo (1968–1978, 1989–2003), USA: NBC, ABC.
Dharma & Greg (1997–2002), USA: ABC.
Ellen (1992–1999), USA: ABC.
Everybody Loves Raymond (1996–2005), USA: CBS.
Frasier (1993–2004), USA: NBC.
Friends (1994–2004), USA: NBC.
How I Met Your Mother (2005–2014), USA: CBS.
Law & Order (1990–2010), USA: NBC.
Mad About You (1992–1999), USA: NBC.
Maude (1972–1978), USA: CBS.
Mom (2013–present), USA: CBS.
New Girl (2011–2018), USA: Fox.
Rhoda (1974–1978), USA: CBS.
Scrubs (2001–2008, 2009–2010), USA: NBC, ABC.
Seinfeld (1989–1998), USA: NBC.
The Big Bang Theory (2007–2019), USA: CBS.
The Comeback (2005, 2014), USA: HBO.
The Fresh Prince of Bel-Air (1990–1996), USA: NBC.
The Honeymooners (1955–1956), USA: CBS.
The Mary Tyler Moore Show (1970–1977), USA: CBS.
The New Adventures of Old Christine (2006–2010), USA: CBS.

The Office—An American Workplace (2005–2013), USA: NBC.
Will & Grace (1998–2006, 2018–present), USA: NBC.

Film

Minnelli, V. 1955. *The Cobweb*. USA: Metro-Goldwyn-Mayer.
Welles, O. 1941. *Citizen Kane*. USA: RKO Radio Pictures.

5

The One with the Emblematic Problematic Fave: *Friends* and the Politics of Representation

The strong ongoing interest in *Friends* noted earlier in this book has been largely playing out via two parallel strands: on the one hand, there is the considerable fan celebration of favourite moments, with countless GIFs, videos and quotes being circulated with remarkable frequency on social media. The interest in continuity errors and spatial inconsistencies discussed in Chapter 4 is part of this celebration, generally marked by amused fondness. On the other hand, there is the equally considerable criticism the show has been receiving for its representation of different identities, as outlined in the introduction to this book and explored in relation to issues of humour in Chapter 2. As we have noted, there is a parallel between the paratextual criticism and the available scholarly literature, which has predominately understood the programme as reinforcing hegemonic discourses on a number of levels. (Not that such celebratory and critical attitudes are necessarily mutually exclusive; as Kristyn Gorton remarks, 'viewers can have an emotional *and* critical position on a televisual text simultaneously, which contradicts the assumption that emotion disables a critical position' [2009, 68; emphasis in original].) While other 'sitcoms have provided fodder for major cultural controversies and conversations' (Morreale 2003, xii), *Friends* appears strikingly comprehensive in its 'problematicity', with charges ranging from racism, fat-shaming, homophobia, transphobia and sexism to sexual harassment, as well as becoming implicated in the #MeToo movement.

Such a thorough failing strikes us as remarkable given Joanne Morreale's argument concerning sitcom's potential to 'allow for a multiplicity of discourses' (2003, xii) that facilitate contradictory relationships with social change, and the complexity and contestability of meaning within the genre potentially introduced by the presence of humour (Mills 2009). With its continuing popularity in a historical moment marked by notions of wokeness and high-profile attention to issues concerning diversity and inclusion, *Friends* has become the emblematic 'problematic fave' (to draw on a term associated with social justice blogging and the 'Your Fave is Problematic' Tumblr). In her dissection of the paratextual framing of another 'problematic fave', Faye Woods has noted that 'commentaries on *Girls* became a cottage industry, driving page-views across the Internet, with this critique doing valuable work in bringing concerns around television representation from the niche spaces of women's websites into mainstream press discourse' (2015, 45). The same can be said for the by now well established backlash to *Friends*, both in that at least some of the criticism will be motivated by procuring readership, and in that significant cultural space is being made available for the engagement with televisual representation, albeit on an amplified level and, as we will explore, with less nuance than has been the case with *Girls*.

The One with the Paratextual Patterns

There are three further points worth noting about this backlash, which was framed and accelerated by the show's 2015 Netflix US acquisition. Firstly, this recent and ongoing paratextual framing shows a shift in terms of *Friends*' wider critical reception. Gray notes 'the all-important early frames through which we will examine, react to, and evaluate textual consumption' (2010, 26), but early discussions of *Friends* rather differ from those, for example, of *Girls*, which were strongly invested in engaging with representational issues (Woods 2015). Early reviews of *Friends* focused instead on issues of genre, especially in terms of the craft of scriptwriting and the performance skills by the main cast (e.g. Tucker 1994; O'Connor 1994). Where there were any references to representational issues, these were brief and focused on gender and sexuality. (For example, Scott commented that the show 'touts promiscuity' [1994].) There would be some criticism during the show's original broadcast run (e.g. Fairfax Media Australia 2003)—probably the most high-profile example is Oprah Winfrey's 'I'd like y'all to get a black friend' comment on *The Oprah Winfrey Show* in 1995—but overall, the programme's early and mid-term frames were not dominated by critiques of *Friends*' representational politics.

So, while scholarship has mostly continued to focus on the problems with the show's approach to representation, this significant shift in the paratextual framing shows the continued significance of the latter beyond the 'the all-important early frame' (Gray 2010, 26), which may become supplanted for programmes with enduring popularity. The paratextual shift also reflects a broader movement in recent mainstream cultural discourses towards more engagement with debates around representation, informed by increasing intersectional awareness. Her continuing emphasis on *Friends* being 'about that time in your life when your friends are your family' notwithstanding, Marta Kauffman has been responsive to this shift. She readily acknowledges her own dissatisfaction with some of the show's representational approaches, especially as far as Chandler's parent, Helena Handbasket, is concerned. As Kauffman put it to us, 'we didn't have the vocabulary to identify that this is a transsexual character, so we kept referring to her as Chandler's father', noting that with her contemporary awareness, she would be taking a different approach now; a view shared by Kevin S. Bright during our interview with him.

The second point worth noting about the backlash to *Friends* is that the shift in recent years towards critically re-evaluating the series has not been driven by the most established anglophone television critics, highlighting 'the impact of spreadable (Jenkins et al. 2013) television commentary in the web 2.0 era' (Woods 2015, 38). Within the vortex of critical commentary on *Friends*, there has been relative silence from key cultural critics and platforms, including Kendra James, Emily Nussbaum, James Poniewozik, Alyssa Rosenberg, Mo Ryan, Dodai

Stewart, Jenna Wortham, as well as *Jezebel*, *Racialicious*, (the now defunct) *The Hairpin*, *The New Yorker* and *The New York Times*. Alan Sepinwall and Willa Paskin each reflected on the show in 2014, as part of the ten-year anniversary of the broadcast of the final episode, but without castigating its representational track record. It is certainly interesting that these key cultural commentators have had little to nothing to say about *Friends*' politics of representation. This is in stark contrast to the thoughtful, in-depth debates several of them have offered on problematic programmes—and we cannot help but notice that these tend to be single-camera shows—such as *Girls* and also *Friends*' 1990s contemporary *Sex and the City* (on which Nussbaum offered attentive reflections in 2013). Whilst the backlash to *Friends* is to be welcomed in that it reflects a widespread interest in issues of diversity and identity, it also—and this is not unrelated to the relative silence of key critical stakeholders—bears out a strikingly strong (if not easy) critical consensus, lacking a certain degree of nuance.

This leads us to the third point to be made about the backlash, which is that what has begun to emerge is something of a backlash to the backlash, and this anti-backlash has been led by comedians. Aziz Ansari featured in his preparatory shows for his 2019 *Road to Nowhere* stand-up tour a set-piece that 'imagines police persecuting white people for their love of Friends and their irresponsible use of farmers' markets' (Logan 2018). As a comedian of colour with long-standing links to discourses of wokeness, who in early 2018 became linked to the #MeToo movement when allegations of sexual misconduct were published online, Ansari's recent material seeks to locate the criticism of *Friends* within the broader movement to 'competitive virtue-signalling online and the Twitter rush to judgment on anyone deemed insufficiently PC' (ibid.). In the summer of 2018, a sketch from *Tracey Breaks the News* titled 'You Woke?' went viral, in which Tracey Ullman hosts a 'support group for people who are so woke that they're finding it impossible to have any fun at all'. As their homework, the 'overly virtuous' young group members were supposed to watch and enjoy 'that old people's sitcom', *Friends*, which is (of course) judged 'deeply problematic' by one of the group members. Articulating the competitive virtue-signalling of interest to Ansari, Ullman's sketch not dissimilarly takes issue with the outrage cycles and 'call out' culture that have come to dominate swathes of social media and cultural discourses more broadly.

Ansari and Ullman's (albeit brief) comedic attention to such issues link to the wider contemporary debates about the role of comedy in the 'age of liberal outrage'. These debates have engaged comedians such as Lisa Lampanelli, Jim Norton, Chris Rock and Jerry Seinfeld, who, their different approaches to comedy notwithstanding, share concerns about the importance of creative risk-taking at a time when offence seems to be taken quickly (if not readily) and is certainly shared widely with more ease than was the case before the advent of digital technology. Interestingly, the ideas put forward by Ansari, Ullman and the other comedians have some resonance with ideas expressed within ideologically conservative discourses, with British right-wing tabloids such as *The Sun* pouring scorn on the 'permanently offended members of Generation Snowflake' (Harrison 2018) for their criticism of *Friends*.

The One where They Emphasise the Importance of Context and Tone

It is beyond the scope of this chapter to consider the fundamental questions about the purpose and status of comedy raised by the *Friends* backlash and the critical response emerging to it (see also Chapter 2), which are further framed by a charged socio-political landscape that includes the rise of white supremacism in the USA, as well as shifts to the ideological far-right within several European countries. (Such questions received some attention during the Lyle v. Warner Brothers Television Productions lawsuit [Heuman 2016].) What in this chapter we instead intend to do is engage with *Friends*' politics of representation and its backlash through close analysis of a specific aspect of the politics of representation as they play out within and across the series. In the introduction to this book, we identified a lack of in-depth textual analysis of *Friends* within the limited scholarship that exists on the show, and the critical engagement of the programme's politics of representation is no exception. Much of the work here has displayed tendencies to not engage in detail with the use of style and performance. This lack of attention to textual detail has sometimes been accompanied by a level of sloppiness, with curious factual errors. The focus usually remains on the level of narrative and dialogue, the latter of which tends to get quoted as 'evidence' for representational failings. There is also a pattern of conflating the perspectives articulated and/or embodied by individual characters with the show's overall critical position. And where attention has indeed been paid to the fact that the programme is a comedy, this usually manifests in the form of brief references to 'irony', without unpacking this any further. (Chapter 2 undertakes in-depth analysis of how humour works within the programme.) Our argument may be simple, but for that no less effective, in that we will emphasise that critical scrutiny of *Friends* has an important and worthwhile contribution to make to engagement with the show and television culture more broadly, but that such scrutiny can only be illuminating if it is informed by attentive, nuanced attention to textual detail and alert to context and tone.

Some of the critique of the series—including from the students we have taught—has tended to include references to contemporary sitcoms such as *The Good Place*, *Brooklyn Nine-Nine* or *One Day at a Time* that have received praise for their inclusive casting and progressive politics of representation. This is very likely informed by consuming these shows via streaming services—British viewers may see them all lined up next to each other on the Netflix UK home screen—which facilitates a joint reading that for younger viewers supplants those earlier joint readings by US viewers of *Friends* with its 1990s NBC schedule brethren, especially *Seinfeld* (see Chidester 2008). Such comparative critique is a touch ahistorical, risking imposing a contemporary lens onto past representations, and does not give sufficient consideration to the importance of context, both socio-culturally and in terms of the creative industries. To directly compare a US network show that began broadcasting on NBC during the 1990s culture wars to network shows that premiered in the different socio-cultural climate of the mid-to-late-2010s (*The Good Place* and *Brooklyn Nine-Nine*), or to an original Netflix production (*One Day at a Time*), is to miss out on the significance of the contexts that shaped *Friends*. It also misses out on the contexts that have shaped the other series in question; for example, Mareike Jenner (2018) has detailed how Netflix—whose original programming further includes Kauffman's *Grace and Frankie*—has embraced particular definitions of diversity for the purposes of brand distinction.

Furthermore, much of the criticism of the 'actually pretty shocking things Friends couldn't get away with today' (Baxter-Wright 2017) has also tended to ignore that, while US television in particular has received acclaim in recent years for on and/or off-screen diversity exemplified by the sitcoms above or *Black-ish*, its long history of problematic approaches to representation has not ceased. To name just a few examples, *2 Broke Girls*, its diverse mix of characters notwithstanding, has been described by Emily Nussbaum as 'so racist it is less offensive than baffling' (2011, 74); *How I Met Your Mother* featured yellow face in 2014; and there is no shortage of statistics attesting to prevailing under-representation both on and off-screen (e.g. Hunt et al. 2018; Lauzen 2018). While critiquing *Friends* may help with taking stock of important progress that has been made, such critique should not serve to obscure contemporary problems, even unintentionally or implicitly.

So, criticism of *Friends* needs to be alert to context, and be open to the idea that *Friends* can and needs to be considered progressive for its time, at least for some representational issues. Moreover, criticism of *Friends* also needs to be alive to matters concerning tone. An interesting, slippery concept, 'tone' as a term gets mentioned in some scholarship on sitcom (e.g. Mills 2009; Vermeulen and Whitfield 2013), but usually without definitional discussion and in-depth exploration. (Phil Wickham [2013] is a welcome exception.) Tone is more established in film studies, where Douglas Pye has explicated it as being:

> not simply about what is being signified in the dramatic material of the film but about the ways in which the film addresses its spectator and implicitly invites us to understand its attitude to its material and the stylistic register it employs. (2007, 7)

Stressing the inextricable interrelationship between the two, Pye's seminal work importantly distinguishes between tone and mood: mood concerns the general atmosphere of a film; it involves 'a sense of the film's *overall* orientation towards the fictional world and action (serious, comedic, satirical, ironic, and so on), towards its conventions […]

and the audience' (ibid., 30, emphasis added). Tone, however, is 'a term under which to analyse effects created by the film's shifting texture' (ibid., 22). Thus, considerations of tone need to engage with 'more specific tonal qualities [that] are implied scene by scene and even moment by moment by the network of decisions that create the fictional world, its characters and events, and present them to the spectator' (ibid., 30). As Pye's words indicate, engaging with tone requires close textual analysis and in-depth engagement with material detail, rather than lists and cursory references, attentive to how humour may function at any given moment and where a stereotype is present, if it is part of a critical project to interrogate the stereotype.

Driven by an interest in context and tone, this chapter will undertake the still much needed close textual analysis of *Friends* via one major case study, Professor Charlie Wheeler played by Aisha Tyler, before concluding with reflections on what *Friends*' politics of representation and the backlash to it may tell us about the sitcom genre more broadly.

The One with the Dominant Whiteness

With its comprehensive list of representational failings, the major charge that has been made concerns *Friends*' lack of black characters, especially given that it is set in a city as culturally and ethnically diverse as New York. Here, paratextual criticism has moved beyond earlier charges that the show 'doesn't appear to contain black people' (Fairfax Media Australia 2003) towards articulating that the black characters who do appear are both limited in number and occupy marginal roles. A high-profile example of this can be found in DocFuture's video 'A semi-alphabetical listing of Black actors with speaking roles on Friends' (2010), which charts the fleeting presence of black identities on the show, albeit with a number of omissions. (It is somewhat reminiscent of, but displays more reflexivity than, Tijana Mamula's *Homophobic Friends: 'The One With All The Gay Jokes'*, which cuts together 50 minutes' worth of scenes from the series to shed 'new light on homophobic attitudes in contemporary TV culture' [politicalremix 2011].) What may be gleaned from this video is some support for the argument by

Entman and Rojecki that 'in shows favored by White audiences, the interchanges between Blacks and Whites are restricted by unequal power relationships' (2000, 149), with the predominant subordinate/superior dynamics working to preclude any level of intimacy between these characters and the six white friends, as Lisa Marie Marshall (2007) and Shelley Cobb (2018) agree.

Friends is, to be sure, marked by whiteness, as Jillian Sandell (1998) and Phil Chidester (2008) discuss in their influential scholarly responses. Sandell argues for a close interconnection between the show's emphasis on 'the "alternative family" of friends and the unmistakeable whiteness of this family' (1998, 149), whereby the existence and visibility of the former 'is made possible only by simultaneously rendering invisible' (ibid., 143) the latter. A decade later, Chidester proposes that:

> *Friends* incorporates the closed circle as a core visual metaphor to represent whiteness as a marker of privilege, and that it does so in two crucial ways. First, the sitcom reinforces whiteness's exclusive freedom to convert its public spaces to private ones; and second, it argues for whiteness's continued right (and concurrent responsibility) to maintain its core sense of purity against racial outsiders by limiting and regulating contacts with the racialized Other. (2008, 160)

Both note that the show is devoid of any explicit discourse on race, including on its own whiteness. While the show does include identities that have historically not been ascribed the status of whiteness (i.e. Jewish and South European immigrant identities), the complexity of whiteness that is inscribed into its core group is not explicitly addressed or explored within the programme. (This is the case even on those few occasions where Monica and Ross's, as well as Rachel's, Jewishness—the latter having received considerable paratextual discussion—or Joey's Italian-American heritage are directly touched on by the narrative.)

The dominant and (within the show) uninterrogated whiteness of *Friends* must be understood as located within the context of the US television industrial landscape in the 1990s. Needing to respond to increasing competition and shifting demographics, networks were becoming more amenable to including LGBTQ+ identities within their programming, and *Friends* was no exception, receiving a GLAAD Media Award in 1995. Over the same time period, new broadcasters such as Fox and then later UPN strategically pursued series 'specifically hailing the Black audience' (Lotz 2005, 140). This saw a concomitant shift by the three established networks, which 'gradually reduced their use of series designed to attract an ethnically mixed audience and instead developed comedy series with overwhelmingly White casts (*Seinfeld*, *Friends*, *Frasier*)' (ibid.). The networks' engagement with the contentious issue of race was most vividly to be found in their news coverage of the 'domestic media spectacles of the 1990s' (Harrison 2010, 102), such as the 1992 Los Angeles riots and the 1995 trial of O. J. Simpson. This emphasis on on-screen racial diversity within the less established competitors in the 1990s would prove to be temporary, and it would be prudent for current praise of US television for its investment in diversity to bear in mind how context-dependent and cyclical such investment has shown itself to be over time. (Netflix's March 2019 cancellation of *One Day at a Time*, which it awkwardly attempted to justify with woke-ish rhetoric, is a case in point.) Moreover, as Beretta E. Smith-Shomade has importantly pointed out, 'Black women failed to benefit substantially from the colorized onslaught of 1990s comedies' (2002, 31), with black sitcoms such as *The Fresh Prince of Bel-Air* or *Martin* preoccupied with their male protagonists.

Something of an exception to this preoccupation was *Living Single* (Fox 1993–1998), a sitcom created by Yvette Lee Bowser, about a group of six black friends—four women (played by Erika Alexander, Kim Coles, Kim Fields and Queen Latifah) and two men (Terrence C. Carson and John Henton)—living together in two different apartments within the same Brooklyn brownstone. If this premise sounds familiar, then it will not be surprising to hear that, with the release of the *Moonlight* video providing fresh impetus, recent years have seen charges that *Friends* is 'No More Than a White Ripoff' (Haughton 2018) of *Living Single*, embodying 'the gentrification of Black art' (ibid.). Given the specificity of the personal experience that informed the creation of *Friends*, as attested by our interviewees

Marta Kauffman, Kevin S. Bright and John Shaffner, this seems highly unlikely to us. Indeed, it is worth bearing in mind the close intertextual links between genre exponents, and that *Living Single* was previously 'called [...] *Designing Women* in black' (Smith-Shomade 2002, 53) because of certain shared attributes.

The more important point to be made concerning the relationship between *Living Single* and *Friends* is that the former was also a Warner Bros show, but received much less promotional support by its studio and network than the latter. (It was also scheduled by Fox against *Friends* [see Braxton 1996].) This vividly demonstrates 'wide-scale institutional defaults to whiteness' (Woods 2015, 47) within the US television industry. It also links back to *Moonlight* in that, as Lauren Cramer has argued:

> One of the pleasures of watching the video is recognizing the impressive list of films/TV shows these actors, writers, and comedians have been a part of and how those works connect to each other. For example, Tessa Thompson stars in the upcoming film *Sorry to Bother* [sic] (Riley, 2018) with Lakeith Stanfield, who was in *Get Out* (Peele, 2017) with Lil Rel Howery. In its most recent season, Howery joined the cast of *Insecure*[.] (2018)

It seems more than plausible to suggest that the cast of *Living Single* did not receive the same type of, or as many, professional high-profile opportunities from *Living Single*'s hampered run than the black creative practitioners named above have been able to access and actualise in recent years. (It remains to be seen how on-screen and off-screen diversity in US television will fare once the current moment of 'peak television' has crested.) That *Living Single* is far less widely remembered than its white brethren *Friends* certainly echoes the high profile bestowed onto Lena Dunham's *Girls* and not Mara Brock Akil's *Girlfriends* within broader cultural discourses. Overall, *Friends*' unprecedented cultural visibility and ubiquity are firmly located within whiteness as an institutional norm that continues to go far beyond *Friends* as an individual show.

The One where Aisha Tyler Plays a White Woman on *Friends*

Into this context of whiteness, *Friends* would eventually introduce three women of colour in narratively more significant roles: Julie, played by Lauren Tom, in seasons 1–2; very briefly Kristen, played by Gabrielle Union, in season 7; and finally, Charlie Wheeler, played by Aisha Tyler, in seasons 9–10. There are a number of issues that frame (if not overshadow) Charlie's presence that have been identified in critical responses to the show. One such issue is that Charlie's presence is 'too little, too late' (Fairfax Media Australia 2003). It is little in that Tyler appears in 9 out of 236 episodes—which is still more than Tom and Union combined—receiving approximately 54 minutes of screen time. It is late in that Tyler first appears towards the end of the show's penultimate season, which Todd Boyd has understood as an empty gesture and a 'gimmick' (in Fairfax Media Australia 2003) aimed at gathering attention.

Here, it is worth bearing in mind the parameters and restrictions placed on network shows in the 1990s, especially those with an earlier slot in the prime-time schedule, such as *Friends*. For example, Marta Kauffman recalled for us the fight about the word 'nipple' in an early *Friends*' script, and the objections from Standards and Practices to showing a condom foil. At the same time, it is equally worth bearing in mind that *Friends* would become so crucial to NBC's ratings success that it seems very unlikely that the network would have objected to earlier attempts to introduce more significant on-screen diversity. A link may be drawn here between the introduction of Charlie and that of Donald Glover's character Sandy in *Girls*, another show critiqued for being set in a very white New York, albeit on premium cable HBO and premiering 18 years after *Friends* began its broadcast run. Both Tyler's and Glover's presences have been understood in terms of their respective shows responding to criticism (see Marghitu and Ng 2013)—only *Girls* did so much sooner, at the start of its second season—and as a perfunctory gesture towards more inclusivity.

In addition to this whiff of tokenism, what also marks Charlie's presence is the charge that Ta-Nehisi Coates articulated in a piece on *Girls*:

I think back to Friends, which for years, was dogged by criticism of its all-white cast. When its creators finally relented they casted two great talents – Aisha Tyler and later Gabriel Union – but didn't even bother to write separate story-lines. They simply recycled the same plot, and plugged in a new black girl. (2012)

While Coates gets the time-line wrong and misspells Union's first name, he rightly identifies—as does DocFuture's (2010) video—that to some extent, Charlie's plot function is a clumsy echo. Cobb notes that Kristen's brief appearance 'quite clearly and succinctly recapitulates the plotting of the initial (and brief) inclusion and subsequent exclusion of both Julie and Charlie' (2018, 715) as part of her overall argument that the main narrative function of the latter two women of colour is to ensure and confirm the postfeminist fated-ness of Ross and Rachel as a couple.

So, it is clear that Charlie Wheeler's introduction on *Friends* is certainly fraught with some difficulty. We now wish to contribute to the existing debates on her presence, which further include brief attention by Chidester (2008) and Marshall (2007), through our in-depth analysis, which takes at its starting point a comment made within recent television culture. This hook, which will enable us to unpack a number of important critical issues, is a joke by Kimmy Schmidt (Ellie Kemper), when considering her roommate Titus Andromedon's (Tituss Burgess's) plan to play a Japanese woman in his play: 'Well, if Aisha Tyler can play a white woman on *Friends*, then I guess it's okay' (2.3). At the risk of sounding churlish, but given that *Unbreakable Kimmy Schmidt* has made more than one quip about *Friends*' representational politics, it is not amiss to note that the former has received quite hefty criticism for its approach to representing a number of minority identity groups, with *TIME* calling it—and, remarkably, not *Friends*—'TV's Most #Problematic Show' (D'Addario 2016).

The joke that Aisha Tyler plays a white woman can be unpacked on several levels. Firstly, it can be understood as a comment on a very present absence within *Friends*. This absence is in stark contrast to Glover's two-episode appearance on *Girls*, some of which is hinged around discussions between him and Lena Dunham's character Hannah about the fact that he is black (and she is white). In *Friends*, however, Chidester has identified:

> a refusal to speak race [which] becomes even more noticeable with the introduction of Aisha Tyler to the cast in 2003. While much was made in the popular press of NBC executives' decision to include an African American character in the regular *Friends* cast for the first time, no mention is ever made of the character's race in the actual sitcom, despite the fact that neither Joey nor Ross had ever been romantically linked to an African American woman during the sitcom's run. (2008, 164)

Whilst he neglects Gabrielle Union's appearance, Chidester rightly recognises that Charlie's race is never explicitly addressed (though, as we will consider below, one episode does so implicitly). This chimes with Sandell's point that 'for a show to have only white characters, and for them to never acknowledge their whiteness, indicates a certain level of disavowal' (1998, 152).

This apparent disavowal could be linked to Aisha Tyler's comments that the role 'wasn't written as a woman of color' (in Hunter 2018) and that she during her auditioning process 'read against women of every ethnic background' (ibid.). It is interesting here to consider the references to Tyler's height within the script. It is unclear if the role was written for a tall actor or whether—given that *Friends* is known for reworking its scripts even during production—these references were added after Tyler was cast. Either way, these comments referring to a specific aspect of Tyler's on-screen presence do not extend beyond her height. Tyler has articulated her own position on this lacuna as follows:

> I think why it worked was that they didn't make it into a "very special episode of *Friends*," where the friends suddenly confront issues of race, or try to somehow counterbalance the previous eight seasons' relative lack of diversity. I was just a character on the show, with her own appeal and quirks and foibles[.] (ibid.)

She is not wrong in implying that one or a few episodes that depart from the show's modus operandi and explicitly address racial issues would likely have been received as heavy-handed and/or disingenuous.

(*Friends*' attempt to tackle economic disparity in 'The One with Five Steaks and an Eggplant' [2.5] has been called 'cringe-worthy' [Rosa 2018].) This is a far cry from the praise a show such as *Black-ish* has received for its ongoing commitment to devoting particular episodes to such topics as police brutality against unarmed black citizens.

Tyler's remarks, including her comments that 'they happened to hire a black woman' (in Hunter 2018) and 'hopefully, I was cast on the merits' (in Fairfax Media Australia 2003) link her presence within *Friends* to debates concerning colour-blind casting. These have circulated in recent years around the showrunner Shonda Rhimes's body of work, which has much more diverse fictional worlds than that of *Friends*. Kristen J. Warner (2015) has argued that the programmes made by Shondaland, despite their representational achievements, need to be also understood as not engaging with the lived experiences of people of colour. A further link can be made between Warner's argument here and the important criticism that has been levelled against *The Cosby Show*. This significant sitcom has been understood as failing to acknowledge the structural inequalities and social obstacles faced by black people, with its upper-middle-class family firmly focused on individual work and effort as the means to succeed. Located within a colour-blind fictional world, such assimilationist discourse (Gray 1995) chimes with American Dream rhetoric. Sut Jhally and Justin Lewis (1992) argue that this show represents a form of 'enlightened racism' that legitimates post-racial claims, referencing Henry Louis Gates's comment that the Huxtables' privileged lives are so disconnected from the realities and struggles faced by so many black people that they are 'in most respects, just like white people' (1989). This last point, namely that the middle-class Huxtable family 'happens to be black' (Gray 1995, 80), is, as Herman Gray has argued, very much part of the show's appeal. He further points out that *The Cosby Show* was not atypical, and that in post-*Cosby* black-cast sitcoms such as *Family Matters*, 'blackness was seldom privileged or framed as vantage point for critical insights, guides to action, or explanation for what happens to African American people in modern American society' (ibid., 83).

As far as engaging with the lived experience of black people is concerned, it would be interesting to ask what aspects of misogynoir (Bailey and Trudy 2018) would Charlie Wheeler, as a woman of colour, be likely to have experienced. What daily micro-aggressions or structural inequalities would she have had to negotiate working as a palaeontology scholar at a US university shortly after the turn of the millennium? As Charlie's first introduction in 'The One with the Soap Opera Party' (9.20) reflexively suggests, the assumption by Ross is that his new colleagues will 'be a couple of old windbags wearing tweed jackets with suede elbow patches'. Despite his protestation that his own tweed jacket's elbow patches are made from a different material, the implication is that this white male palaeontology scholar conceives of his new colleagues in his own image (albeit older and [supposedly] less cool), and certainly not as a younger—and black—woman. What other reductive expectations or social practices might a woman of colour show up within such an environment?

These are questions not explored within the post-racial world of this sitcom, in which, as Naomi Rockler comments, identity issues are 'problems of the past that have been eradicated and replaced with equality' (2006, 454). It is worth adding here that scholars such as Gray (1995) and Smith-Shomade (2002) pay attention to the significance of Afrocentric markers in sitcoms such as *The Cosby Show* and *Living Single*, including 'Black-specific artwork' (Smith-Shomade 2002, 57) and clothing. No such presence can be found in *Friends*, as no scenes are set in Charlie's accommodation, and while Gabrielle Union's character Kristen is introduced at the point of moving into the neighbourhood, we only get brief glimpses of relatively nondescript furniture, and the contents of her moving boxes are never properly revealed. (For an engaging discussion of a black woman's enjoyment of white culture, see Robinson 2016.) Likewise, there are no other cultural specificities, including clothing, that may speak to black viewers, with Tyler's and Union's costumes very much interchangeable with those worn by Jennifer Aniston and especially Courteney Cox.

So, Kimmy Schmidt's joke can be read via the argument debated in relation to *The Cosby Show*, namely that because of the focus on black identity with class privilege that circumvents the specificity of black lived experience, Tyler 'just happens to be black' in *Friends* (see Smith-Shomade 2002, 34). This echoes Warner's criticism of Shonda Rhimes's politics of colour-blindness, whereby the privileging of her characters' individual quirks at the expense of structural inequalities as well as their location within discourses of assimilation facilitate their 'racial transcendence' (2015, 80). It furthermore resonates with Warner's concern about 'plastic representation' (2017)—whose coinage of the term emerged from her reflections on the *Moonlight* video—namely, that Tyler's presence adds a body of colour to the show, but that this in itself does not necessarily achieve meaningful representation.

A very different response to Kimmy Schmidt's quip is that Aisha Tyler plays a white woman on *Friends* in the sense that her presence is not marked with the common stereotypes that have long plagued the representations of black women. Patricia Hill Collins has noted that a number of controlling images, all linked to black women's sexuality, 'are designed to make racism, sexism, poverty, and other forms of social injustice appear to be natural, normal, and inevitable parts of everyday life' (2000, 69). Unfixed and evolving over time (Springer 2008), these images prominently include the Jezebel, the Mammy, the Sapphire and the Welfare Queen (the latter itself an evolution of the Welfare Mother).

As an unattached, well-dressed, confident, highly successful professional, Charlie bears out—via her visual construction and storylines—no links to the 'subordinate, nurturing, self-sacrificing Mammy figure' (West 2018, 142) or the Welfare Queen's connotations of moral aberration, economic dependency and drain on state resources (Lubiano 1992). She offers empathy and help to others, especially Ross in Barbados when his conference keynote speech needs to be rewritten, but such emotional and intellectual labour is not shown to come at the expense of her own well-being. In this way, she also does not evoke one of the more recent developments of the Mammy, the Strong Black Woman. Her character is not deployed in such a way that requires her to demonstrate any particular strengths, especially of endurance. Instead, she receives positive, helpful input from others (e.g. Joey takes her sight-seeing; Rachel, albeit at Joey's suggestion, takes her shopping), and she is shown to enjoy herself and have fun, such as when she persuades Ross to ditch the (older, white, male and boring) colleague, or they sip cocktails in Barbados.

Throughout her time on the show, Charlie shows herself to have a generally relaxed and affable manner. This distinguishes her from a number of recurring characters, including and especially potential love interests for the six friends, such as Rachel's boss Joanna (Alison LaPlaca), Joey's roommate Janine (Elle Macpherson) and Ross's second wife Emily (Helen Baxendale), each of whom displays dislikeable traits. Indeed, there are several references by some of the six friends that emphasise that she is 'cool', that is, pleasant, easy-going company. There is no attempt to extract humour from presenting her as angry, domineering or aggressive; so, she is far removed from 'the loudmouthed Sapphire' (Springer 2008, 78) or its widespread contemporary invocation (West 2018), the Angry Black Woman. The latter, Cobb (2018) points out, is evoked by Rhonda (Sherri Shepherd), a tour guide at the museum where Ross works, in 'The One with Phoebe's Uterus' (4.11).

Within the narrow parameters delineated by the controlling images, black women's sexuality is policed by the extremes of the 'desexed' (Hill Collins 2000, 84) Mammy to the promiscuous Jezebel. The latter perhaps intersects the most interestingly with Charlie, who is brought into the show with a tricky narrative whereby she dates Joey and Ross in very quick succession, being set up as potentially splitting the main in-group that underpins the 'sit' in this sitcom. However, there are two significant factors that put a stop to reading her in terms of the Jezebel. Firstly, while she displays sexual desire and agency, this is not linked to notions of deviancy. Charlie and Ross kiss after she has ended her relationship with Joey, and at Ross's suggestion, they agree to not pursue their interest in each other further until he has spoken to Joey. Rachel's comment in 10.1 that Charlie 'is really making her way through the group' is quickly followed by the acknowledgment 'eh, who am I to talk?' before kissing Joey. When Charlie rekindles her relationship with Benjamin Hobart (Greg Kinnear) with Ross present, she shows some concern for Ross. And importantly, Tyler is also not fetishised within the show. Several characters note Charlie's physical attractiveness—Ross and Joey refer to her as 'hot' and Monica calls her 'a hottie'—but this is again no different to the appearances by other recurring characters, such as Janine or Tag (Eddie Cahill). Tyler wears fashionable, form-fitting clothes very much in line with the other actors on the show, and neither her performance nor the way in which she is framed through camera and editing single out or draw particular attention to her physicality.

So, as the above shows, Aisha Tyler can be understood as playing a white woman on *Friends*, because, while her character's lived experience as a black woman is not being engaged with, she is also not trapped within the dominant and highly reductive stereotypes that shape the representations of black women. This may be because the role, as Tyler has indicated, was not written for a woman of colour, but even so, this is a noteworthy enough presence given the ways in which representations of black women continue to be limited and policed across different media and genres (Springer 2008). Hill Collins has pointed out: 'Denying Black women status as fully human subjects by treating us as the objectified Other within multiple binaries demonstrates the power that binary thinking, oppositional difference, and objectification wield within intersecting oppressions' (2000, 71). Charlie's presence is not marked by a binaristic, overdetermined 'see-saw' discourse commonly found in representations of marginalised identities, which dictates that one textual attribute must inevitably necessitate and/or deny another textual attribute. She is affable, neither markedly aggressive nor placid. She has sexual desire, but is presented as neither licentious nor overly virtuous. She is, in the terms of the show, 'hot' and 'cool'. Within her brief appearance, Charlie is ascribed a degree of complexity and roundedness, not reduced or flattened to narrow, extreme parameters—in other words, privileges most commonly linked to whiteness (see Dyer 1997).

The One where Aisha Tyler Doesn't Play a White Woman on *Friends*

Another response to Kimmy Schmidt's joke that Aisha Tyler plays a white woman on *Friends* is that what makes Kimmy's comment a joke is, of course, the fact that Tyler is a black woman. Indeed, not only is she a black woman, but she is a black woman who certainly would not pass the 'paper bag test' (see Kerr 2006), with a much darker skin tone than, for example, *The Fresh Prince of Bel-Air*'s Karyn Parsons, whose character Hilary Banks 'symbolized what the American Dream looked like in Black' (Smith-Shomade 2002, 61). (What she shares with Parsons and other black female actors is a physical adherence to dominant white Eurocentric standards of beauty.) Smith-Shomade notes that 'the vast spectrum of Black women's coloring' (ibid., 60) gained more public visibility in the 1980s and 1990s, but lighter-skinned actors would, and continue to, benefit from colourism in terms of casting. Moreover, the characters played by dark-skinned actors are often subject to further marginalisation, both in terms of audio-visual style and storytelling.

As Richard Dyer has argued in his seminal work, lighting for film was developed to privilege and construct whiteness (1997, 89), and recent years have seen a rise in cultural debates about successful lighting for black skin, linked to the achievements of such films and programmes as *Moonlight* (2016) and *Insecure*. It is worth noting that Aisha Tyler is well lit in *Friends*: her facial features and expressions are as readable on screen as are the white actors' around her. This balancing of light is maintained when she is framed in the same shot with other actors—something which some contemporary single-camera shows, such as *Stranger Things*, fail to achieve. This links to the overall modulated approach to multi-camera lighting in *Friends* that we noted in Chapter 4, which in the case of lighting for Tyler's skin means that the series avoids an overly bright lighting scheme, which recent debates on lighting for black skin have identified in sitcoms such as *The Cosby Show* and *The Fresh Prince of Bel-Air* (see Harding 2017). That this is something *Friends* works to achieve is confirmed by Kevin S. Bright, who directed the episode and gives particular credit to director of cinematography Nick McLean. It is reflexively signalled by the one moment involving Tyler where the lighting works less successfully for her skin tone: in Barbados, when Charlie and Ross have finished restoring his speech, they briefly encounter Joey and Rachel in the corridor, and Tyler's face receives more shadows here. Overall, however, her skin is shot in such a way that it often glows, especially when she wears white tops, such as in several scenes in the episodes set in Barbados. Such glow, as Dyer discusses, 'remains a key quality in idealised representations of white women' (1997, 132), and is achieved here through the lighting (particularly the use of gels), costuming and make-up (including the use of moisturiser) working together. This glow is even evident when Tyler is literally cheek-to-cheek with Schwimmer in a corner when their characters are hiding from the other conference attendants in Barbados in 9.24, as Fig. 5.1 shows. So, there is a concerted effort to give Tyler a stylistic privilege traditionally bestowed on white female skin, rendering Tyler not marginalised in terms of the aesthetics of representation.

As far as storytelling is concerned, Tyler's dark complexion makes her and the characters she is cast for more likely to become subject to experiences of misogynoir and stereotyping that frequently highlight their bodies and/or emotions. This makes it only more noteworthy that Charlie Wheeler is not presented as a Jezebel and also that she works successfully as a scholar within the field of earth science. As Smith-Shomade has argued, in sitcoms, a high number of black female characters work in fields linked to performance, creativity and emotionality: 'Very few Black doctors, factory workers, lawyers, administrative assistants, teachers, or scientists are shown—and seldom are they Black

Fig. 5.1 Glowing skin: Ross (David Schwimmer) and Charlie (Aisha Tyler) in 'The One in Barbados, Part 2' (9.24)

women. Many of these occupations require college degrees, vision and/or an ability to thrive, not just survive' (2002, 49). With her educational and professional achievements, Charlie is presented as certainly more than just surviving within a fictional world generally marked by aspirational upward mobility.

An intellectual, high-achieving, middle-class black woman, Charlie intersects with a variant of the Mammy (Hill Collins 2000, 81), namely the Black Lady: the image of the hardworking black professional woman, 'designed to counter accusations of black female licentiousness' (Springer 2008, 78) and marked by middle-class respectability. Indeed, Cobb calls Charlie '*Friends*'s "black lady"' (2018, 716) who 'epitomizes the ongoing postracial politics of respectability' (ibid., 708) and 'must be better than even Ross to be good enough for him and the group' (ibid., 716). (It is unclear to us in what ways Charlie is better than Ross, given that they are educated to the same level, and there is no indication within the programme that she is more advanced in her career. While she can spell the made-up paleontological term Mboscodictiasaur that Ross struggles with, she also expresses her appreciation of his research on several occasions.) We want to suggest that Charlie does not map against the Black Lady image as clearly as Cobb finds.

As we have already noted, Charlie skips a professional engagement to have fun, with no indication that she 'works twice as hard as everyone else' (Hill Collins 2000, 81). Hill Collins remarks that 'Black ladies have jobs that are so all-consuming that they have no *time* for men or have forgotten how to treat them. Because they so routinely compete with men and are successful at it, they become less feminine' (ibid., emphasis in original). Cobb acknowledges that Charlie's success is not grounded in asexuality, but suggests that 'rather, her sexuality is linked to her high achievements because she has only ever dated men who have achieved even more than she has' (2018, 716). This, of course, changes when Charlie begins a romantic relationship with Joey. Drawing on Springer (2008), Cobb suggests that 'in the end, Charlie is figured as a snob when she chooses a Nobel-prize winner over Ross' (2018, 719), but this is debatable, not least because there is no indication within the programme that Charlie chooses Benjamin Hobart because he is so high-achieving. Overall, Aisha Tyler plays neither a white woman nor a

Black Lady, but a dark-skinned black woman who is both intellectually high-achieving with a love of high culture (such as the Kronos Quartet) as well as emotional and passionate.

The One with Representation, Performance and Tone

The Black Lady image raises the issue of class, which in turn brings us to the instance within the show when Charlie's identity as a black woman is, finally, implicitly addressed. In 'The One after Joey and Rachel Kiss' (10.1), one of the storylines involves Monica's hair expanding in volume and taking on a frizzy texture because of the Barbadian humidity. Here, it is worth taking a moment to note that Charlie's straight hair appears totally unaffected by the humidity. The challenges experienced by black women when caring for their hair in different weather conditions have been highlighted in socio-cultural debates in recent years (see Obama 2018), and Aisha Tyler in her first book refers to the 'chemical nexus between black women's hair and environmental moisture' (2004, 13, Note 3), recalling a memory where she 'start[s] to sweat, which makes [her] hair slowly but surely puff out toward an inevitable Afro shape' (ibid., 13). However, this finds no articulation within *Friends* with Charlie—is Tyler wearing her own, straightened hair? A weave? A wig?—who shows no concern about weather conditions and moreover invites Ross to shower with her in 10.5.

While Tyler's dark skin is lit well in *Friends*, there is a lacuna about black women's hair and its 'forcefully symbolic dimension' (Mercer 1987, 35) within the scripts; a lacuna that could have been addressed through the presence of a woman of colour, one possessing the relevant capital to be able to speak out about this, in the writers' room (from which Amaani Lyle was fired a few years earlier). So, on *Friends*, Aisha Tyler plays a black woman within a storyworld framed by the assumptions of the predominately white production personnel. (Pasadena Playhouse artistic director emeritus Sheldon Epps, who directed the episode in which Charlie first appears, is the most high-profile black creative practitioner to have worked on the show.) Written, respectively, by

Andrew Reich and Ted Cohen, and Dana Klein, what finds articulation in episodes 10.1 and 10.5 is Dyer's argument that 'white people create the dominant images of the world and don't quite see that they thus construct the world in their own image' (1997, 9), 'not realising, that for much of the time they speak only for whiteness' (ibid., xiv).

When Monica's hair gets affected by the humidity in 'The One after Joey and Rachel Kiss', she gets her hair put into braids with decorative shells. (She later acknowledges that this is in reference to Bo Derek's hair in *Ten* [1979]—whose 'Bolero' she gets mixed up with 'Ride of the Valkyries', which implies a level of cultural ignorance—but then also wears a Rastafarian hat and refers to singing *No Woman, No Cry*, thus displaying an uneven awareness of racial connotations.) Monica's new hair style causes strong responses from Phoebe, Chandler and Ross in 10.1, none of whom indicate any awareness that this is, in fact, an act of cultural appropriation. Chandler's and Ross's comments in particular—that her scalp is visible and that she has 'shell fish in your head'—frame her hair style as an anomaly and thus represent an act of Othering from a white-centric perspective that is not questioned or challenged within or by the text. This is particularly noteworthy for Ross, given that his character was shown reading Studs Terkel's *Race: How Blacks and Whites Think and Feel About the American Obsession* (1992) in 3.13. Evidently, this ostensible interest in racial issues did not create a lasting sensitivity.

Charlie is also present, and her first response is the comment: 'It's, uh, it's something', immediately followed by: 'You go, girlfriend!' She is then asked by Ross 'You've never said that in your life, have you?' to which she replies 'Not once', which receives a 'I thought so' from him. This moment has received some attention in both paratextual criticism and scholarship. For example, one of the Canadian students—possibly adopting a pen-name to reference Phoebe's fake name Regina Phalange—writing the blog criticalinsightintofriends.wordpress.com commented that:

> The phrase 'you go, girl' has been coined in popular culture by African American women. So, by her not associating with the term she distances herself from the typical African American women – pushing herself closer to the 'safety' that is whiteness. (Phalange 2016)

This has some resonance with the following argument articulated by Shelley Cobb:

> Charlie cannot use the black diction that Rhonda did. The classism, racism, and patriarchy that Charlie is required to negotiate as a black character who must assimilate to keep her space among the friends is made explicit. It is a *white* man who makes it clear that she is unable to perform blackness, precisely because, for the friends, she has *never been* black. That they all tiptoe around Monica's inappropriate appropriation and commodification of the braids is in direct opposition to Ross's outing of Charlie as not really black, and his implication that she makes a fool of herself by trying to be so. As I argue above, to hang out with the *Friends* Charlie must be better than all of them in terms of education and achievement so that she is not classed as too black. And then, she is critiqued for performing her own racial identity even as she is confronted with the spectacle of a white woman who has commodified it and who is found amusing for doing so. (2018, 718, emphases in original)

It is our argument that the material detail of the text here supports a different reading, especially when the use of performance and tone throughout the scene are engaged with in depth, which links particularly to the work of Tyler as actor and Bright as not only director of the episode but also, in the words of James Burrows, 'master editor' for the show. When Charlie first sees Monica's new hair style, her immediate reaction is a stunned look (see Fig. 5.2), with Tyler's lips slightly parted and her eyes wide, though not as parted or wide as Schwimmer's mouth and eyes, who is next to her within the frame. Indeed, her reaction is the most muted, with Tyler's initial silence and lack of movement indicating an internal response, that her character needs a moment to take in what she is seeing. By the time that Monica exclaims 'Don't you just love it?', Tyler has a slight smile on her face, but this to us does not read as her 'apparently find[ing] humorous [Monica's] cultural appropriation of a hairstyle associated with black women' (Cobb 2018, 717). Instead, given that her smile appears frozen and does not reach her eyes, and is further accompanied by her eye brows moving up at Monica's question, Tyler's performance signals that her character is processing a situation that she (unlike the other characters) recognises as awkward because of the links to issues of race.

Fig. 5.2 Looking stunned: Charlie (Aisha Tyler) and Ross (David Schwimmer) in 'The One after Joey and Rachel Kiss' (10.1)

This sense of awareness on the level of her character is further conveyed by Tyler when she delivers her first vocal response with an elongated 's' in the first 'it's', the hesitant 'uh', several blinks and a widening smile. Her acting choices indicate that Charlie is buying a little extra time to be able to come up with a response that is tailored to the social context of the moment, while remaining lost for words, as the 'something' reflects. That her delivery of the sentence-ending 'something' does not have the strong upward-rising intonation and vocal stress that mark Matthew Perry's 'scalp' and David Schwimmer's 'head' further sets her reaction apart as one marked by awareness that there is something more significant at stake. While her lines are likely to be as they were in the shooting script, Tyler inflects the 'something' with a slight vocal twang, which hints that the 'something' is a placeholder for a more negative response. Not only does Tyler's performance within the space of seconds indicate that her character recognises the awkward underlying racial issues, but she also conveys that her character recognises that the social situation needs managing: she moves her right hand in a downward flap, which can be read as a supportive gesture towards Monica (who is, after all, her new romantic interest's sister), as well as Charlie symbolically wiping away her own internal reaction in her gear shift towards handling the social situation, accompanied by her smile broadening further.

We want to suggest that there is an interestingly ambiguous tone that is worth highlighting. Charlie's response to Monica can be read both in terms of a straightforward expression of support and female solidarity. It can also be read as Charlie offering something to Monica that to the latter may read as supportive, but which actually has a double meaning. Charlie uses a phrase with racial connotations, which could suggest that she is wishing to address Monica in the terms of black women's culture which Monica has so cluelessly appropriated, subtly picking Monica up on the racial connotations. The ambiguity here is partly facilitated by Tyler's acting choices, especially her vocal delivery of 'You go, girlfriend' in a lower pitch from the immediately preceding 'It's, uh, it's something', as well as the fact that her hand gesture is unusual for her within the context of her physical presence within the show. These choices add a performative quality to Charlie's response, signalling that this is a conscious adopting of a mode of discourse that she would not normally use, which suggests that there may be an element of discomfort for her. The ambiguity marking this moment is further amplified by the fact that the performative quality is subtle, with the vocal delivery of 'You go, girlfriend' right on the cusp of becoming heightened, and the hand gesture not becoming a fully embodied movement and instead remaining at the level of a flick; both of which stop Charlie's response turning 'sassy'. The ambiguous tone is further reinforced by the absence of Monica's reaction to Charlie's comments: while the viewer is shown Monica's responses to Chandler's and Ross's comments, there is no reaction shot of Monica being delighted with Charlie's response. It would not have been difficult to include a quick cut to Monica, which would have confirmed that Charlie's comments were (entirely) operating on the level of female solidarity, or at least were received as that. However, no reaction shot is forthcoming in the episode directed and overseen by

Bright, and thus such confirmation of female solidarity is withheld and the meaning of the moment is less firmly secured.

Instead of Monica's reaction, the viewers are shown Charlie's smile and then her quick exchange with Ross. Her smile might indicate that she is feeling pleased that she has managed to recover sufficiently to deal with the (for her) awkward social situation without embarrassing the clueless others, remaining on good terms with her new romantic interest, his sister and close friends. When Ross asks her about having used the expression 'You go, girlfriend' before, he does so not with 'a skeptical look' (Cobb 2018, 717), but with a dry vocal delivery that strongly suggests that Ross knows that she has not used that phrase before. While he showed a lack of sensitivity concerning racial issues earlier in the scene, he is here picking up on the slight performative quality of Charlie's response to Monica, which would be enabled on the level of characterisation and storytelling by the fact that he has spent some time with her and thus has some knowledge of her behavioural modus operandi. The immediacy of Tyler's final response to him demonstrates that Charlie expected that she would get a question of this kind from him, knowing that he is familiar enough with her to recognise her response to Monica as performance. Tyler delivers the 'not once' assertively, with her smile hardening a touch as if to say: 'No, I've not been put in this ridiculous situation before, so why would I?'

That is a question worth unpicking in more detail. The programme both explicitly (through the script) and implicitly (through subtle acting choices) suggests that Charlie's response to Monica is a moment of performance for the former, and that the specific black female discourse that she adopts here briefly is not part of her modus operandi. Is this her distancing 'herself from the typical African American women—pushing herself closer to the "safety" that is whiteness' (Phalange 2016)? Is Charlie here 'unable to perform blackness' (Cobb 2018, 718)? Does Aisha Tyler effectively play a white woman on *Friends*, after all? We suggest that an intersectional reading that takes at its starting point that black identity is not monolithic can provide a different argument. Smith-Shomade has noted that in 1990s sitcoms, black female characters spoke standard English, 'wed[ding] Black women to whiteness' (2002, 58). However, she also highlights that other factors, especially class, function as important 'perpetuator[s] of difference' (ibid., 56) and are increasingly significant in relation to dialect. Charlie is presented as a middle-class or upper-middle-class black woman. Given the professional success she has achieved at a relatively young age, and with a family that includes a father who is 'a raging alcoholic', it seems likely that she comes from a socio-economically privileged background. So, she would be likely to have had a particular socialisation, one that makes it plausible that 'you go, girlfriend'—a term with working-class connotations—is not part of this black woman's sociolect and cultural capital (Bourdieu 1984). To us, to understand Charlie as 'performing her own racial identity' (Cobb 2018, 718) is to risk falling into the essentialism that, as bell hooks has argued, has marked much of black feminism, warning that evocations of a fixed, essentialist notion of black identity risk excluding 'individuals from "blackness" whose perspectives, values, or lifestyles may differ from a totalizing notion of black experience' (1992, 52). So, Charlie is not so much unable to perform blackness, but, as acted by Aisha Tyler, performatively engages with a particular type or aspect of blackness that does not correspond to her. (It would have been interesting to see if, had *Friends* had any further black characters, especially from different speech communities, for Charlie to interact with, she would have attempted any further code-switching.)

So, the exchange between Ross and Charlie entails an acknowledgment about Charlie's identity not so much in terms of race, but in terms of class, specifically habitus (Bourdieu 1984). Charlie is a black woman who is very invested in palaeontology, which is regularly framed by the show as a 'nerdy' and 'uncool' science, and who fleetingly draws on a mode of speech that has further connotations of pop cultural coolness (see Pountain and Robins 2000 for a discussion of the African-American origins of the latter). This, we want to suggest, is what is recognised and commented upon by fellow nerd Ross, who has an impressive track record of unsuccessfully trying to be cool, such as when he wears leather pants in 5.11 (see Chapter 3) or adopts a fake English accent to impress his students in 6.4. The attempt and ultimate failure to deliver a performance of coolness by members of the main in-group is a strand of the programme's farcical comedy. Indeed, a very similar joke appeared on the show previously: in 2.19, Monica, responding to Rachel being fired up by a self-help book, says to her 'You go, girl!' before turning to Phoebe with the comment: 'I can't pull that off, can I' Reflecting the appropriation of black slang by white mainstream popular culture (Springer 2008, 88), which is heightened through Monica snapping her fingers, this joke here operates not on the level of race, but coolness: Monica recognises that such coolness does not suit her, just as Ross recognises this in Charlie. Ross's recognition, specifically his final comment ('I thought so'), is delivered by Schwimmer with a slight smile detectible within the closer framing. This to us does not constitute an 'outing of Charlie as not really black, and [Ross's] implication that she makes a fool of herself by trying to be so' (Cobb 2018, 718), but instead opens up the possibility of reading this as Ross recognising something of himself in Charlie's performative attempt at (pop cultural) coolness.

Cobb's point about Charlie being outed 'as not really black' (2018, 718) or characterised 'as inauthentically black' (ibid., 717) deserves further reflection, especially as this has resonance with the actor cast for the role, Aisha Tyler, whose career includes successes as a comedian, actor, voice actor, podcaster, director and talk show host. Tyler has spoken of her continuing experiences of being critiqued for being 'not black enough' (in Ghomeshi 2014) and the 'pressures [...] to conform' (in Redd 2014) that she has felt in relation to this. (Such experiences have been dramatised in *The Fresh Prince of Bel-Air*, in which Carlton Banks [Alfonso Ribeiro] received repeated criticisms pertaining to being 'not black enough' or 'not really black', because of his upper-middle-class identity and taste codes.) She has articulated that, because she does not fit into the 'stereotype of how a black female comedian should be' (Ghomeshi 2014), because she doesn't 'have the accent' (Tyler in Ghomeshi 2014), cannot move her body in ways that meet such expectations, and has a different comic sensibility (in Anderson 2017), the creative industries and audiences (including black audiences) 'struggled to get' her (in Ghomeshi 2014). Understood in terms of being a comic who is black, but not a 'black comic' (Anderson 2017), Tyler self-identifies as a 'black nerd', or 'blerd', who loves SF, fantasy and video games, but has struggled to be received via this frame, which has been much more readily ascribed in recent years to such creative individuals as Issa Rae, indicating a shift in 'the prevailing societal sense of what a black woman should be and do' (hooks 1992, 57). (In 2012, she posted a widely shared response on Facebook to claims that she is 'not a real gamer', which lists her credentials within video game sub-culture and comments 'You think you know. You don't know' [Tyler 2012], signalling her awareness of the gap between her cultural capital and socio-cultural expectations of black women.) So, there is an interesting resonance between Tyler's star image (Dyer 1998) and the role she plays in *Friends*, which may inform readings of the scene analysed above for viewers with broader knowledge of Tyler's career. Both Tyler and the character she plays in *Friends* are productively understood not as 'not black enough', but as 'differently black'.

While the scene in 'The One after Joey and Rachel Kiss' overall draws humour from the (very objectionable) reactions to Monica's hair style, its meanings and tone are complicated by Tyler's performance and the absence of Monica's reaction shot, both of which intersect with Bright's work as director and executive producer. These creative choices produce an ambiguity and uncertainty for a scene that may have looked rather different and much more straightforward in the pages of the script. As it appears on screen, the scene manages to keep an interesting tension about the awkwardness subtly signalled by Tyler, whose acting choices as Charlie here are noticeably different to her vocal performance as the strong-willed and short-tempered Lana Kane on adult animated sitcom *Archer*. It is easy to picture how such a scene would be handled by a single-camera mockumentary sitcom such as *The Office—An American Workplace*, namely a quick zoom towards Charlie looking at the camera, which would signpost her awareness and flag the racial awkwardness of the moment, with a sense of the racial awkwardness thus having been 'handled' by the text. Through the ambiguity deployed in the scene explored above, *Friends* makes viewers work to pick up on the awkwardness and at the same time does not let them off the hook about it. Keeping tension, this scene demonstrates how multi-camera sitcoms, notwithstanding the fact that the non-diegetic laughter may signal humour somewhat indiscriminately, may harbour considerable tonal complexity that is worth unpicking in detail. Highlighting the potential for tonal complexity within multi-camera sitcom is a worthwhile undertaking, not least because this genre has frequently been dismissed as straightforwardly ideologically regressive, as we will go on to consider next.

The One where They Come Full Circle on Intimacy: Re-evaluating *Friends* and the Genre of Sitcom

Hoping to have demonstrated the insights into *Friends* that can be gained from close analysis that is carefully engaged with issues of tone, we will begin to move towards concluding this chapter by reflecting on why *Friends* has become such a key site in which ideas about representation and culture are being so fervently debated. This will allow us to broaden out the discussion and think through established conceptions of sitcom as an inherently conservative genre.

Given that we are in what is understood to be the age of 'peak television', with an unprecedented number of programmes readily available for consumption, why is it that one of several successful multi-camera sitcoms from the 1990s has been subject to so much debate? Paratextual criticism of *Friends* often includes acknowledgment that '*Friends* is no different than any number of television texts that likewise unfold in situations marked by the absence of the racial Other' (Chidester 2008, 161), but this usually appears in the form of a brief aside, only for the focus to insistently turn back to *Friends*. To be sure, other programmes have been subjected to paratextual critique. For example, *Jezebel* has mapped 'Every Non-white Character on *Sex and the City*' (Reynolds and Rothkopf 2018), which is reminiscent of DocFuture's (2010) video. Interestingly, while Chidester reads *Seinfeld* as a positive counter-example to *Friends*, arguing that the former's 'NYC presents its characters with innumerable opportunities to encounter and understand the racial Other' (2008, 169), paratextual criticism has shown itself less positively inclined towards Jerry Seinfeld and Larry David's programme. Nevertheless, it is *Friends*—and not US television's overall norms of whiteness—that 'has been the main lightning rod for such perceived shortcomings, especially since it became available on Netflix [US] in January 2015' (Butler 2016).

Friends has been singled out not just because of its high profile that lends itself to clickbait, or, as per the criticism, its many representational issues. As we have noted in the introduction to this book, the series is both part of current 1990s nostalgia and marked by a degree of timelessness, and the latter may make it more likely that it will be understood and judged via a contemporary, and not contemporaneous, socio-cultural sensibility. Such a sensibility may take any representational achievements as a given and not give enough recognition to the fact that, as Marta Kauffman recalls, NBC was (justifiably) expecting much more complaints about 'The One with the Lesbian Wedding' (2.11; which some affiliates refused to broadcast) than it eventually received. Most crucially, however, it is our view that the fervent criticism of *Friends* is partly caused by a feeling of disappointment, a sense that the show and its characters should have been more progressive. Such feelings of disappointment are considered, for example, by Ruth Graham (2015), whose criticism of Chandler Bing (see Chapter 2) is marked by the urge to critically distance herself from a programme watched during her formative years. As such, perhaps, some critical commentators have felt the need to 'unfriend' *Friends*. The disappointment in the show links to its discourse of inclusion—which is focused on supportive friendship and explicitly articulated by its theme tune, especially the line 'I'll be there for you'—and its strategy of intimacy that, as previous chapters have demonstrated, is achieved on a number of levels. Here, performance deserves a particular mention, because the realist acting by the core cast means the persistent performative quality to be found in, for example, *Seinfeld*, is absent, and the *Friends* main characters engender more emotional resonance for and investment from viewers. Viewers, in turn, may thus find the characters' ideological failings more objectionable, and moreover feel—repeatedly or momentarily—excluded from the programme's intimacy if they find their own interests in identity not represented or misrepresented within it.

It is worth thinking further about the intimacy that underpins so much of the success of the show. This intimacy is hinged around an in-group that is carefully controlled in terms of the disruptions it experiences by outsiders, who usually get expelled by the end of one or a few episodes. This links to both Chidester's visual metaphor of the closed circle in *Friends*, which has been influential on subsequent scholarship on *Friends*' representation of race, and established debates on sitcom more broadly. Chidester argues that 'the circle serves as a visual boundary between included and excluded, as a perimeter to be doggedly defended against anyone who might challenge the in-group's physical solidarity and cultural unity' (2008, 163). This metaphor is embodied in the circular arrangement of the core cast on the couches in Central Perk and Monica's apartment. According to Chidester, this circle is much more open to white outsiders than to outsiders of colour: 'Over the course of the series, a number of white romantic interests are easily and freely welcomed into the circle by both male and female members of the group' (ibid., 165).

Chidester's circle of whiteness—a closed ring of six white friends that expels people of colour—finds some resonance with established scholarly criticism of sitcom in its schematic neatness. Sitcom has been seen as typically defined by 'the half-hour format, the basis in humor, [and] the "problem of the week" that causes the hilarious situation and that will be resolved so that a new episode may take its place the next week' (Feuer 1992, 146). It has been understood in terms of being marked by formula and predictability and offering reassurance to its viewers (Newcomb 1974), and as Brett Mills notes, is 'often presented as a *problem* whose humour contributes (unwittingly?) to stereotyped representations of underprivileged groups, turning such social issues into nothing more than something worthy of laughter' (2009, 10; emphasis in original). Indeed, the very name of the genre, *situation* comedy, seems to signal an unchanging status quo with attendant ideological staticity. Informed by a formalist approach that looks at structure but certainly not tone, this understanding of the genre has an ongoing influence on scholarship, as is attested by Hannah Hamad's repeated and uninterrogated reference to sitcom's 'inherent conservativeness (2018, 696). It has been running side-by-side with a more nuanced understanding of the genre, which has been articulated in Morreale's work that pays attention to the potential presence of a 'multiplicity of discourses' (2003, xii). Jane Feuer has written that, the genre's simplicity and repeatability notwithstanding, 'it has been the ideological flexibility of the sitcom that has accounted for its longevity. The sitcom has been the perfect format for illustrating current ideological conflicts while entertaining an audience' (2015, 100–101). Building on Feuer's work, Frederik Dhaenens and Sofie Van Bauwel note that:

some hegemonic ideas within a sitcom might be challenged or reversed over the course of seasons. Hence, an inquiry into the meanings of a single sitcom starts from an acknowledgment of its own particularities and conventions in relation to the interpretive community in which it is produced and consumed. (2018, 301)

We wish to emphasise that, just as sitcom has been established to be more complex than some of the existing arguments would suggest, so *Friends*, once you carefully engage with its particularities and conventions, also bears out more nuance than Chidester's overly neat visual metaphor of the closed circle can account for. One of the key particularities of the show is *how* it handles the disruptions to the main in-group that constitutes the core of its notion of intimacy. We are not convinced by Chidester's claim that white outsiders find much more ready inclusion than outsiders of colour. Similarly, we are not convinced by the point made by Sandell (who acknowledges the complexity of the sitcom genre) that 'indeed, the recent romance between Ross and his white English girlfriend Emily suggests once again that difference can only be accommodated when it is "safe" and will not upset the fragility of the group' (1998, 152–153). Instead, we want to highlight that the programme tends to dispose of outsiders often quite harshly, but it reserves the hardest expulsions for white characters.

For example, Joey breaks up with Janine off-screen, after she repeatedly expresses a dislike for Monica and Chandler. In the very final moments of their marriage, when Ross and Emily speak on the phone, she is framed in a close-up against a pale-yellow wall, which contrasts with the shot of Ross on Monica's balcony, in front of the texture of the brick wall and Monica's warm apartment. This visual separation then turns into their actual break-up, which takes place while Ross can only be glimpsed in the background, with the focus on the five other friends arranged by the couch. So, the programme makes no emotional investment into the actual break-up or Emily's response; only Ross's matters, as he receives a group hug from the others. Charlie and Julie, by contrast, are expelled from the circle differently: we see the beginning of Joey and Charlie's (rather amicable) break-up, and in the break-up between Ross and Charlie, the latter shows some concern for the former's well-being. The break-up between Ross and Julie takes place off-screen, but she returns after two episodes, briefly articulating her emotions. Cobb argues that Charlie and Julie's 'disruptive breaches of the closed circle become neutered when they are paired up with men who are just another version of Ross, or a better version of Ross' (2018, 719), and Marshall suggests that, apart from Ross, 'the ensemble did not care about losing Julie' (2007, 113). We think a different argument is possible, namely that the programme treats both of them with more empathy than it does many other outsiders, which, in the terms of the show, means that neither is cast aside, but expelled by becoming part of an outside heteronormative couple.

It is because of the empathy shown to these particular outsiders that we are also not convinced by Chidester's claim concerning 'Charlie's active visual exclusion from the center' (2008, 164). He comments that:

> Tyler's Charlie does manage to insert herself twice into the coffee-shop scene during her short run on the program, but on both occasions she is joined by only a few members of the central cast. She is allowed to interact with members of the core circle, in other words, but never to be seen as *belonging* to that group of insiders as a whole. (ibid., emphasis in original)

What Chidester here does not consider sufficiently is that a significant amount of Charlie's presence in the programme is set in Barbados, so her limited appearances within the circular arrangements of the actors around the couches is less meaningful than it otherwise would be. Living in close proximity to Monica's apartment and Central Perk, Janine is integrated into one substantial circle within the latter, and Emily is not once, despite appearing on the show between episodes 4.14 and 5.6. Most importantly, however, the notion of belonging to the in-group is more significantly linked to factors other than the physical blocking of the actors within the space.

Charlie and Julie, because of their compatibility with Ross in terms of their careers and interests, pose a substantial potential threat to Ross and Rachel as the 'fated couple' (Cobb 2018), which makes it only more significant that Charlie and Julie are presented as likeable. We

5 The One with the Emblematic Problematic Fave … 205

have explored Charlie's likeability earlier in this chapter, and Julie is also presented as generally affable and good-natured. This actually works to make Rachel's comments about her—for example, when Julie helps her tie up her apron in 2.2, Rachel calls her a 'bitch'—funny in such a way that the joke is on Rachel and her petty jealousy. This raises issues with Chidester's reference to 'the viciousness with which [Julie] is treated as an interloper' (2008, 164), which fails to distinguish between the level of character, which is where the viciousness is located, and the level of programme. Through their likeability, the two women of colour differ quite significantly from characters such as Janine or Emily, as we noted earlier. There is little to no investment made in establishing a connection between these white women and the viewers. This is apparent from, for example, Emily's very introduction in the show in 4.14: as can be gleaned from Fig. 5.3, clothed in black, wet from the torrential rain and quickly grumpy, she evokes the Wicked Witch from *The Wizard*

Fig. 5.3 Evoking the Wicked Witch: Emily (Helen Baxendale) in 'The One with Joey's Dirty Day' (4.14)

of Oz. It continues even within scenes that would lend themselves to exploring Emily's emotional well-being, such as after Ross says Rachel's name at the altar (in 4.24 and 5.1) or when she discovers that he is about to go on their honeymoon with Rachel at the airport (in 5.1). In such cases, the use of camera, editing and performance passes up opportunities to construct a stronger emotional engagement—indeed, intimacy—with Emily, reserving much more interest for Rachel's emotional responses.

Charlie bears out a connection to the in-group through two other means. Charlie is shown to be funny—as is Julie, who, in her first moments within the show in 2.1, responds to Rachel's assumption that she is a foreigner by mirroring Rachel's loud and slow mode of speaking to inform her that she is from New York. For example, episode 10.2 features an attempt at socialising by the new couples Charlie and Ross, and Rachel and Joey, during which Ross behaves increasingly erratically and drinks too much. When a weepy Ross does not want her to leave, Charlie assures him: 'This has been lovely!' Tyler's performance—especially the slight pause between 'This' and 'has' and her near unbroken eye contact—makes it clear that her character is trying to be nice to Ross after what she recognizes as a socially disastrous evening. Seconds later, when Ross lets it slip that Charlie had concerns about the likely awkwardness of the double date and never liked Rachel, she quips 'You're on fire!', with Charlie's amusement evident on Tyler's face. There are more instances, but the above should suffice to show a difference between Charlie's function in relation to humour and what Smith-Shomade has identified in relation to 1990s black-cast sitcoms, namely that in shows such as *The Fresh Prince of Bel-Air*, *Martin*, *Moesha* or *Living Single*, black women are positioned 'as perpetual objects of laughter' (2002, 5). Informed by Tyler's comedic skills (especially in relation to timing), Charlie's comedic agency importantly extends to transgressing social norms. Earlier during the disastrous double date, she makes a comment about her father being 'a raging alcoholic', and when Rachel and Joey look somewhat taken aback, she shoots back with a sarcastic vocal inflection: 'Oh, I'm sorry, have I made this evening uncomfortable?!' This complicates the argument that the main characters' regular 'transgression of social norms is made possible by the privileges of their whiteness, a privilege that is simply not available to (or possible for) those who are marked as the racial other' (Cobb 2018, 714–715). If there is any implication here by Joey or Rachel that she, as a black woman, should not transgress social rules, then it is being challenged by Tyler's Charlie in a way that encourages the audience to laugh *with* her, not *at* her. This is substantially different to the function of characters such as Janine in relation to humour, and deserves to be understood as a privilege granted by the text.

Charlie also has moments of connection with the other characters in ways that engender a level of intimacy between her and the members of the in-group as well as the audience more broadly. The scene in 10.1 discussed in-depth earlier in this chapter ends with a shared look between Ross and Charlie (see Fig. 5.4), who smile at each other

Fig. 5.4 Sharing a look: Charlie (Aisha Tyler), Ross (David Schwimmer), Chandler (Matthew Perry), Monica (Courteney Cox) and Phoebe (Lisa Kudrow) in 'The One after Joey and Rachel Kiss' (10.1) (set lights visible due to DVD aspect ratio)

as Monica does a silly dance to make her shells click against each other. This is not the only such shared look between them; for example, in 10.5, they do so when Rachel's sister Amy (Christina Applegate) fails to remember him, despite the fact that she is the aunt of Ross and Rachel's child. Such shared looks between characters suggest that they share an awareness of what is going on, as well as a sensibility in terms of how they judge it—here, the ridiculousness of Monica and Amy, respectively. This can extend to the viewers, who may share with them an understanding that is not available to the other characters (Monica and Amy) present. So, Charlie is invested with a notion of being 'in the know' and 'in on' situations with Ross. In addition to this knowingness, she also has moments of emotional connection, particularly when in 10.1 she tells Ross that she has broken up with Joey and begins to confess her feelings for him. This is a brief but emotionally affective moment, in which Tyler very effectively performs Charlie's nervousness and emotional vulnerability, especially by having her character struggling to keep Ross's gaze.

Certainly, *Friends* begins and ends with a circle of whiteness, which becomes expanded in the final season to accommodate Phoebe getting married to Mike, who, cast with Paul Rudd, is not only also white, but in terms of his physicality fits quite seamlessly into the in-group. However, the presence of Charlie and Julie is nevertheless marked by more complexity than working to 'reinforc[e] the group's intimacy when they leave, […] [and] functioning to confirm the fated-ness of Ross and Rachel as a couple, as well as the whiteness of the postfeminist tropes of fate and retreatism' (Cobb 2018, 715). Tyler's Charlie is invested with a level of intimacy—one of the key privileges for *Friends* to bestow—that meaningfully connects her with the in-group, without necessarily being physically part of a closed circle.

As for the closed circle, Chidester himself acknowledges that 'to contend that the core visual metaphor of *Friends* is the closed circle is to ignore the fact that the circle is not visually closed at all. In the case of both the apartment couches and the couches in Central Perk, the furniture circle is open to the screen' (2008, 167). However, he does not see this as possibly indicating more ideological ambiguity; on the contrary, he asserts that:

the viewer is visually invited to close the circle, to make up the fourth side of the racial border to be patrolled and defended. Not enough can be made of the rhetorical power of the invitation to identification […] that this visual consistently and persistently extends to the audience member. (ibid.)

While we have argued in Chapter 4 that an intimate link between viewers and space in multi-camera sitcom may be engendered by a regime of looking in across a shared threshold, we do not share Chidester's views concerning the interpellative effect of this link, especially because it fails to engage with issues of tone.

Instead, we want to suggest that the circle can be understood as open, because sitcom is dependent for its very existence on continual engagement with what is outside of the given in-group. As Dhaenens and Van Bauwel (2018) rightly note, the genre may challenge hegemonic ideas over time, especially if its storytelling involves serialisation; but even the more episodic narrative structure depends on continual engagement with disruption—otherwise, there is, after all, no show. How an individual sitcom constructs what is inside and outside of the in-group and manages the disruptions is an important, but separate question. But it strikes us that there is a tension embedded within sitcom, with a complex relationship of expulsion and dependence that may produce contestable but not necessarily straightforward or simple politics of representations, which may be productively understood in terms of John Ellis's notion of 'working through' (2002).

Conclusion

In one of the few paratextual pieces that does not condemn *Friends* for its representational failings, but instead seeks to highlight that the show deserves more recognition for certain representational achievements, Sarah Gosling in *The Guardian* points out that, while the show has its issues, 'the conversations remain relevant' (2018), which links to Ellis's notion of 'working through' noted above. She goes on to ask: 'How are we to progress into an educated, truthful place if we swap comedic dialogue for a monologue of prescribed rhetoric?' (Gosling 2018). This resonates with Wesley Morris's 2018 think piece in *The New York Times*, in which he raises important questions about the status of entertainment culture and how audiences and critics engage with it in the current political climate. Observing that discussions about artistic achievement have been supplanted by debates about the moral worth of culture, he articulates some concern about 'how blindingly monolithic the thinking about representation and diversity has become' (Morris 2018). As Morris puts it, 'the conversations are exasperated, the verdicts swift, conclusive and seemingly absolute' (ibid.), accompanied by a good amount of 'shushing', where certain ideas or questions apparently cannot be raised anymore. Just as it is not okay to not praise *Insecure*, or ask questions about Beyoncé, so it seems that it is not okay to not comprehensively criticise a show such as *Friends*.

These ideas and concerns have been with us as we have written this chapter. The critical consensus that *Friends* is entrenched in reinforcing hegemonic discourses is so strong that seeking to open up the debate about the show's politics of representation feels somewhat risky. This is especially so as we have focused on the representation of a black woman, and we are both white, so do not share the relevant lived experience nor possess the moral authority that, as perceived by some, would make our arguments more likely to be found permissible. We accept that some readers may find our take on the programme to be generously inclined in ways that it, to them, has not earned. But we hope that they will agree that our discussion is based on attention to textual detail, and that readers will recognise that we could have chosen to tackle much safer ground and explored some of the show's representational issues more readily understood as achievements, such as *Friends*' inclusion of surrogacy, adoption and the experiences of blended families within its storyworld.

Instead, we have focused on *Friends*' most persistently problematic representational track record, namely its engagement with issues of race. It would be easy to judge *Friends* as a show that does not 'see race' because it is blinded by its white privilege. Given how well-realised *Friends* is in so many respects, it is frustrating that the programme is not, put simply, better at representation. We have no issue with the fact that Marta Kauffman and David Crane co-created a show that spoke to their specific experience, a show that no-one could have known would be more than 'just another sitcom' (Tucker 1994), more than one of many new programmes with an uncertain future in the US TV landscape of the 1990s. But certainly, we wish there had been a concerted effort towards diversity with a more lasting presence within the show once it was on the way towards becoming the juggernaut that it now is; a juggernaut that 'perform[s] important cultural and ideological work in terms of how such issues [of race, class, gender or sexuality] are represented' (Sandell 1998, 153). In our interview, Kevin S. Bright noted that, even with the same core cast, it would be possible to introduce 'more stories with diverse characters, and put the friends in situations and environments we've never seen them in before'. He added that, if he were to make the programme today, it would 'feel incumbent upon [him] to make it a more diverse show'; a view shared by Marta Kauffman.

There was an opportunity to make a significant contribution towards representational normalisation, where recurring characters of colour are characters who are of colour. Charlie Wheeler cannot be such a character, because, as Jonathan Gray has remarked, where little representation is provided, 'those few characters that do exist become densely loaded with expectation and representational weight' (2008, 111). This burden operates in relation to Charlie on a broader level, namely the wider US TV landscape of her time, and specifically in relation to *Friends*. As much as her character may be marked by a degree of white privilege, Aisha Tyler does not play a white woman or 'just a character' (Tyler in Hunter 2018) on the show in the way that the white actors cast for other recurring or one-off roles do. Charlie cannot access the same space of individuality, with the burden of representation weighing heavily on her. That, however, does not obliterate the intersectional complexity inscribed into her within her brief existence within the show: she is a black, middle-class woman who is professionally and intellectually high-achieving and enjoys fun, desiring and desirable (and not fetishised), ultimately expelled, but invested with a level of intimacy. Charlie does not adopt what are widely recognised as types of black modes of being, but in the scene explored in depth in this chapter draws on black female discourse. In doing so, she can be productively understood not as 'inauthentically black' or 'not black enough', but as offering a contribution to 'the representation of differences within blackness' (Gray 1995, 81), resonating with Aisha Tyler's star image. This difference is shaped by the programme's contextual frameworks and significantly informed by tone, which is marked by noteworthy complexity and ambiguity, not least because of Tyler's performance.

Being alive to tonal complexity and ambiguity in this way is an important critical undertaking, both because sitcom continues to be reductively understood as ideologically straightforwardly conservative, and because engagement with representations of black women or other marginalised identities needs to consider what heterogeneity (if any) may be present, and not inadvertently further the limiting and narrowing that stubborn stereotypes perform. In highlighting the complexity and ambiguity to be found in the representation of Charlie Wheeler as performed by Aisha Tyler, our work shows a kinship with Cynthia Baron's (2018) exploration of the significance of Viola Davis's acting choices in *How to Get Away with Murder* for challenging historic representations of black women, as well as Dhaenens and Van Bauwel's analysis of the discourses on sex in *Friends*, which finds 'much more ambiguity' (2018, 307) than previous scholarship. Such complexity and ambiguity run counter to the strong critical consensus in paratextual and scholarly discussions, making for much less 'neat' judgements (and certainly no clickbait-friendly lists) on the show.

They also speak to the heterogeneous viewing positions occupied by the considerable range of demographics who watch *Friends*. Much of the scholarly (and some of the paratextual) criticism of the series refers to *Friends*' success with white viewers and lack of success with black viewers during its initial broadcast run. According to James Sterngold, in the 1998/1999 prime-time season, *Friends* was 'the No. 1 comedy and No. 2 show overall in white households, [but] ranked just 91st for blacks' (1998, A01). Chidester sees the show's popularity rooted partly 'in its efforts to defend whiteness's hegemonic privilege in contemporary America' (2008, 160), referring to the series as 'a safe media haven for those viewers most heavily invested in preserving a sense of whiteness as an unspoken marker of privilege' (ibid., 168). What would be interesting here would be to take a step back from this focus on what is another white circle—the show is 'marked by its whiteness. It is also a show consumed primarily by white viewers' (Sandell 1998, 151)—and consider further the considerable ongoing popularity of *Friends* with audiences across the globe (and beyond the binary of black and white audiences). Of course, white privilege may find resonance with structures of dominance in other contexts, but as the ethnographic work by Ketan S. Chitnis et al. (2006) and Katherine Dillion (2009) has shown, audiences in non-anglophone national contexts engage with *Friends* in complex ways.

While Chapter 6 considers *Friends*' place within a transnational television landscape, some of the reasons for its global appeal and some of the issues raised by its reception in different national contexts, actual ethnographic study is beyond the scope of this book. We hope that future scholarship will explore the show's ongoing popularity with audiences across the globe, and how they receive its representations, testing out strong claims, such as Chidester's (2008) that the viewer is instrumental in closing *Friends*' circle of whiteness. We hope that more scholars of colour will enter the fray and join the debates on *Friends*' contestable politics of representation. We also hope that the current 'outrage culture'—which our students tell us impedes their involvement in issues concerning diversity and inclusion, for fear of making a mistake and being 'called out'—will make more space for reflective dialogue. Here, scholarship has a responsibility to engage with broader cultural conversations about representations, to help ensure we do not end up with the 'monocriticism' that Morris (2018) is concerned about. And finally, we hope to have shown in this chapter that *Friends*' representation of race is marked by several issues that need to be acknowledged and thought through, but in ways that are alert to context and tone, which in turn may reveal complexity, ambiguity and nuance that are worth uncovering. More of its contestable complexity awaits to be explored, as *Friends* offers a productive space for engaging with television and the politics of representation.

Bibliography

Anderson, Tre'vell. 2017. Aisha Tyler Isn't a 'Black Comic.' She's a Comic Who Is Black. *Los Angeles Times*. https://www.latimes.com/entertainment/la-ca-black-women-comedy-aisha-tyler-20170720-htmlstory.html. Accessed 14 April 2019.

Bailey, Moya, and Trudy. 2018. On Misogynoir: Citation, Erasure, and Plagiarism. *Feminist Media Studies* 18 (4): 762–768. https://doi.org/10.1080/14680777.2018.1447395.

Baron, Cynthia. 2018. Viola Davis: A Context for Her Craft and Success in Series Television. In *Exploring Television Acting*, ed. Tom Cantrell and Christopher Hogg, 79–94. London: Methuen Drama.

Baxter-Wright, Dusty. 2017. 11 Actually Pretty Shocking Things Friends Couldn't Get Away with Today. *Cosmopolitan*. https://www.cosmopolitan.com/uk/entertainment/a38817/11-times-friends-sexist-homophobic/. Accessed 14 April 2019.

Bourdieu, Pierre. 1984. *Distinction: A Social Critique of the Judgment of Taste*. Cambridge: Harvard University Press.

Braxton, Greg. 1996. 'Single' Looks for a Little Help Against 'Friends'. *Los Angeles Times*. https://www.latimes.com/archives/la-xpm-1996-02-01-ca-30941-story.html. Accessed 14 April 2019.

Butler, Bethonie. 2016. Should We Forgive 'Friends' for Feeling a Little Offensive in 2016? *The Washington Post*. https://www.washingtonpost.com/lifestyle/style/should-we-forgive-friends-for-feeling-a-little-offensive-in-2016/2016/02/18/e8d47280-d0d3-11e5-b2bc-988409ee911b_story.html?noredirect=on&utm_term=.a1e17020e9c4. Accessed 14 April 2019.

Chidester, Phil. 2008. May the Circle Stay Unbroken: *Friends*, The Presence of Absence, and the Rhetorical Reinforcement of Whiteness. *Critical Studies in Mass Communication* 25 (2): 157–174. https://doi.org/10.1080/15295030802031772.

Chitnis, Ketan S., Avinash Thombre, Everett M. Rogers, Arvind Singhal, and Ami Sengupta. 2006. (Dis)similar Readings: Indian and American Audiences' Interpretation of *Friends*. *The International Communication Gazette* 68 (2): 131–145. https://doi.org/10.1177/1748048506062229.

Coates, Ta-Nehisi. 2012. 'Girls' Through the Veil. *The Atlantic*. https://www.theatlantic.com/entertainment/archive/2012/04/girls-through-the-veil/256154/. Accessed 14 April 2019.

Cobb, Shelley. 2018. 'I'd Like Y'all to Get a Black Friend': The Politics of Race in *Friends*. *Television & New Media* 19 (8): 708–723. https://doi.org/10.1177/1527476418778420.

Cramer, Lauren. 2018. Spotlight, Moonlight… The New Grammar of Black Visual Culture. *MediaCommons*. http://mediacommons.org/fieldguide/question/how-does-increase-manifesting-blackness-through-african-american-representations-televisi-7. Accessed 14 April 2019.

Crenshaw, Kimberlé. 1989. Demarginalizing the Intersection of Race and Sex: A Black Feminist Critique of Antidiscrimination Doctrine, Feminist Theory and Antiracist Politics. *University of Chicago Legal Forum* 1989 (1): 139–167.

D'Addario, Daniel. 2016. Review: *Unbreakable Kimmy Schmidt* Is TV's Most #Problematic Show. *Time*. http://time.com/4292506/unbreakable-kimmy-schmidt-season-2-review/?xid=time_socialflow_twitter. Accessed 14 April 2019.

Dhaenens, Frederik, and Sofie Van Bauwel. 2018. Sex in Sitcoms: Unravelling the Discourses on Sex in *Friends*. In *The Routledge Companion to Media, Sex and Sexuality*, ed. Clarissa Smith, Feona Attwood, and Brian McNair, 300–308. London and New York: Routledge.

Dillion, Katherine. 2009. *Friends Watching Friends: American Television in Egypt*. Newcastle upon Tyne: Cambridge Scholars Publishing.

DocFuture. 2010. A Semi-Alphabetical Listing of Black Actors with Speaking Roles on Friends. YouTube. https://www.youtube.com/watch?v=oUc0vbSlanM. Accessed 14 April 2019.

Dyer, Richard. 1997. *White*. London and New York: Routledge.

Dyer, Richard. 1998. *Stars*. 2nd ed. London: BFI.

Ellis, John. 2002. *Seeing Things: Television in the Age of Uncertainty*. London and New York: I.B. Tauris.

Entman, Robert, and Andrew Rojecki. 2000. *The Black Image in the White Mind*. Chicago: University of Chicago Press.

Fairfax Media Australia. 2003. Colour Is Not the Issue Here, Girlfriend. *The Age*. https://www.theage.com.au/entertainment/tv-and-radio/colour-is-not-the-issue-here-girlfriend-20030501-gdvmrj.html. Accessed 14 April 2019.

Feuer, Jane. 1992. Genre Study and Television. In *Channels of Discourse, Reassembled: Television and Contemporary Criticism*, ed. Robert C. Allen, 2nd ed., 138–159. London: Routledge.

Feuer, Jane. 2015. Situation Comedy, Part 2. In *The Television Genre Book*, 3rd ed, ed. Glen Creeber, 100–101. London: BFI.

Gates, Henry Louis. 1989. TV's Black World Turns—But Stays Unreal. *The New York Times*. 12 November, 1.
Ghomeshi, Jian. 2014. Aisha Tyler Is 'Not Black Enough'. *Q*. https://www.youtube.com/watch?v=vQ_WQbtFdKU. Accessed 14 April 2019.
Gorton, Kristyn. 2009. *Media Audiences: Television, Meaning and Emotion*. Edinburgh: Edinburgh University Press.
Gosling, Sarah. 2018. Don't Knock Friends. It's Still Relevant, and Progressive, Too. *The Guardian*. https://www.theguardian.com/commentisfree/2018/jan/19/friends-tv-dated-sexuality-masculinity-young-people. Accessed 14 April 2019.
Graham, Ruth. 2015. Chandler Bing Is the Worst Thing About Watching *Friends* in 2015. *Slate*. https://slate.com/culture/2015/01/friends-chandler-bing-and-his-homophobia-are-the-worst-thing-about-watching-the-nbc-sitcom-in-2015.html. Accessed 30 January 2019.
Gray, Herman. 1995. *Watching Race: Television and the Struggle for 'Blackness'*. Minneapolis: University of Minnesota Press.
Gray, Jonathan. 2008. *Television Entertainment*. New York and London: Routledge.
Gray, Jonathan. 2010. *Show Sold Separately: Promos, Spoilers, and Other Media Paratexts*. New York and London: New York University Press.
Hamad, Hannah. 2018. The One with the Feminist Critique: Revisiting Millennial Postfeminism with *Friends*. *Television & New Media* 19 (8): 692–707. https://doi.org/10.1177/1527476418779624.
Harding, Xavier. 2017. Keeping 'Insecure' Lit: HBO Cinematographer Ava Berkofsky on Properly Lighting Black Faces. *Mic*. https://mic.com/articles/184244/keeping-insecure-lit-hbo-cinematographer-ava-berkofsky-on-properly-lighting-black-faces#.gXfwOvwuV. Accessed 14 April 2019.
Harrison, Colin. 2010. *American Culture in the 1990s*. Edinburgh: Edinburgh University Press.
Harrison, George. 2018. Think Friends Is Offensive? Snowflakes, You'll Want to Look Away from All These Sitcoms Too. *The Sun*. https://www.thesun.co.uk/news/5362323/friends-offensive-snowflakes-sitcoms/. Accessed 14 April 2019.
Haughton, Ashleigh. 2018. 17 Reasons 'Friends' Is No More Than a White Ripoff of 'Living Single'. *Odyssey*. https://www.theodysseyonline.com/white-ripoff. Accessed 14 April 2019.
Heuman, Josh. 2016. What Happens in the Writers' Room Stays in the Writers' Room? Professional Authority. *Lyle v. Warner Bros. Television & New Media* 17 (3): 195–211. https://doi.org/10.1177/1527476415594887.
Hill Collins, Patricia. 2000. *Black Feminist Thought: Knowledge, Consciousness, and the Politics of Empowerment*, 2nd ed. New York and London: Routledge.

hooks, bell. 1992. *Black Looks: Race and Representation*. Boston: South End Press.

Hunt, Darnell, et al. 2018. *Hollywood Diversity Report 2018: Five Years of Progress and Missed Opportunities*. Los Angeles: Ralph J. Bunche Center for African American Studies at UCLA. https://socialsciences.ucla.edu/wp-content/uploads/2018/02/UCLA-Hollywood-Diversity-Report-2018-2-27-18.pdf. Accessed 14 April 2019.

Hunter, Gené B. 2018. Aisha Tyler Looks Back at the 'Colorblind Casting' That Got Her on *Friends*. *InStyle*. https://www.instyle.com/aisha-tyler-friends-colorblind-casting. Accessed 14 April 2019.

Jenkins, Henry, Sam Ford, and Joshua Green. 2013. *Spreadable Media: Creating Value and Meaning in a Networked Culture*. New York and London: New York University Press.

Jenner, Mareike. 2018. *Netflix and the Re-invention of Television*. London: Palgrave Macmillan.

Jhally, Sut, and Justin Lewis. 1992. *Enlightened Racism: The Cosby Show, Audiences, and the Myth of the American Dream*. Oxford and Boulder: Westview Press.

Kaplan, Ilana. 2018. Friends: 10 Times the Classic Sitcom Was Problematic. *The Independent*. https://www.independent.co.uk/arts-entertainment/films/friends-netflix-sitcom-problem-sexism-men-joey-phoebe-chandler-ross-rachel-a8168976.html. Accessed 14 April 2019.

Kerr, Audrey Elisa. 2006. *The Paper Bag Principle: Class, Colorism, Rumor and the Case of Black Washington*. Knoxville: University of Tennessee Press.

Kessler, Kelly. 2006. Politics of the Sitcom Formula: *Friends*, *Mad About You* and the Sapphic Second Banana. In *The New Queer Aesthetic on Television: Essays on Recent Programming*, ed. James R. Keller and Leslie Stratyner, 130–146. Jefferson: McFarland.

Lauzen, Martha M. 2018. *Boxed in 2017–18: Women on Screen and Behind the Scenes in Television*. Center for the Study of Women in Television & Film. San Diego: San Diego State University. https://womenintvfilm.sdsu.edu/wp-content/uploads/2018/09/2017-18_Boxed_In_Report.pdf. Accessed 14 April 2019.

Logan, Brian. 2018. Aziz Ansari Suggests 'Wokeness' Can Go Too Far at Surprise Gig. *The Guardian*. https://www.theguardian.com/stage/2018/oct/08/aziz-ansari-surprise-standup-gig. Accessed 14 April 2019.

Lotz, Amanda D. 2005. Segregated Sitcoms: Institutional Causes of Disparity Among Black and White Comedy Images and Audiences. In *The Sitcom*

Reader: Viewed and Skewed, ed. Mary M. Dalton and Laura R. Linder, 139–150. Albany: State University of New York Press.

Lubiano, Wahneema. 1992. Black Ladies, Welfare Queens, and State Minstrels: Ideological War by Narrative Means. In *Race-ing Justice, En-Gendering Power*, ed. Toni Morrison, 323–363. New York: Pantheon.

Lyle v. Warner Brothers Television Productions. 2006. Supreme Court of California. S125171 Ct. App. 2/7 160528. Los Angeles County Super. Ct. No. BC239047.

Marghitu, Stefania, and Conrad Ng. 2013. Body Talk: Reconsidering the Post-Feminist Discourse and Critical Reception of Lena Dunham's *Girls*. *Gender Forum: An Internet Journal for Gender Studies* 45: 108–125. http://www.genderforum.org/issues/special-issue-early-career-researchers-i/body-talk-re-considering-the-post-feminist-discourse-and-critical-reception-of-lena-dun-hams-girls/. Accessed 14 April 2019.

Marshall, Lisa Marie. 2007. 'I'll Be There for You' If You Are Just Like Me: An Analysis of Hegemonic Social Structures in 'Friends'. Unpublished PhD thesis, Graduate College of Bowling Green State University.

Mercer, Kobena. 1987. Black Hair/Style Politics. *New Formations* 3: 33–54.

Miller, Kelsey. 2018a. *I'll Be There For You: The One About Friends*. London: HQ.

Miller, Kelsey. 2018b. The Ruling in This 'Friends' Lawsuit Set Back the #MeToo Movement By Years—Now the Woman at the Center of It Speaks Out. *Bustle*. https://www.bustle.com/p/the-ruling-in-this-friends-lawsuit-set-back-the-metoo-movement-by-years-now-the-woman-at-the-center-of-it-speaks-out-12636045. Accessed 14 April 2019.

Mills, Brett. 2009. *The Sitcom*. Edinburgh: Edinburgh University Press.

Morreale, Joanne. 2003. Introduction: On the Sitcom. In *Critiquing the Sitcom: A Reader*, ed. Joanne Morreale, xi–xix. Syracuse: Syracuse University Press.

Morris, Wesley. 2018. Should Art Be a Battleground for Social Justice?: The Morality Wars. *The New York Times*. https://www.nytimes.com/interactive/2018/10/03/magazine/morality-social-justice-art-entertainment.html. Accessed 14 April 2019.

Newcomb, Horace. 1974. *TV: The Most Popular Art*. Garden City, NY: Anchor Books.

Nussbaum, Emily. 2011. Crass Warfare: Raunch and Ridicule on 'Whitney' and 'Two Broke Girls'. *The New Yorker*, 28 November, 72–74.

Nussbaum, Emily. 2013. Difficult Women: How 'Sex and the City' Lost Its Good Name. *The New Yorker*, 29 July, 64–67.

Obama, Michelle. 2018. *Becoming*. New York: Crown.

O'Connor, John J. 1994. Television Review: Yes, More Friends Sitting Around. *The New York Times*, 29 September, C18.

Paskin, Willa. 2014. Attractive People Being Funny While Doing Amusing and Sometimes Romantic Things. *Slate*. https://slate.com/culture/2014/09/friends-20th-anniversary-the-nbc-sitcom-was-truly-great.html. Accessed 14 April 2019.

Phalange, Roberta. 2016. 'The One with Racial Discrimination'—A Contemporary Look into Friends. https://criticalinsightintofriends.wordpress.com/2016/02/01/the-one-with-racial-discrimination-a-contemporary-look-into-friends-2/. Accessed 14 April 2019.

politicalremix. 2011. Homophobic Friends—By Tijana Mamula. YouTube. https://www.youtube.com/watch?v=SsQ5za-J6I8&feature=player_embedded#. Accessed 14 April 2019.

Pountain, Dick, and David Robins. 2000. *Cool Rules: Anatomy of an Attitude*. London: Reaktion Books.

Pye, Douglas. 2007. Movies and Tone. In *Close Up 02*, ed. John Gibbs and Douglas Pye, 1–80. London: Wallflower Press.

Redd, Nancy. 2014. Why Aisha Tyler Is So Proud to Be a 'Black Nerd'. *HuffPost Live*. https://www.huffingtonpost.co.uk/entry/why-aisha-tyler-is-so-proud-to-be-a-black-nerd_us_5b4f6627e4b004fe162f8980. Accessed 14 April 2019.

Reynolds, Megan, and Joanna Rothkopf. 2018. Every Non-white Character on *Sex and the City*. *Jezebel*. https://themuse.jezebel.com/every-non-white-character-on-sex-and-the-city-1826192709. Accessed 14 April 2019.

Robinson, Phoebe. 2016. *You Can't Touch My Hair: And Other Things I Still Have to Explain*. New York: Plume.

Rockler, Naomi R. 2006. *Friends*, Judaism, and the Holiday Armadillo: Mapping a Rhetoric of Postidentity Politics. *Communication Theory* 16 (4): 453–473. https://doi.org/10.1111/j.1468-2885.2006.00278.x.

Rosa, Christopher. 2018. Revisiting the *Friends* Episode in Which Everyone's Awkward About Money. *Glamour*. https://www.glamour.com/story/friends-episode-five-steaks-and-an-eggplant-money. Accessed 14 April 2019.

Sandell, Jillian. 1998. I'll Be There For You: *Friends* and the Fantasy of Alternative Families. *American Studies* 39 (2): 141–155.

Scott, Tony. 1994. Friends. *Variety*. https://variety.com/1994/tv/reviews/friends-4-1200438471/. Accessed 14 April 2019.

Sepinwall, Alan. 2014. The One Where 'Friends' Ended 10 Years Ago Tonight. *Uproxx*. https://uproxx.com/sepinwall/the-one-where-friends-ended-10-years-ago-tonight/. Accessed 14 April 2019.

Smith-Shomade, Beretta E. 2002. *Shaded Lives: African-American Women and Television*. New Brunswick and London: Rutgers University Press.

Springer, Kimberly. 2008. Divas, Evil Black Bitches, and Bitter Black Women: African American Women in Postfeminist and Post-Civil Rights Popular Culture. In *Feminist Television Criticism: A Reader*, ed. Charlotte Brunsdon and Lynn Spigel, 2nd ed., 72–92. Maidenhead: Open University Press.

Sterngold, James. 1998. A Racial Divide Widens on Network TV. *The New York Times*, 29 December, A01.

Terkel, Studs. 1992. *Race: How Blacks and Whites Think and Feel About the American Obsession*. New York: Anchor Books.

Tucker, Ken. 1994. TV Show Review: Winning 'Friends'. *Entertainment Weekly*. https://ew.com/article/1994/10/21/tv-show-review-winning-friends/. Accessed 14 April 2019.

Tyler, Aisha. 2004. *Swerve: Reckless Observations of a Postmodern Girl*. New York: Dutton.

Tyler, Aisha. 2012. Dear Gamers. *Facebook*. https://www.facebook.com/notes/aisha-tyler/dear-gamers/10151040991508993. Accessed 14 April 2019.

Vermeulen, Timotheus, and James Whitfield. 2013. Arrested Developments: Towards an Aesthetic of the Contemporary US Sitcom. In *Television Aesthetics and Style*, ed. Jason Jacobs and Steven Peacock, 103–111. London and New York: Bloomsbury.

Warner, Kristen J. 2015. *The Cultural Politics of Colorblind TV Casting*. New York: Routledge.

Warner, Kristen J. 2017. In the Time of Plastic Representation. *Film Quarterly* 71 (2): 32–37. https://doi.org/10.1525/fq.2017.71.2.32.

West, Carolyn M. 2018. Mammy, Sapphire, Jezebel, and the Bad Girls of Reality Television: Media Representations of Black Women. In *Lectures on the Psychology of Women*, 5th ed, ed. Joan C. Chrisler and Carla Golden, 139–158. Long Grove: Waveland Press.

Wickham, Phil. 2013. British Situation Comedy and 'The Culture of the New Capitalism'. Unpublished PhD thesis, University of Exeter.

Woods, Faye. 2015. *Girls* Talk: Authorship and Authenticity in the Reception of Lena Dunham's *Girls*. *Critical Studies in Television* 10 (2): 37–54. https://doi.org/10.7227/CST.10.2.4.

Television

Archer (2009–present), USA: FX.
Black-ish (2014–present), USA: ABC.
2 Broke Girls (2011–2017), USA: CBS.
Brooklyn Nine-Nine (2013–2018, 2019–present), USA: Fox, NBC.
Designing Women (1986–1993), USA: CBS.
Family Matters (1989–1998), USA: ABC/CBS.
Frasier (1993–2004), USA: NBC.
Friends (1994–2004), USA: NBC.
Grace and Frankie (2015–present), USA: Netflix.
Girlfriends (2000–2008), USA: UPN/The CW.
Girls (2011–2017), USA: HBO.
How I Met Your Mother (2005–2014), USA: CBS.
How to Get Away with Murder (2014–present), USA: ABC.
Insecure (2016–present), USA: HBO.
Living Single (1993–1998), USA: Fox.
Martin (1992–1997), USA: Fox.
Moesha (1996–2001), USA: UPN.
One Day at a Time (2017–2019), USA: Netflix.
Seinfeld (1989–1998), USA: NBC.
Sex and the City (1998–2004), USA: HBO.
Stranger Things (2016–present), USA: Netflix.
The Cosby Show (1984–1992), USA: NBC.
The Fresh Prince of Bel-Air (1990–1996), USA: NBC.
The Good Place (2016–present), USA: NBC.
The Office—An American Workplace (2005–2013), USA: NBC.
The Oprah Winfrey Show (1986–2011), USA: ABC.
Tracey Breaks the News (2017–present), UK: BBC One.
Unbreakable Kimmy Schmidt (2015–2019), USA: Netflix.

Film

Edwards, B. 1979. *10*. Burbank, CA, USA: Warner Bros.
Fleming, V. 1939. *The Wizard of Oz*. New York, NY, USA: Loews.
Jenkins, B. 2016. *Moonlight*. New York, NY, USA: A24.
Peele, J. 2017. *Get Out*. New York, NY, USA: Universal Pictures.
Riley, B. 2018. *Sorry to Bother You*. West Hollywood, CA, USA: Mirror Releasing.

6

The One with the Orbit of Failure: The *Joey* Spin-Off, Other Adaptations and the Global Reception of *Friends*

If *Seinfeld* is, as television mythology has it, a show about 'nothing', then *Friends* might be a show about (almost) 'everything'. Part of its enduring success is its seemingly endless 'quotability'—of verbal jokes, of catchphrases, of situations. For, indeed, *Friends*' narrative set-up seems universal: it addresses situations, dynamics and conflicts which are instantly recognisable to its audiences around the world. As Kevin S. Bright observed for us, the show is about young adulthood, which 'people are either about to experience, are experiencing, or have experienced'. That the show speaks easily and strongly to viewers from diverse socio-cultural contexts is evident in the extensive, ongoing paratextual engagement—numerous Facebook groups and Instagram accounts from across the globe post their favourite moments, fan art and cherished trivia on a daily basis—which seems to go beyond the usual patterns of fan loyalty.

One of the reasons for this particular demand for intertextuality and online engagement might be the fact that *Friends* was a show produced during the end of TVIII (Rogers et al. 2002), an era dominated by national broadcasters and commercial channels, but most significantly, still as part of a linear television discourse. For most of its initial audience, *Friends* happened at a fixed point in time, in their living room in front of a television set, not on their laptops, tablets or smartphones. While, as Todd (2011) has explored, there was significant online fan discourse during its original broadcast run, the show went without in-character social media accounts, and the production process was not made transparent online or on social media. In fact, there is surprisingly little 'making of' material available, and from the second season none of the main actors particularly engaged with celebrity culture. (The DVD edition released in 2004, after the series' finale, features a 45-minute 'making of' feature, chronicling the production of 6.1, in September 1999.) Yet, the desire by fans of *Friends* to explore and engage with various aspects of the show's characters, narrative and aesthetics is obvious and prevalent across the plethora of today's digital landscape.

How, then, can we approach the apparent (and evident) universality of *Friends*' distinct appeal with audiences around the world? As can be gleaned from our analysis of the *Friends* backlash in Chapter 5, and as Simone Knox points out in her reflections on transnationalisation and television, 'the universal' is a far from unproblematic concept, 'especially from a post-colonial, feminist, queer and/or any other traditionally marginalised perspective' (2013, 104–105). Furthermore, the discipline of television studies, including this book, has rightly made pertinent claims as to the importance of context, be that historical, cultural, aesthetic, industrial or otherwise, and has actively refuted the equalisation of dominant heterogeneous discourses with a singular definition of universality. However, a television show such as *Friends*—whose popular impact extends beyond the spatial and temporal reach of its initial broadcast and, which, 25 years after its first release, can be described as still one of the few global reference shows—has to be discussed and analysed precisely because of its universal appeal. As we have argued in the introduction to this book, there is little previous scholarship on *Friends*, and the existing work is characterised by scepticism towards its universal qualities, mostly neglecting the fact that 'the universal' is also a concept that has strong currency within industry discourses and enables a 'more nuanced understanding of the global' (Knox 2013, 105). As such, we argue that *Friends* serves as an illuminating case study of the notion of universality, for scholarly insight and as a relevant framework for practitioners across the creative industries.

6 The One with the Orbit of Failure …

This chapter will look beyond *Friends* to consider the show's different intertextual brethren, whose various degrees of failure help to cast a light on the factors that facilitated *Friends*' considerable success. With *Mad About You* character Ursula being retconned as Phoebe's evil twin following a cross-over appearance in *Friends*' first season, and Joey's role of Dr Drake Ramoray on the fictionalised version of *Days of Our Lives* starting in the second season, *Friends* had relatively open intertextual borders since its beginning. Rumours concerning potential spin-offs began circulating during the programme's initial broadcast, and NBC was understandably concerned to find a replacement hit when *Friends* started to come to its end. However, the *Joey* spin-off focusing on Matt LeBlanc barely lasted two seasons following its highly anticipated premiere in the former timeslot of its antecedent. In addition to this, NBC had already experienced a lack of success with the short-lived US format adaptation of the British sitcom *Coupling* in 2003 (hereafter referred to as *Coupling USA* and *Coupling UK*), which had been intended to replace *Friends*. This chapter will consider how these failures may throw a reflexive light on *Friends*' success.

Continuing with the theme of failure, the chapter will moreover bring in a more explicitly global (and less anglophone) outlook by considering why *Friends* was a comparatively lesser success in Germany during its initial broadcast there. Noting the problems the sitcom experienced with its scheduling by broadcaster Sat. 1, we will discuss a number of issues with the German dubbing of *Friends*. Despite the German dubbing industry's high level of expertise, the German *Friends* is generally acknowledged to have been problematic; and our analysis will tease out how issues concerning casting and performance can contribute to our understanding of *Friends*. We will conclude the chapter by considering how *Friends* has influenced international television comedy productions, with a number of shows drawing on *Friends* with varying degrees of explicit admission. Our key examples here are the Iranian programme *Eshgh Ta'til Nist*, which recreates Monica's apartment to a striking level of similarity, and the Chinese sitcom *iPartment*, which featured a will-they-won't-they storyline between a shy male scientist and a woman who runs away from her privileged background and eventually starts to work in fashion. We will discuss how the presence of such loose, 'unofficial' adaptations in very different socio-cultural contexts may reflect on the American ideology and transnational resonance of *Friends*.

Before we proceed with our case studies, we would like to specify our conceptualisation of 'failure' and why we consider it a relevant framework for this chapter. Within the field of scholarly research on cultural products across formats and genres, there is a tendency to focus on 'success stories', or, in other words, successful processes of creative execution, commerciality or legitimisation by audiences and cultural curators, such as critics and journalists. As interesting and relevant as these explorations of achievement are, in particular when they reveal insights in strategic approaches which might be beneficial for both industrial application and further research, they only represent a small fraction of cultural products being executed and launched. As the editors of a noteworthy special issue on failure in *The Velvet Light Trap* argue, 'media history is lined with failures, flops, and false starts across the areas of aesthetics and style, technology, social and political representation, media studies' methods and models, and industry and business' (2009, 76). In particular, the global television industry is littered with unsuccessful format pitches, unrealised scripts or cancelled pilots. A brief glance at the end of Nell Scovell's 2018 memoir *Just the Funny Parts* vividly attests to this: the creator of *Sabrina the Teenage Witch* (1996–2003), and with her writing credits further including *The Simpsons*, *Murphy Brown* and *Charmed*, Scovell's curriculum vitae is peppered with 'unshot' pilots. As such, *Friends* is an exception to the rule, or as Jason Mittell puts it, 'television creativity itself is immersed in failure, and failure needs to be seen as the default norm, not the exception' (2009, 76). Here, it is important to stress that for most constituents of the television industry, success and consequently failure are first and foremost measured in quantitative (audiences) and economic terms (revenues). Even though *Friends* was (and still is) a success in both of these categories, we are not explicitly interested in the failures of its spin-off, its global adaptions or the German dubbed version as quantitatively measurable successes (or lack thereof) on their respective television markets, but mostly as antitheses of an initial concept drenched in aesthetic, narrative and commercial achievement and popularity. These failures are of empirical value for the industry and offer a reflective understanding of *Friends*' ongoing success with audiences around the globe. For, in general, 'failures help us understand the limits of the system as well as the possibilities that got passed over, and thus they need to be viewed alongside clear successes and within the gray area in between' (ibid., 77).

The One where the *Joey* Spin-off Doesn't Work

As Todd Gitlin has noted, the history of the sitcom genre has no shortage of spin-offs, as part of a wider recombinant culture that follows the dictum that 'nothing succeeds like success' (2000 [1983], 64–69). *Joey* premiered in September 2004 as part of NBC's prestigious Thursday night Must-See TV schedule, taking over the original *Friends* slot (8 p.m.). The premise of the programme is a direct continuation of the character's story arc from *Friends*: Joey moves from New York to Los Angeles to pursue a Hollywood acting career. His sister Gina (Drea de Matteo)—who had not appeared in *Friends* (at least not played by de Matteo)—works as a hair stylist and arranges a flat for Joey which he eventually shares with his nephew, Gina's 20-year-old son Michael (Paulo Costanzo). Gina, who initially shares Joey's attitudes to promiscuity and hedonism, is very protective of her son and disapproves of Joey's bad influence as part of their shared bachelor-pad living arrangement. The next-door neighbour Alex (Andrea Anders) first befriends Joey and from the end of the first season becomes romantically involved with him. Other storylines and subplots see Joey pursuing an acting career by going to auditions, filming pilots and eventually staring in movies, facilitating a variety of celebrity guest appearances (e.g. Jay Leno, Lucy Liu, Ellen DeGeneres).

The series was created and produced by former *Friends* showrunners Scott Silveri and Shana Goldberg-Meehan and executive produced by Kevin S. Bright. Even though it was marketed as the official spin-off, *Friends*' co-creators and initial showrunners Marta Kauffman and David Crane were not actively involved in the production of *Joey* (but are acknowledged in the closing credits). In addition to a variety of regular *Friends* writers and executive producers, David Schwimmer made a guest appearance and directed two episodes in the first season (1.5 and 1.13). Both actors Adam Goldberg (playing Michael's father Jimmy

Costa) and Jennifer Coolidge (playing Joey's agent Bobbie) had previously appeared on *Friends* in different roles, Goldberg as Chandler's psychotic roommate Eddie (in the second season), and Coolidge as Monica's friend Amanda (the one with a fake British accent) in 10.3. Relying on experienced creative personnel behind the camera is a legitimate strategy to ensure the new format's narrative, aesthetic and commercial success; however, in hindsight, recasting the same actors in different roles across the intertextually intertwined universes of both shows seems counterproductive and a likely means to alienate established fans. Despite scheduling *Joey* in an established 'premium' slot and numerous promotional appearances by Matt LeBlanc in talk shows and other programmes prior and during its launch, *Joey* did not connect meaningfully with audiences and critics. However, it is worth noting that the ratings for the show were considerably stable, averaging at around 7 million viewers during its second season (Thomas 2019). At the time, though, NBC was still relying on bigger audiences for its Must-See TV Thursday market dominance and ensuring investments and revenues by high profile advertisers. Thus, this explains why the network consequently evaluated *Joey* as a failure and cancelled the show in March 2006 during its second season after 46 broadcast episodes, with eight episodes left unaired. This decision, based on quantitative and commercial factors alone, seems very much of its time. In TVIV, an era dominated by digital platform distribution redefining the meaning of 'niche' programmes through the impact of fragmented audiences, as well as a preponderance for spin-offs, crossover shows and reboots, *Joey* not only might have found an audience, but would be considered a success. As David Crane has argued in reference to *Joey*, 'if that show was on today, it would be the highest-rated show on television. Everything has changed so much. We had shows cancelled years ago that today would be crazy ridiculous numbers' (in Gajewski 2017).

As we have established in the introduction to this chapter, we are not interested in the commercial failure of the show per se, at least not in terms of its direct market value. Rather, we are trying to explore whether the failure of *Joey* to connect with (larger) audiences might tell us something about the failure or reversion of the successful strategy of intimacy employed by *Friends* and outlined in detail in previous chapters. A good place to begin our analysis is the show's opening credits sequence, which is comprised of a variety of fast-paced shots of Joey driving through sunny Los Angeles in a cabriolet, using the song *Sunny Hours* by American pop-ska band Long Beach Dub Allstars featuring will.i.am. The opening shots introduce images of a variety of buildings and facades of a distinctly urban yet touristy Los Angeles, positioning Joey as the central character and the programme's distinct focus (the other main characters are not featured). Interestingly, and perhaps unintentionally, this introduction enhances the feeling of isolation with regards to the Joey character; he is exploring Los Angeles as an outsider, a tourist, aimlessly cruising through the streets, 'abandoned' by his friends back home in New York.

In terms of *Joey*'s aesthetics, the show employs a classical multi-camera set-up and was recorded in front of a live audience. Linking back to our analysis of *Friends*' use of style in Chapter 4, it is noteworthy to what extent *Joey*'s approach to set design and lighting does not achieve the same effect of inclusive intimacy compared to its antecedent. Joey and Michael's condo, one of the main sets of the series, is lit with much harsher and brighter light and exposes the living room area as a wide floor with lots of unused space. The furniture seems pushed back upstage, which might have been a conscious decision to give more room for the physical performances in the foreground but lacks a structuring perpendicular element such as the couch in Monica's apartment. In terms of texture, the condo seems much less detailed and strikingly empty compared to the filled cupboards, decorated walls and embroidered pillows in Monica's place, evoking the sense of an unused basement. As Fig. 6.1 shows, there are intertextual references to the *Friends* set, for example the Magna Doodle at the door; however, the most striking difference is the use of an entirely different colour palette. Whereas Monica's apartment was characterised by the unusual but inviting colour purple, Joey's LA apartment is dominated by earthy colours using mostly brown and yellow tones. As such, his place is rendered as a stereotypically traditional gendered space—a bachelor pad—which, through a combination of the harsh lighting, empty main space and darker colour palette, does not generate a notion of intimacy.

Fig. 6.1 Unfamiliar surroundings: Michael (Paulo Costanzo), Joey (Matt LeBlanc) and Gina Tribbiani (Drea de Matteo) in *Joey* ('Joey and the Student', 1.2)

On a narrative level, Joey's new home, Los Angeles, is established as a place of falseness, inauthenticity and broken dreams already in the pilot episode: Joey's sister Gina is proud of her 'fake boobs', Alex describes the inhabitants of the neighbourhood as 'everybody is an actor here' and the Hollywood sign is not fully visible from the patio of the apartment and referred to by Joey as the 'ollywo' sign. This context instils the series with a more satirical and cynical tonality and, as such, lacks the warmth, kindness and universality of *Friends* both in terms of how the story world is constructed and how the characters interact with each other. Even though the show taps into media-savvy global audiences' knowledge of and interest in the stereotypes related to Hollywood, putting the focus on the challenges and repercussions of working in the entertainment industry might have had an alienating effect in a generic context that benefits from emotional inclusion for its comedic sensibility to work.

For the most part, Joey is the butt of the joke, with his intellectual limitations and hedonistic approach to life regularly ridiculed, but as we have argued in our reflections on *Friends*' use of humour in Chapter 2, Joey's comedic personality needs a regulatory framework in the shape of a commentator, in other words, an adult to his inner (and outer) child. Here, it is interesting how *Joey*'s ensemble cast is trying to replicate the psycho-social constellation of the main characters in *Friends*. His nephew Michael inherits some of the character traits ascribed to Chandler and Ross (the inexperience with women, the geekiness), his sister Gina, though irresponsible in her own right, serves as an authoritative figure similar to Monica, his neighbour Alex is established as a friend-turned-lover in the same vein as Rachel functions as a love interest for Joey throughout the later seasons, and his agent Bobbie inherits some of the absurdist humour and the ditsyness of Phoebe. Still, despite relying on a similar character constellation and diegetic framework, the comedic sensibility of *Joey* has slightly shifted. This, we suggest, can be explained by two discursive dynamics. First, the ensemble performance quality of *Friends* is not replicated in *Joey*, first and foremost and obviously, because of its different cast. As a consequence, Joey's character traits take more centre stage (literally) and are not counterbalanced by the nuanced performances of the other *Friends* actors, making the show's humour seem less sophisticated and more superficial.

Second, the dominance of Joey's comedic tropes marks the show's humour. For example, Joey's negotiation of gender relations is more problematic and less balanced. In the pilot episode, the numeric rating of females by Joey, Michael and Gina—'She is a 9' or 'I got a phone number from a solid 5'—although presented as immature, is established as a legitimate way of describing the opposite sex and consequently used as a direct source for situational humour and not as a means to ironise or satirise chauvinist sexism as, for the most part, was the case in *Friends*. Ultimately, it seems that Joey's prediction (in *Friends*) of being able 'to turn anything dirty', even an innocent phrase such as 'grandma's chicken salad' (5.3) has finally come true. In our interview, Kevin S. Bright articulated the reasons for *Joey*'s failure in relation to the fundamental change of Joey's character as follows:

> That's what happens when the creative ball is passed from one writing team to another. And the new writing team doesn't necessarily accept or want to continue any of the conventions or foundations that the character had before. So, it's the new Joey […]; 'We want Joey to really fall

in love, and be married, and have kids' [...] and I'm hearing this in the beginning and my heart is falling on the floor [...]. It's a very basic premise: Joey gets laid, people are happy, what are you trying to change the formula for? [...] So, Joey never started out as the Joey we knew from *Friends*.

We suggest that 'the failure' of *Joey* manifests itself first and foremost through a comedic and performative absence; Joey is literally lacking his *Friends*. Furthermore, the show does not employ the strategic approach to facilitating intimacy through its aesthetics, narrative and to a lesser degree also its comedic performance.

At the time of the series' cancellation, industry commentators and critics focused mostly on the commercial failure and the ratings drop from 18.6 million viewers watching the first episode to 4 million watching the final episodes of the second season in March 2006 (Banham 2006). The lack of enthusiasm for and engagement with the show can be gleaned from this excerpt from the industry paper *Entertainment Weekly*:

> Perhaps the bigger question is why NBC stuck with *Joey* in the first place, despite a mediocre first season (10.1 million viewers) and an icy reception from critics. LeBlanc declined to speak to EW for this story, but sources say canning *Joey* before the end of the second season would have proved incredibly costly – with stiff penalties to be paid to Warner Bros. TV, plus $700,000 an episode to LeBlanc for two seasons' worth of shows, regardless of how many were actually filmed. On top of that, NBC likely wanted to avoid a predictable chorus of *I told you so*'s from an industry already pessimistic about spin-offs. (Rice 2006)

Perhaps *Joey* seemed particularly anachronistic at the time of its initial implementation, with 'hybrid sitcoms' (Schwind 2015) such as *Curb Your Enthusiasm* or *Arrested Development* heralding a shift in aesthetics, storytelling and tonality. In other words, sitcoms had started to look and feel different; furthermore, these single-camera shows had to address the fragmentation of television audiences worldwide. That said, multi-camera sitcoms were still reliable schedule tent poles in the early 2000s, in particular for CBS, with programmes such as *Two and a Half Men* and *How I Met Your Mother* scoring high with audiences (both nationally and internationally), affiliates and advertisers. What NBC had to negotiate, then, was the fostering of a new comedic and aesthetic sensibility in its sitcoms, catering to a younger demographic by deliberately avoiding the multi-camera discourse that was increasingly perceived as dated and anachronistic. Interestingly, *Joey* is not available on Netflix or any other mainstream digital platform at the time of writing. It would be interesting to see whether the perception of the show would be different as part of the fragmented but global reach of *Friends* on the platform. As such, the broadcasting legacy of *Joey* still seems to be very much affected by what Mareike Jenner has called 'a cultural distinction within the genre that was established during the TV III era' (2018, 145), meaning that it is perceived as a dated and formulaic multi-camera sitcom.

To this date, Matt LeBlanc seems to be the member of the *Friends* cast who is most willing to both subvert and confirm his established image as iconic multi-camera sitcom star. He is offering yet another version of his multi-camera comedic persona in the CBS sitcom *Man with a Plan* (2016–present), in which he plays a father who has to take care of his three children after his wife decides to start working again. Despite (or possibly because of?) the rather anachronistic premise, the series has found its audience, with its stable ratings proving, once again, that the multi-camera situation comedy is very much a functioning and reliable discourse. However, in *Episodes* (2011–2017) LeBlanc plays a fictional version of himself, ruining the career ambitions of two British comedy writers (played by Stephen Mangan and Tamsin Greig) by being cast as the lead in the American version of their sitcom. *Episodes* draws humour from both the actual and assumed cultural differences and the clash of UK and US television production. The series successfully avoids the risk of being one giant industry-inside joke and manages to both caricature LeBlanc's off-screen persona and satirise the discourse of transnational format adaptation.

It is noteworthy how Matt LeBlanc approaches performance here, opting for a more restrained style of acting as the fictional 'Matt LeBlanc' in the single-camera show *Episodes* compared to his work in the multi-camera shows *Friends*, *Joey* and *Man with a Plan*. For example, his speaking voice in *Episodes* is characterised by a lower pitch and slower speech patterns, closer to his actual speaking voice, audible in, for instance, his numerous talk show appearances and interviews. Consequently, *Episodes* serves as an interesting comparative meta-case study and suitable transition to our analysis of the next 'failure' in the aftermath of *Friends*, namely the NBC adaptation of the British format *Coupling*. For, as Elke Weissmann has argued in her discussion on the transatlantic adaptation dynamics:

> *Episodes* thus constructs two very different industries: the UK system, which remains dedicated to the creative vision of the writer/creator, who is often perceived as artist and hence given reign over the development of a story, and the US industry, which is based on economic incentives and hence restricts the creativity of the artist in favour of well-established rules and conventions. (2012, 2)

The One with *Coupling*: Cultural Proximity, National Specificities and a Lack of Intimacy in Transnational Media Spaces

If the comedy of the single-camera sitcom *Episodes* 'is typical of how both industries look at themselves' (Weissmann 2012, 2), then the NBC format adaptation of the multi-camera sitcom *Coupling* could be read as pastiche or parody of an über-Americanised adaptation of a British show. *Coupling USA* was broadcast in 2003, from 25 September until 23 October, and cancelled by NBC after only four episodes, with six episodes left unaired. The British 'original' ran from 2000 to 2004 on BBC Two and BBC Three, and all 28 episodes were broadcast on BBC America in the USA. Both *Coupling UK* and *Coupling USA* were created, written and overseen by British showrunner Steven Moffat, who based the original premise of the show on his real-life experiences of socialising with friends in the urban environment of London and dating his later wife Sue Vertue (a producer of the British programme and executive producer of *Coupling USA*). The series focuses on the relationships and love lives of three male and three female characters and was characterised by its often raunchy and risqué dialogue-based comedy finding humour in the sexual relationships and mishaps of its main protagonists. Given its character constellation and set-up, as well as its time of inception, *Coupling UK* is clearly inspired by the success of the concept of *Friends*, which was among the most popular American sitcoms on British television during its original broadcast run (Pile 2004). From the beginning, the similarities and televisual co-existence invited comparisons and led to both British and American journalists referring to *Coupling UK* as 'the British *Friends*' (Sanson 2011, 43). When NBC was looking for a new sitcom concept to be developed alongside *Friends* for Must-See TV, to eventually take over its slot, the producers turned to Moffat and colleagues to adapt *Coupling UK* for the USA.

To this day, *Coupling USA* rates among the biggest failures of USA–UK transnational format adaptations, both in scholarly research on format adaptations (e.g. Sanson 2011; Mikos 2015; Schwind 2015) as well as online commentary. For example, the YouTube channel Mojo rates *Coupling USA* among the ten worst remakes of British shows, calling it 'a horrible Americanization of a truly brilliant British show' (2014). Carlen Lavigne and Heather Marcovitch rightly point out that fiction format adaptation 'does not follow a single prescribed path, nor are there systemic criteria for what comprises success or failure in this process' (2011, xii), but it is certainly possible to identify a set of reasons for *Coupling USA*'s particular kind of failure. However, before we provide an analysis of its distinct failure, it is important to explore the historical and theoretical framework of transnational format adaptations between the UK and the USA. Thus, we start by addressing some relevant concepts of scholarly research on the specificities of format adaptation.

The One with the Conceptualisation of the Television Format

Albert Moran and Justin Malbon offer a useful definition of the television format 'as that set of invariable elements in a programme out of which the variable elements of an individual episode are produced' (2006, 20). Furthermore, they conceive of a television format as being the result of a collection of processes, which can be summed up in the three phases of 'devising', 'developing' and 'distributing' a format

(Moran and Malbon 2006). More specifically, Moran understands the format as shaped and defined by a conglomerate of knowledge, providing a set of 'knowledge components' constituting the fundamental structure of a television format (Moran 1998, 18). Julie Christie, CEO Touchdown Productions, neatly summarises these components as follows: 'a format is all about the rules you put on an idea' (in Moran and Malbon 2006, 39).

In terms of television scholarship, we strongly agree with Heidi Keinonen who claims that, as a still emerging field, 'format study […] necessitates theoretical and methodological cultivation' (2016, 2). She (ibid., 4) has also identified the need for more programme-specific research on format adaptation that pays attention to not just the final product but also to relevant processes of production. In her study of the format flow of television dramas between the United States and the UK, Elke Weissmann (2012) suggests rethinking the flow of televisual formats, concepts and ideas away from a rather archaic dynamism shaped by the mythology of travelling, a journey from origin to destination, and instead to conceptualise them as fundamentally transnational, as two sides of the same coin. This proposes an interesting approach to our analysis since it suggests that:

> most dramas – where they do not address specific national moments, in which case they are often repackaged for the international market – are now produced with international audiences already in mind […] creating a production environment in which very specific national elements are often reduced or exaggerated to stereotype in order to cater to tourist sensibilities. (Weissmann 2012, 6–7)

That said, the genre of sitcom complicates this dynamic. As we have explored in more detail in Chapter 2, social analyses of humour have repeatedly stressed the importance of establishing a connection between the joke teller and the receiver, an intimacy that establishes common linguistic, semiotic or social grounds for the joke, or the humoristic exchange, to function. In other words, for the jokes of a sitcom to work in different countries, the comedic sensibility is likely to be in need of adjustment.

This process is reminiscent of the broader process of format adaptation, to which Joseph Straubhaar's theory of cultural proximity speaks as follows: 'audiences seem to prefer television programs that are as close to them as possible in language, ethnic appearance, dress style, humour, historical reference, and shared topical knowledge' (2007, 26). Straubhaar (1991) originally developed this concept to explain the success of the cross-country adaptations of Latin American telenovelas to Spain and Portugal. The identification of linguistic and socio-cultural similarities as a result of a shared colonial past worked as a blueprint for other geographical regions and was also used to describe the format flow between English language countries such as the United States and the UK. Despite raising valid points, the theory could not explain the many failures of format adaptations from within a similar cultural proximity. As a result, Straubhaar himself has criticised his concept as 'too simplistic and has pointed to the multiple cultural proximities that exist for each viewer in every nation' (Weissmann 2012, 7).

Indeed, when watching television, viewers may enjoy a programme not just because of their nationality or ethnicity, but also—and probably even more—because of more differentiated and diversified social contexts. Again, television comedy in general, and sitcom in particular, serve as a good example, for the enjoyment of mediatised forms of humour is related to highly individual social conceptualisations of 'the self' as well as the more complicated processes of legitimising and cultural elitist connotations of taste (see Newman and Levine 2012). Consequently, we argue for a more thorough examination of what Knox (2018) terms the 'push-pull' of factors involved in transatlantic fiction format adaptation. The adaptation process of *Coupling*, then, has to be considered against the backdrop of both the theoretical conceptualisations of television formats travelling within a transnational media space as well as the specificities of the cultural exchange and format trade between US and UK television markets. Here it is important to note that theories of American cultural imperialism, such as Herbert Schiller's influential study *Mass Communication and American Empire* (1969), have to be refined and expanded in order to fully comprehend the contemporary relationship of Anglo-American cultural exchange. Indeed, as many scholars have argued, the notion of cultural imperialism serves as first and foremost a 'starting point' when assessing the global effects of the dominant 'Hollywood entertainment industry' on local television markets and indigenous discourses (Sinclair et al. 1996). Just as prevailing notions of US American cultural ignorance have to be addressed, European conceptions of a homogeneous and uniform 'American culture', too, should be re-evaluated and re-assessed. As Christopher Hogg argues in his discussion of the adaptation of the British (drama) format *Cracker* to the US market:

> such a conception of an 'all-American' cultural uniformity masks the far more diverse consumer tastes and desires which do exist within the socio-cultural fabric of a richly multiplicitous America, increasingly catered for in a televisual sense by the myriad narrowcast cable, satellite, and digital providers now operating beyond the confines of mainstream US broadcasting. (2013, 121)

The One where *Coupling* Gets Lost in Transnational Media Space

Returning our attention to the *Coupling* format, it is important to note that *Coupling USA* was devised and produced at a decisive time of transition for NBC. From around 2002/2003, the broadcaster was beginning to recalibrate both its drama and comedy production, anticipating the fragmentation of audiences and the rise of more specialised and nuanced taste cultures enabled by digital and non-linear distribution platforms such as HBO, and later Netflix. More significantly, this was done before the transnational success of the US version of *Shameless* or *The Office—An American Workplace,* of which in particular the latter represented a new approach to the localisation and distribution of British formats on the US market (Schwind 2014, 2015). For what had become increasingly noticeable for the television industry but also audiences on both sides of the Atlantic was a growing awareness of the existence of the programmes about to be adapted and localised. In his analysis of the *Coupling* format Kevin Sanson argues:

the increasingly visible circulation of transatlantic television formats, as originals and remakes, muddles any natural link between culture and geography and, in the process, makes easy distinctions between the foreign and domestic difficult to maintain. [...] *Coupling*, then, not only expanded the cultural space where certain national differences were played out and performed but also facilitated an equally compelling transatlantic dialogue about creative ownership, appropriation, and a network's responsibility to its audiences. (2011, 40)

In other words, to a certain extent, the transparency of the adaptation process of the *Coupling* format had overshadowed the programme's implementation on the US market as an original and relevant new show to watch. Simultaneously, more detailed knowledge of television genres on a global scale had come to the fore, meaning that both successes and failures around the world would go less and less unnoticed. We have already addressed *Coupling*'s relationship with *Friends* earlier in this chapter, in terms of both shows' thematic emphasis on extracting humour from the core group's relationships as well as their extra-textual transatlantic correspondence and the difficulties of negotiating audience and industry expectations. After the immanent failure and surprisingly hasty cancellation of *Coupling USA*, Steven Moffat expressed his frustration and clearly identified a cause for the format's failure in the USA:

> I can answer it with three letters: N-B-C. Very, very good writing team. Very, very good cast. The network fucked it up because they intervened endlessly. [...] US Coupling was commissioned by NBC, promoted as the new Friends by NBC (we asked them not to), promoted as the sexiest show on TV by NBC (we begged them not to), promoted as 'the show you're all talking about' (no one had seen it, how could they be talking about it?), scheduled by NBC, noted to death by NBC, cancelled by NBC, and publicly blamed and disowned by NBC [...]. It's not Coupling that sucks, it's NBC. (in Paine 2003)

Moffat's lament contains several aspects that we would like to explore in more detail, having identified a number of possible reasons for the distinct failure of *Coupling USA*, both as a television format lacking the support of its broadcaster and a connection with audiences. First, as we have already argued, the prevalent awareness of the British source material on the US market did not help the implementation of *Coupling USA*. In fact, BBC America, which became more and more of a focal point for American networks in terms of where to find 'hip' foreign shows (Becker 2007), had already been broadcasting *Coupling UK* prior to its adaptation and was later counter-programming the show against its remake in order to profit from the buzz surrounding the format. Thus, 'instead of seeking inspiration from a successful idea in Britain, NBC identified a series with an established track record and trendy reputation in America' (Sanson 2011, 47). Here, the awareness of and proactive signposting to the British material subverted the process of establishing a distinct, self-sufficient identity for the adaptation. Furthermore, the deliberate linkage of the disproportionately successful *Friends* as a thematic and aesthetic sibling to *Coupling UK* did not facilitate a smooth transition to the US market and prevented a more successful reception of *Coupling USA*. As a result, both the British and the American *Coupling* were repositioned as syncretic forms rather than authentic domestic productions (Sanson 2011, 43). They were, to draw on Linda Hutcheon (2012, 9), not only second, but also secondary.

Despite exploring the ramifications of the 'push-pull factor' (Knox 2018) affecting this particular transnational adaptation process, it is important to scrutinise the format's problematic internal dynamics as well. Various commentators have pointed out that both the casting and visual style of *Coupling UK* had already been commented on as 'too good looking' and 'too colourful and bright' compared to most British comedies (Shannon 2003; Sanson 2011). Obvious stylistic and narrative similarities between *Friends* and *Coupling UK* played an important role in the reception of the latter in Britain and later on also on BBC America. As Sanson suggests:

> Both series are very much embedded within a highly romanticized urban milieu populated with other people who look very much like the cast itself: white, affluent, twenty-to-thirty-somethings. A central proscenium, either the sofa in the New York coffee shop or the sofa in the London wine bar, is a prominent staging device in a number of episodes. (2011, 44)

However, as our close analysis of *Friends'* performance and style in Chapters 3 and 4 reflexively confirms, neither *Coupling UK* nor *Coupling USA* achieve the same level of intimacy with their audiences. A comparison of the first episode of both versions will now reveal the different creative choices made in relation to casting and visual style, especially since they are both based on (almost) the same script by Steven Moffat.

The first British episode (titled 'Flushed') is characterised by a combination of exterior shots and street scenes with more 'theatrical' main sets such as the wine bar and the restaurant, whereas the American episode (titled 'The Right One') plays out almost entirely in interior sets, emulating *Friends'* more traditional set structure (one set per plotline). Furthermore, in 'The Right One', the opening scene—a cross-cutting between the men and the women on their way to the bar—is shortened and repositioned into a cold open, aligning itself with the standard structure of sitcoms on US television. Here, we can identify one of the main sites of structural and narrative adjustments between UK and US formats, based on the pragmatic necessities of linear scheduling. This observation echoes Christopher Hogg's (2013) analysis of the process of UK–US (drama) translation, in which he notes potential structural incompatibilities between British script and US production practices and broadcasting contexts (e.g. the need to accommodate a particular number of commercial breaks), which can have significant repercussions for the programme's narrative structure and tonality. Certainly, the themes of 'men as boys' and 'women as judgemental adults' are established in both versions, for instance by dedicating a lengthy dialogue exchange to the explanation of the concept of 'porn buddies', a friend who removes his recently deceased friend's pornography 'before his parents can find it' (Jeff, in both versions). However, the scene in the lady's room cubicle where Steve is making out with Jane is shot and blocked almost identically in *Coupling USA*—even replicating the same overhead camera angle to establish the narrow space—but less explicit in its portrayal of the rattling door suggesting intercourse between the two characters. Moreover, the episode's cumbersome and contrived finale in which Susan shows her right breast to the rest of the group to make a pseudo-empowered feminist statement is replicated in *Coupling USA*, however, without the line 'I want you all to know, I intend this breast satirically'. This hints at a different comedic sensibility of the British version, which offers a more ironic and sarcastic perspective on its characters and, as such, seems more in tune with the comedic dialogue of *Friends*. (Could 'satirical breasts' *be* any more Chandler?)

Although theatrical and farcical in its set-up, the British version conveys a more successful 'comic event' (Roof 2018) and believable comedic performance by its main ensemble cast, as well as establishing a closer 'cultural proximity' (Straubhaar 2007) through its use of exterior London street scenes and variations in interior scenes actually shot on location, for instance Susan and Jeff's office. In contrast, as Sanson points out in his analysis of *Coupling USA*: 'both fans and critics criticized the network for not localizing the format enough, leaving audiences with an inferior copy of a superior original. [...] This articulation expresses a desire for more attention to the socio-cultural specificities of space and place' (2011, 48). (Here, we suggest that the lack of engagement with issues of representation also contributed to the failure of *Coupling USA*. It seems that *Coupling USA* was neglecting the opportunities [and challenges] related to multi-ethnic casting, which by the early 2000s would have been more likely to come across as outdated and non-inclusive and sat more awkwardly within the US television landscape following the latter's strong bifurcation in the 1990s.) Portraying characters from a privileged social class and milieu, both versions suffer from a rather undefined and uncharismatic ensemble cast. Most of the characters are not given specific enough comedic types (see Chapter 2), and in particular in *Coupling USA*, the characters seem interchangeable. In the words of one critic: 'none of the characters have Chicago accents or Midwestern quirks, they are all homogenized Hollywood actors with plastic good looks' (Stanley 2003).

Here, it is important to note that the American version was not given the opportunity to develop a more functioning ensemble performance style and more defined and nuanced characters. This, incidentally, was a similar critique directed towards the American version of *The Office* during its first season (Schwind 2014), which was granted more room for development by NBC by producing a second season, during which *The Office—An American Workplace* eventually found its distinct comedic performance trajectory, a chance never given to *Coupling USA* which was cancelled after four aired episodes. However, in this comparative assessment of the format's approach to performance, it is important to note a long-standing bias towards British actors in the USA, informed by 'the prestige connotations of the British stage and British drama school training' (Knox and Cassidy 2019, 182). So, the visible co-existence of the British version, featuring British actors endowed with superior cultural capital and ranked higher within the taste hierarchies of certain US audiences, was another factor that impeded the successful implementation of *Coupling USA*.

Focusing on the actors in both versions of *Coupling*, we argue that, what they lack, in particular in comparison to the main cast of *Friends*, is not only 'star quality', but more significantly, what Dyer (1998) has called the 'ordinary/extraordinary' paradox of stardom, namely that a star is simultaneously constructed as 'typical' and 'special'. Both the main cast of *Coupling*, and also the supporting cast of *Joey*, seem to fall between these two categories, adding to an impression of superficiality and blandness in their appearance and performance. In this way, their presence works very differently to that of, for example, David Hyde Pierce's distinctive and award-winning performance of Niles Crane in *Frasier*, which helped to bestow additional textual identity to the *Cheers* spin-off, 'lessening the role of the [...] progenitor as the discursive point of reference' (Knox 2018, 18). The 'ordinary/extraordinary' binary is important, in particular in sitcom, because it is a decisive factor in facilitating intimacy—not only for an audience's para-social engagement with the programme's narrative and characters, but also for a distinctive ensemble-based performance style to emerge. In the case of *Friends*, the main cast was chosen because of their acting skills, attractiveness and potential star 'quality', but also because they were relatable as 'ordinary' characters, both to each other and to its audience. This, in turn, generates a distinctive comedic sensibility which distils humour not only from 'written' verbal jokes, but draws from character dynamic. Other multi-camera sitcoms which have achieved this effect of intimacy, but are beyond the scope of this study, are *Friends*' 1990s companions *Seinfeld* and *Frasier*, but also more recent shows like *The Big Bang Theory*. Here, the main characters are inextricably intertwined with their actors' star images, which have evolved during the initial broadcasting run of these shows and serve as a decisive factor in their continued appeal in the age of TVIV and beyond.

Concluding our discussion of *Coupling*, although *Friends* constitutes the most relevant point of reference, the temporal and thematic co-existence to the HBO single-camera show *Sex and the City* might have caused additional problems for the successful implementation of *Coupling USA*. At the time, and prior to the its final season in 2004, *Sex and the City* was at the height of its domestic and global success. With a clearly defined comedic sensibility and framework, the humour of *Sex and the City* is verbal and dialogue-based but, most significantly, addresses themes and issues related to sex and relationships through the use of taboo and risqué language, in a similar way to what *Coupling USA* was attempting. And even though the comedy of *Coupling USA* was actively trying to revoke traditional gender roles and draw humour from outdated stereotypes of male–female relationships, the more specific and, at the time, more progressive feminist sensibility of *Sex and the City* rendered *Coupling USA* as already more dated and anachronistic at the time of its initial launch on NBC.

In retrospect, despite its initial internal shortcomings, *Coupling USA* could have been a success or at least had a more prolonged life as a somewhat traditional multi-camera sitcom on NBC. It seems that it was the lack of support and interference with the creative process by the network that caused Moffat's frustration and brought a successful adaptation process to an abrupt halt. This is a striking echo of what his mother-in-law Beryl Vertue, whose production company Hartswood Films' roster includes not only *Coupling UK* but also *Sherlock*, experienced in the mid-1970s: Vertue produced *Beacon Hill*, a format adaptation of *Upstairs, Downstairs*, for CBS and had to contend with 'interference from which the programme could not recover' (Knox 2019, 17). As Vertue has reflected on the show's mid-season cancellation: 'I remember thinking at the time, how strange actually to be a failure with 23 million people' (in ibid.). In the television industry, *plus ça change*, it would seem. In his analysis of *Coupling USA*, Sanson concludes: 'while NBC might have been acting in accordance with what they perceived as their audience's desire for national specificity, the network failed to estimate the increasingly complicated ways viewers and critics can position themselves in an expanded audio-visual space' (2011, 51). That is a valid point to make; however, it is important to note that despite these misjudgements, we can assume that it was not the intention of NBC to facilitate a failure. Rather, it seems that, at the time of the *Coupling* adaptation, sufficient knowledge and understanding, more specifically a set of knowledge components (Moran 1998) and standardised practices informing the adaptation process, were either not available to or not utilised by the creative and executive personnel involved. However, the dynamics of this specific 'push-pull' process are also influenced by a certain level of 'myth-making' with regards to cultural hierarchies between the USA and the UK as well as assumed higher levels of sophistication and quality attached to the discourses of British comedy and humour. (For example, leading figures of British comedy production, such as renowned BBC producer Jon Plowman, have continually nurtured a bias and view of more nuanced and sophisticated British comedy compared to its US counterpart [Walters 2005].) As such, as Sanson argues, 'despite the network's earlier claims to the contrary, there was something quintessentially British about the series that these commentators were reclaiming as their own against the dislocating processes of globalization' (2011, 48).

With *Coupling*, then, representing an attempt to transfer the *Friends* concept within a similar and recognisable cultural space, we will now expand our attention beyond the proximity of Anglo-American format exchange and address different approaches from other linguistic and cultural contexts to translate, copy or develop aspects of the series.

The One with *Friends* Across the Globe: Narrative Transparency and Reception

Since its formation, the products of the US entertainment industry have dominated the global media arena and represent an aesthetic discursive hegemony which local cultural industries are continually forced to address. Television in particular, due to its decisive role as a domestic mass medium with a far reach into the private sphere of its viewers, has played an important role in representing and promoting US lifestyles and values in many parts of the world. Thus, following the cultural critique of the Frankfurt School, scholars have critiqued the effects of the capitalist excess in American mainstream entertainment. As Ketan Chitnis et al. argue, 'past studies suggest that when consumed over a period of time, American media products may influence the way an audience member in a foreign country may feel, dress and act' (2006, 132). Given its narrative, cultural and aesthetic focus on family and/or workplace settings, the sitcom genre plays a vital role in creating discourses of representation that foreign audiences constantly encounter and negotiate in relation to their own experiences of how US shows and their protagonists look like, manage conflicts, consume food and conduct relationships. However, as we have established in our conceptualisation of the dynamics of global television format adaptation and, more specifically, in our discussion of the *Coupling* case, foreign audiences respond in heterogeneous and nuanced ways to assumed Hollywood hegemony and US cultural imperialism. As we will illuminate now, their reception and enjoyment of US entertainment is characterised by a process of appropriation in which these programmes may be simultaneously embraced and celebrated as well as critically assessed and contextualised. Furthermore, it is important to note the extent to which US programmes have become increasingly diversified because of the fragmentation of production and distribution within the US market. In turn, these programmes, across forms and genres, enter the global television circuit, in particular through streaming platforms, where they have an impact on traditional and hegemonic societies and values. For instance, exploring the Indian television market, Ruchi Kher Jaggi (2018) argues that, on the Indian television market, TVI and TVIV exist simultaneously, resulting in a complex framework for issues of representation.

Connecting the Indian cultural context to our study, *Friends* has been part of Indian television since its initial inception and continues to rate among the most popular programmes in English. A more detailed discussion of the reception of *Friends* in India is beyond the scope of this book; however, Chitnis et al. (2006) have studied (dis)similar readings in Indian and US audiences' interpretations of *Friends*, providing insights into the diverse responses global audiences can have towards the show. Interestingly, the authors apply Scott Robert Olson's (1999) narrative transparency theory, which speaks to how audiences of different cultures may project their own cultural references onto a foreign text in order to facilitate a successful relocation process. As they argue:

> a cross-cultural understanding of the text may take place because the audience interprets a foreign text using their own cultural beliefs and values. Transparency theory claims that to understand the popularity of global media, one has to understand both the media text and the audience members, local and foreign, who consume them. (Chitnis et al. 2006, 133)

In other words, viewers interpret the programme differently based on their own cultural context and social situation, and Chitnis et al. explore several elements of transparency, focusing on textual attributes that allow for a transparent reading and cultural relocation of the *Friends* episode being discussed (2.18 'The One where Doctor Ramoray Dies').

Particularly noteworthy is the ways in which the Indian respondents actively negotiate cultural proximity to the narrative or the characters. This becomes especially evident in their comments on the scene in which Monica and Rachel argue over who gets to use the last condom, which contrast with the US viewers' appreciation of the safe sex message the episode's narrative promotes. Here, it is interesting to speculate on the culturally specific interpretation of the comedic intent of the sequence. We suggest that while the American audiences might find humour not in the fact that Monica and Rachel fight over the last condom, but, rather, in the exaggerated ways they are negotiating and trying to work out who gets the contraceptive, Indian audiences might laugh at the 'absurdity' of the situation and the passivity of the male characters. This interpretation is supported by the study's findings, in which many of the Indian respondents found discussions related to protection and consensual sex between members of the opposite sex unreal and improbable.

Working from a similar hypothesis while exploring another cultural context, Katherine Dillion (2009) studies the reception of *Friends* in Egypt, establishing the series' relocation as particularly problematic given the troubled political and socio-cultural relationship between the

USA and the Middle East, particularly post-9/11. Drawing from interviews with mostly female viewers, Dillion claims that despite an increase in anti-US sentiment throughout the country, the popularity of *Friends* (and other American sitcoms) helped to present a counter-image and had the 'potential of giving a "different face" to Americans' (2009, 57). The study, though in parts anecdotal and simplistic in its interpretation of transnational comedic discourses, raises some valid points with regards to *Friends*' global (and indeed universal) appeal: 'people in developing nations could see the faces of six Americans who were not aggressive or power hungry, but rather who often shared some of the same frustrations as Egyptians and indeed people everywhere: trouble with jobs, money, and relationships' (ibid.). This links back to our analysis of *Friends*' inclusive comedic sensibility in Chapter 2, which not only invites in global audiences by focusing on a humour based on character specificities but also presents a transparent and accessible cultural context where the protagonists fail in naming all 50 American states (7.8) or comment on the US imperialistic undertones of a G.I. Joe toy solider (3.4).

Dillion also applies Olson's (1999) narrative transparency theory, offering a detailed interpretation of four elements of Olson's theory which allow *Friends* to become 'a globally transparent text' (2009, 81); namely inclusion, virtuality, negentropy and circularity. With regards to inclusion, Dillion concludes that *Friends* invites its Egyptian viewers to be part of the group. Not only through direct identification with the core group, but also through the 'womblike' sofa, which 'becomes a comforting icon that signals the viewer that no matter what else happens in the next half hour, these six friends will likely meet back on the same sofa to regroup from any conflict that has come up in the course of the show' (ibid., 82). This corresponds with our analysis of the series' set design (Chapter 4) and supports our reservation about Phil Chidester's (2008) argument concerning *Friends*' closed circle of whiteness as discussed in Chapter 5. The attribute of virtuality expands the notion of intimacy by a focus on the virtual family the main characters constitute and the family values they propagate: 'this familial element has particular appeal in Egypt and the rest of the Middle East since Muslim societies place special emphasis on the importance of family' (Dillion 2009,

83). The term 'negentropy' describes the sense of order and control an audience can experience by watching a show defined by its clear and predictable generic structure such as that of a sitcom. Dillion shows to what extent negentropy can help to overcome cultural differences via her focus group's discussion of the episode in which Phoebe does not approve of her young brother Frank wanting to marry his older teacher (3.18). Even though age-discrepant marriage is considered problematic in Egypt, the respondents can accept the episode's conclusion, 'because it still maintained a sense of order, even if that order was different from what they wanted' (ibid., 84). Finally, 'circularity' refers to the narrative and aesthetic order *Friends* conveys through its narrative and stylistic choices, whereby 'the sofa again becomes the material embodiment of the principal [sic] of circularity' (ibid.), and we would add that recurring characters (e.g. Richard or Janice) or themes (e.g. a focus on food and eating, or Thanksgiving) establish circularity as well.

Obviously, these divergent readings point to the challenges of the global distribution of culturally specific content and particularly the ways in which humour and comedy are interpreted in different parts of the world. Furthermore, this dynamic complicates the notions of 'universality' and 'failure' which we have explored earlier in this chapter: for what is a 'global success' when different cultural readings render a programme such as *Friends* a palimpsest of contradictory meanings? Is this particular quality of the show and its transparency most usefully understood as an achievement or a shortcoming? And to what extent can or should creators and producers be aware of this multiplicity of meaning? More extensive comparative case studies will hopefully contribute to a more nuanced understanding of these dynamics, with more space given to exploring and mapping out more specific cultural contexts and comparisons. Despite being in parts over-simplistic, in particular by ignoring the narrative and aesthetic specificities of the episodes discussed, studies such as Dillion's and Chitnis et al.'s show to what extent a 'global media product such as *Friends* can be become a culturally sharable and transparent text' (Chitnis et al. 2006, 143) and how different cultural contexts negotiate the globally established canon and vocabulary of American sitcoms.

Chitnis et al.'s analysis was focused on Indian viewers who watched *Friends* during its original Indian broadcast run, for which it was shown without subtitles in a former British colony in which English is a subsidiary official language. However, *Friends* has been shown with Hindi and Punjabi subtitles since, and it was subtitled in Egypt, as Dillion briefly acknowledges. This suggests to us that there is scope for studies of the global reception of programmes to pay more attention to audio-visual translation, and how this may impact on textual meaning and, indeed, narrative transparency. (For example, Inger-Lise Kalviknes Bores sees the laugh track's potential to facilitate 'diverging viewpoints' [Bore 2011, 24], but in the context of audio-visual translation, it may acquire an inclusive and potentially educative function: viewers reliant on the aid of subtitles receive audible cues concerning *Friends*' humour, which can help their process of engaging with the programme.) This is what we will undertake now by exploring a rare case of failure when it comes to *Friends*, namely its dubbed German version.

The One where They Get Lost in Translation: The German Dubbing of *Friends*

Anglophone creative industries and scholarship are characterised by a general lack of awareness about the practices and discourses of dubbing. Only more recently have specific studies exploring relevant issues begun to emerge. For instance, Christina Adamou and Simone Knox usefully argue that:

> Far from being defined by necessity, practicality and constraint, dubbing and subtitling must be understood as transformative practices. Not only do they significantly contribute to determining the meaning of the target text, but they problematise notions of a fixed, stable *core* of textual identity: the idea that, when scheduling, promotion et cetera, are taken out of the equation, there is still somehow the same core of the text there [...] which often underlies thinking about television and television drama. (2011, 17; emphasis in original)

These transformative practices represent historically established and commercially significant strands of the local television industries and screen cultures in various countries around the world, particularly many of the bigger European nations. Here, dubbing emerged as a vital industry practice after World War II and became part of the socio-cultural and political nationalisation of film distribution and television broadcasting. The practice created new job roles such as the dubbing (or voice) actor, the dubbing director and the dubbing script writer. Here, it is useful to clarify that, as our analysis will be focused on German fiction dubbing, our discussion of dubbing will effectively be referring to 'full-cast dubbing', meaning the replacement of the source actors' voices with performances by actors in the target language. It is much more time-consuming and expensive than 'voice-over dubbing'—in which one or two main voices speak and/or read out the translated dialogue, with the original soundtrack still audible on lower volume in the background—and subtitling.

Even though subtitling is a common practice in anglophone countries, dubbing is still considered a peculiar oddity and not sufficiently conceptualised when US or British formats start their journeys around the world. This is a significant oversight in the implementation and adaptation processes of fiction formats designed for the international market, as the practices of audio-visual translation have a major effect on how programmes are received around the world, inflecting both the narrative content and performance. As we are going to show, the audio-visual translation of cultural and linguistic aspects in relation to comedy programmes may generate particular challenges for both the creative personnel behind the dubbing process and the interpretation of the humour in the source text by its target audiences.

Before we scrutinise the problematic dubbing of *Friends* in Germany, it is worth briefly illuminating the relevant broadcasting context. After entering the phase of TVII, with the introduction of commercial television in Germany from the mid-1980s onwards, private channels such as Sat1, RTL and ProSieben often structured their content based on American programming. Thus, a range of genres were increasingly imported and dubbed, and sitcoms such as *Roseanne*, *Who's the Boss?*, *The Golden Girls*, *Married … with Children* and *The Simpsons* were successfully introduced to German audiences. *Married … with Children* in particular, launched in 1992 and despite being randomly moved about in the German television schedule, gathered impressive ratings (Holzer 1999, 94) and helped to establish the multi-camera aesthetics and punchline-driven narrative structures of American sitcoms. However, some globally highly successful shows never managed to achieve the rating successes that German broadcasters expected of them, especially *Seinfeld*, *Frasier* and *Friends* (ibid., 96).

The implementation of the dubbed version of *Friends* in Germany was turbulent. Its initial launch date was 17 August 1996 on commercial channel Sat1, which, at the time, was building a distinct comedy profile, mostly with original sketch shows and the late-night show *Die Harald Schmidt Show*, which was a successful format adaptation of the *Late Show with David Letterman*. Given the success of *Friends* in the US market (by then in its third season) and increasingly in other countries as well, Sat1 acquired the German distribution rights. Incomprehensibly, Sat1 not only frequently changed the scheduling slots for *Friends* but, more significantly, it also did not broadcast most of the episodes in chronological order, making it hard to find the show, let alone follow the overarching storylines. It was not before 2000, when another commercial channel, Pro7, started broadcasting the show in a regular time slot, that the show gained a steady audience and following and, consequentially, was brought to a successful run, with regular re-runs ever since. Furthermore, sales of various editions of the DVD box sets were particularly successful, most certainly because they offered the original audio-track of the show as well. Finally, in November 2016 *Friends* became available on Netflix Germany, where viewers may choose to watch the show in the German dub or in the untranslated English-language version.

From the initial launch of *Friends*, the German dubbing was criticised for the poor quality of its translation resulting in a strikingly high loss of comical references (Holzer 1999, 16). At first glance, one of the reasons for this particular failure is related to the complicated process of dubbing itself, which in the case of translating humour and comedy is particularly challenging since the translators are faced with:

> making the translated joke as funny as possible, on the one hand, and, on the other, finding solutions that will not put the viewer off because there

is an excessive lack of synchronisation; or because the plot, the structure and the coherence of the text are weakened for the sake of certain witty one-liners. (Zabalbeascoa 1997, 332)

As such, we argue that different sitcoms may present different types and degrees of challenges to dubbing: obviously, shows based on mostly visual slapstick humour are easier to translate, but a dialogue-driven sitcom such as *Friends* poses a much greater challenge to the process of dubbing, which we would briefly like to outline in more detail, before examining a few examples.

First, based on the source dialogue script, a translator provides a rough translation of all the dialogue, before it is passed on to the dubbing writer, who then has to produce a script version, which has to take account of such technical elements as 'lip-synchronisation' (Herbst 1994)—that is, a match between the visible lip movements and the audible dialogue—as well as 'synchronisation of gestures' (Kurz 2006). It also has to translate the actual content of the dialogue on a linguistic and semantic level to an extent that 'the audience reacts in the same way the audience of the original version would have reacted, even if one has to add and adjust to achieve this goal' (ibid., 7; our translation). As far as genre is concerned, Matthias Müntefering, (then) head of the dubbing department of Deutsche Synchron, summed it up as follows: 'Action is cheap. Humor is expensive. Culture is impossibly expensive' (2002, 15). As this reflects, the German dubbing industry is aware of the particular linguistic and cultural challenges of translating humour. We argue that the awareness of the specific challenges of translating humour and comedy across linguistic and cultural contexts is essential for the textual analysis of translocated formats in general and the problems of the German dubbing of *Friends* in particular.

In broader terms, the process of dubbing is closely linked to what Jan Pedersen (2007) has termed intra-linguistic and extra-linguistic culture-bound references. Whereas intra-linguistic references are mostly related to idioms, puns and proverbs, extra-linguistic culture-bound references consist of historical, geographical or cultural references. As a palimpsest of visual images and sonic elements, which consist of not only spoken dialogue containing intra- and extra-linguistic references, but also sound effects and music, dubbing is a complicated process that needs to negotiate several challenges simultaneously. What is eventually required are what Lourdes Lorenzo has called synchronisms, namely agreements and harmonies, between the source text and the target text, such as 'content synchronism (agreement between the translated version of the text and the original story line)' (2003, 271) and 'character synchronism (harmony between the voice of the dubbing artist and the appearance and gesture of the actor or actress)' (ibid.).

It is our argument that the German dubbing of *Friends* is productively understood in terms of failure because a number of choices and decisions during the dubbing process impeded synchronisms, to the extent that it is widely known within the social culture of the German dubbing industry that the dubbing company Arena Synchron to this day feels embarrassed that they 'messed up' *Friends*. As we will now explore, the dubbing team struggled to recognise the show's textual sensibility, including and especially its strategy of intimacy, in ways that concern humour and the translation of jokes—which Martin Thauer (2008) and Tanja Vierrether (2017) have already paid some attention to, in line with much existing scholarship's focus on the correctness of audio-visual translation—but also casting and performance (which deserve much more scholarly consideration when it comes to dubbing).

For example, in episode 1.21, Chandler and Joey are trying to come up with a pseudonym for Joey's acting persona, with Chandler proposing: 'Joe … Joe … Joe … Stalin?' In the German version, the dialogue is changed to: 'Joe … Joe … Joe … Einstein?' It seems plausible that the dubbing translator did not find it appropriate to use the name of a dictator associated with World War II crimes for a German audience, opting for a more 'neutral' or politically correct approach by replacing 'Stalin' with 'Einstein'. As such, the allusion to Stalin's first name Joseph—the same as the character Joey's—is lost, as is an implicit duality of *Friends*' comedic sensibility. For, what gets lost in the German dub is Chandler's mockery of Joey who is—as Chandler knows—not intellectually capable of recognising the name of an infamous dictator and Chandler's pleasure in the idea that Joey goes to auditions introducing himself as 'Joe Stalin'. The alteration of the German dialogue takes away the sarcastic and at times viciously playful edge of Chandler's comedic persona and, more significantly, tames the comedic interplay of the Chandler–Joey couple dynamic, a vital component of the show's comedic sensibility.

More examples revealing such noticeable alterations to the source dialogue can be found in Thauer's (2008) and Vierrether's (2017) analyses of the challenges of translating *Friends* into German. For instance, Vierrether demonstrates how in episode 4.13, the joke's original intent is mismanaged when Chandler confronts Joey about his absurd theory that a lack of onstage chemistry is proof of actors having an actual sexual relationship in real life (which Chandler suspects his actor-girlfriend Kathy [Paget Brewster] to have). Joey responds in the source dialogue as follows:

> *Joey*: Wo-ho! That was just a theory. There's a lot of theories that didn't pan out. Lone gunman, communism, geometry.

The German dubbing translates this to:

> *Joey*: Okay, halt, halt, halt, Chandler. Das war nur eine Theorie. Und viele Theorien haben mit der Praxis nichts zu tun. Die Wettervorhersage stimmt nie. Oder ich glaub ich krieg sie rum und dann klappt's doch nicht. Und so weiter.

This back-translates as:

> *Joey*: Okay, stop, stop, stop, Chandler. That was just a theory. And lots of theories have nothing to do with practice. The weather forecast is never right. Or I believe I'll get her and then it doesn't work out. And so on.

Vierrether explains that the 'lone gunman theory' stemming from the assassination of John F. Kennedy was likely dropped because this reference is 'assumably not that well-known among the German audience' (2017, 73). More significantly, she argues that:

> While the second part aims at Joey's reputation of trying to get a different woman almost every day, it does not have the same comic effect as him questioning something as basic as geometry. Additionally, him

questioning his success with women is very unlikely, since he is known for being very successful in that area and never has any problems finding something else to stay over for the night. The part with the weather forecast works very well lip-sync wise and since it ends on 'gunman' and the German words for 'communism' and 'geometry' ('Kommunismus' and 'Geometrie') sound very similar and match the lip movements, it would have been better to directly translate these two[.] (ibid., 73–74)

Through such deliberate misinterpretations, some of the jokes in the German version of *Friends* are effectively turned into 'anti-jokes', sometimes adding a level of absurdist humour to the show, but mostly flattening the comedic moments and altering the show's sense of humour. Whilst Vierrether's conclusion is focused on the degree of 'humour loss' (ibid., 79) within this sequence, we argue that, more significantly still, the translation choices such as those under scrutiny here, through their misrepresentation of characterisation, undermine the comedic sensibility of the show, and especially the textured humour landscape that we have explored in Chapter 2. So, *Friends* is subject to criticism for unnecessary dialogue adjustments, often ruining the original joke setups and punchlines. To be clear, despite the immanent linguistic and semantic challenges of the inter-cultural translation process, German dubbing is generally known for its high standards and strong levels of achievement, and deliberate changes to translating dialogue in relation to humour can work successfully: for example, the 1970s show *The Persuaders!*, starring Tony Curtis and Roger Moore, was significantly altered in its German dubbing, drawing on partially improvised dialogue marked by a self-conscious meta-quality, and as a result, *Die 2* became a cult hit with German audiences. However, such significant pronounced changes are the exception.

Moreover, *Friends* is also subject to criticism for its problematic voice casting (Holzer 1999) and approach to performance, as the German voices chosen for the main cast were perceived as incongruous for both the American actors and the characters. Usually, German dubbing actors are cast because their voices and performance styles resonate with the source actors. There are notable successes here, such as the popularity of the German dubbing actors for *The Golden Girls*, who were cast in character for German radio commercials for a supermarket chain in the 1990s. Becoming very well-known for her vocal performance as Carrie Bradshaw in *Sex and the City*, Irina von Bentheim 'appeared on German chat shows talking about the HBO series, current attitudes towards sex and relationships, and has even given on-stage *Sex and the City* readings' (Adamou and Knox 2011, 13). Franziska Pigulla, who dubbed Gillian Anderson in *The X-Files* with a vocal performance marked by a darker pitch and restrained cadence, has been recognised as contributing significantly to the success of the show in Germany. However, for the German version of *Friends*, the voice casting of all main characters, with the exception of Lisa Kudrow as Phoebe, strike us as misjudged and off-key.

To contextualise, the performances of the German-voice cast bear a strong influence by a normative and traditionalist approach to comedy television entertainment—traditionally, German television production has been characterised by a schism of *E- und U-Unterhaltung* (serious and non-serious entertainment)—with a focus on farcical and exaggerated comedic acting. This acting is very much influenced by sketch and variety show programmes which were much more common on German television, and much less influenced by the thematic and stylistic variety of British or American situation comedies. The German dubbing actors perform in a heightened performative style, with both men and women employing high pitched voices and very little naturalistic nuance in their acting. In particular, Gerald Schaale, the German voice of Ross, performs at such a high register that this counteracts the vocal performance by David Schwimmer, who often modulates his voice for comic effect, and so German Ross sounds undiversified and flat. (A direct comparison of the scene in episode 9.19 in which Ross, high on maple syrup candy, refuses to check out of a hotel room before he has pocketed all 'complementary' items, strikingly illustrates this.) As a consequence, the repetitive cadence and intonation of the German voice actors counteract the nuanced comedic performances and the character-based realism that the US cast works hard to achieve. Furthermore, the German actors interpret *Friends*' core group in terms of only a few of their basic character tropes—for example, Ross as goofy, Rachel as shrill, Monica as harsh and domineering—and approach their vocal performances based on this singularity. (Here, it is worth noting that at the time of the programme's launch in Germany in 1996, two full seasons were available, and usually the German dubbing industry has to make strategic casting decisions based on only a few available episodes.) We do not seek to single out the work of the dubbing performers here, as these problems point to issues in terms of the approach to directing by Janina Richter—but the result is that the German version of *Friends* is transformed into a different type of comedic performance than originally intended and executed.

This immanent lack of performance marked by nuance, realism and intimacy as well as a general sonic flatness are influenced by some technical challenges present in the process of dubbing. Films or television episodes are dubbed by dividing them into smaller units (the industry term is 'take'). These takes are then recorded with an average length of eight seconds, depending on the sentence length. The dubbing actor does not usually get to re-enact the performance arc of an entire scene (or indeed, shot). Usually, both dubbing actors and directors are aware of this challenge and know how to facilitate these arcs; but in the German dub of *Friends*, recreating these organic 'journeys' through scenes is often absent. Furthermore, the overall sound mix of the German episodes seems more frontal and thicker, alienatingly amplifying foley sounds, such as footsteps and movements, and the non-diegetic laughter, which was added in post-production. As a result, the sonic space of the German *Friends* seems empty and flat.

So, despite the usually high standards and performance achievements of German dubbing, the German dubbing of *Friends* was problematic, though it has to be said that both the dialogue translation and to a certain extent also the vocal performances improved over the course of the show's run. Thus, small adjustments were made, but to completely change course would have led to a noticeable break in the German version's verbal humour and acoustic style. *Friends* in Germany eventually became a reasonably successful sitcom despite its initial failures of dubbing. Building on our conceptualisation of failure in this context, we suggest that the comedic sensibility of *Friends*, as it was initially imagined by the show's co-creators and further developed by its actors, was significantly altered. The German *Friends* are superficially funny, not quietly smart, rather, they seem babblingly goofy.

Our discussion of the German version of *Friends* illustrates to what extent audio-visual translations need a particular analytical tool kit, which brings together considerations of specific intra- and extra-linguistic culture-bound references, as well as analysis of casting and performance. In our final exploration of the global impact and reception of *Friends*, we will now turn our attention to the 'unofficial' remakes of the format, or rather, situation comedies that tried to emulate particular aspects of *Friends*' aesthetics and storytelling, with varying degrees of success.

The One with the Unofficial International Adaptations: Iran and China

After *Friends*' initial success and the rapport and connection the series started to build with audiences worldwide throughout the second half of the 1990s and beyond, various attempts at unofficially remaking, or recreating, the show were carried out in a variety of different cultural and linguistic contexts. As we have shown, whereas the *Coupling* format tried to both appropriate the *Friends* formula and relocate the British distillate to the US market, other *Friends* replicas across the globe were picking up on central aspects of the show. It is beyond the scope of this book to discuss each of these unofficial adaptations in more detail, but we will investigate two of them to unpick how they can reflexively illuminate the show's distinct universal appeal.

Interestingly, *Friends*, though never officially broadcast, is a highly popular programme in Iran, consumed first and foremost through illegal downloads. Thus, it represents a relevant reference show for domestic production, and *Eshgh Ta'til Nist* (which roughly translates as 'love goes on') in terms of its set design closely draws on Monica's apartment via the purple wall colour, the empty yellow picture frame, the layout of the furniture, as well as some of the textual density marking cupboards, shelves and tables. In these scenes set in this space, the lighting is also warmer compared to the rest of the show, so clearly, the programme here works towards a strategy of intimacy concerning set design in very similar terms to what we have discussed in Chapter 4. However, some scenes of the show, which was directed by Bijan Birang, are shot from an unusual top-down angle. By exposing the artificiality and theatricality of the sitcom sets, this actively works against establishing intimacy with the programme's viewers. This and a number of other creative choices, which further include the use of non-diegetic laughter—highly unusual in an Iranian context—indicate a desire for a Brechtian *Verfremdungseffekt* facilitating a spectatorial engagement very different to what *Friends* offers.

Furthermore, the episodes reviewed end on a more reflective or melancholic note, with downbeat music playing over a voice-over narrator, or a character talking directly to camera. Here, the programme offers (often lengthy) conclusions enriched with moral and ethical advice for its viewers, which clearly stand in contrast to the shorter comedic dialogue of the rest of the episode, and which, because of their lecturing nature, may also alienate Iranian viewers. And, indeed, it seems, it did: with initially 26 episodes planned and commissioned, the show was cancelled after the broadcast of only five episodes in 2015. We suggest that *Eshgh Ta'til Nist*'s aesthetic and narrative hybridity is motivated by a necessity to negotiate and reconcile a lack of familiarity with the sitcom genre in Iran with a desire to create contemporary and relevant television programming featuring a variety of highly popular star actors.

Both aesthetic and narrative hybridity also characterises the Chinese sitcom *iPartment*—the 'i' in the English title is a reference to *ài* (爱), the Mandarin term for love—which was first shown by Jiangxi TV in mainland China in 2009, pre-dating President Xi Jinping's 'Chinese Dream' discourse. The programme was accused of 'stealing jokes' from American sitcoms, in particular *Friends*. The sitcom tells the stories of seven young main characters in their twenties who live together as roommates or neighbours in an urban apartment block, with a focus on their love lives, work and family relations. Stylistically, *iPartment* is clearly a hybrid sitcom (Schwind 2015) in the sense that it combines single-camera aesthetics shot on locations with a more traditional multi-camera style and set design for the interior scenes in the various apartments. The show's comedic sensibility is defined by character-based verbal humour, but features occasional physical humour and slapstick set pieces as well. Thematically, like most of the unofficial international *Friends* replicas, the programme focuses on the emotional and professional lives of its protagonists; however, what is noteworthy in *iPartment* is the distinct focus on the prospects and challenges of urban housing, as well as a dichotomy of the urban and the rural, which is already established in the first episode.

The fictional world is established by the chance meeting of two of the series' main protagonists, Lin Wanyo (played by Zhao Ji) and Lu Zhanbo (played by Jin Shijia), on a bus at Shanghai's Pudong Airport, which is supposed to take them to the city. Lu Zhanbo's character, a bachelor with a degree in computer science returning from Los Angeles, is deliberately rendered as an outsider, both Chinese but also a foreigner, for example by the detail of not knowing how to pay for the bus. Eventually, they end up in 'the middle of nowhere', on a long, stretched out countryside road. Abandoned by the bus driver, they try to hitch-hike back to the city, with the help of a friendly farmer and his tractor. Despite playing on the classical comedic 'fish out of water' trope, in particular through Lin Wanyo's out-of-place remarks, naïve personality and kooky behaviour, most of the humour in these sequences is distilled from the incompatibility of the rural farmer with the city folk. What is particularly noteworthy is how authority figures, here represented by two traffic policemen, are portrayed and handled comedically by the show. After they stop the couple on the tractor (which by then was towed by a Mercedes car with a drunk and speeding driver), they are reprimanded and morally lectured by one of the policemen: 'The new era? You guys are young. Instead of sitting in the car for your wedding, you choose to sit on a tractor. Don't you care about your lives!' This dialogue does not trigger non-diegetic laughter, which in an interesting aesthetic choice is also present in the exterior single-camera sequences throughout the show, and clearly signals that the moralising lesson of the policeman was not intended to be funny. Given China's problematic and non-democratic socio-political context, this strikes us as an interesting appropriation of comedic tonality, where representatives of state authority are not meant to be joked with, representing (and defending) a firm moral framework that shapes each citizen's character and should not be subverted or even playfully addressed. (This stands in contrast to the treatment of the priest character at a later point in the pilot episode, who is clearly and more ruthlessly ridiculed through classical comedic tropes, which given the largely secularised socio-cultural context of contemporary China seems a far less controversial narrative choice.)

Returning to the theme of urbanity, the basic premise of *iPartment* addresses the distinct socio-cultural reality of its young target audience, namely the challenges of inner-city housing in the country with the highest population on earth. The increasing fluctuation of young people to the bigger cities has left more and more rural villages in mainland China abandoned with some of them being 'at the brink of extinction' (Phillips 2013). The portrayal of *iPartment*'s main characters addresses this interesting duality by simultaneously propagating and satirising their desire to pursue urban lifestyles instead of a more rural and traditionalist existence in the countryside. To own a high-class apartment in Shanghai, where the series is set, is an expensive luxury commodity which is addressed by the pilot episode's narrative, and the fact that unrelated and unknown characters have to share a space as roommates. *iPartment*'s apartment block is rendered both as a practical solution for its tenants and as a space where possible romances might unfold. The couple that used to live there and who is getting married in a nearby park in an extended scene that assembles all the main characters, declares in their speech: 'Our wish is that from this day on, the apartment will be named "Love Apartment"'.

Here, the programme posits the idea of the apartment as a haven for civic security and heteronormative marital bliss, a claim which is never actively and sincerely challenged by any of the series' main characters. Moreover, it is striking to what extent *iPartment* foregrounds a different connotation of the concept of romantic love, namely by linking it to the shared experience of urban spaces and materiality, in particular, in contrast to *Friends* where romantic (and platonic) relationships are presented as the only way to personal fulfilment and happiness. As such, it seems to us that the concept of *iPartment* was very much inspired by the premise of 'friends sharing a common space'; however, the programme appropriated this set-up with added layers of meaning for its Chinese target audience. A similar approach is visible in other formats emerging from the pan-Asian sphere in recent years, for instance the highly popular programme *Terrace House* (2012–present), a Japanese reality show in which a group of strangers share an exclusive luxury property and are observed as they are dating and making a living.

The main characters in *iPartment* represent a variety of figures of a distinctively urban socio-cultural landscape in China, but are nevertheless clearly inspired by the character constellation of *Friends*, most prominently in the characters of Hu Yifei (played by Lou Yixiao), a rather obsessive PhD graduate, Lu Zhanbo, a nerdy network engineer who is shy and awkward around girls, and Lin Wanyo, a rich billionaire's daughter who later starts working in fashion. The will-they-won't-they storyline noted in the introduction to this chapter unsurprisingly features Lu and Lin, and the latter is furthermore also clearly modelled on Lisa Kudrow's portrayal of Phoebe with her quirky, at times absurdist behaviour and humour. As we have noted earlier, basing a show's characters on the *Friends* ensemble is an understandable, yet problematic approach in the challenging contexts of transnational format adaptation. In an increasingly globalised television arena, where local programmes can easily become subject to global scrutiny, it comes as no surprise, then, that *iPartment*—despite being successful with audiences (it won the China TV Drama Award for Most Popular Television Series in 2013)—was met with strong criticism. Commentators have focused on the obvious parallels to *Friends* as well as other shows: 'The characters have some similarities—there's a Ross type, who lectures at a university … though he could also be a Ted Mosby, as critics say entire scenes have been lifted from not only *Friends*, but *How I Met Your Mother*' (Carlson 2012). Moreover, viewers have identified active attempts at plagiarism, according to this newspaper article:

> The series, produced by the Shanghai Film Group, was launched in 2009 and is now broadcast across China on satellite channels. But Chinese television addicts became increasingly suspicious about similarities between the programme and a number of American sitcoms. Incensed, they began posting angry online messages and screenshots comparing what they claimed were virtually identical scenes from shows including How I Met Your Mother, Friends and The Big Bang Theory. (Phillips 2012)

It seems likely that increasing criticism of the show eventually forced the producers to take a stance, in particular after the legal consequences of alleged plagiarism were brought into the debate by industry experts and trade journalists. As Lu Chen wrote in *The Global Times*:

> 'According to Chinese copyright law, translating an original work requires that one first get permission from the author. Otherwise, it may result in copyright infringement,' said Ren Haiyong, a Shanghai based lawyer specialized in intellectual property law. On Saturday, the show's producers sent an apology letter to a famous online joke and screenplay writer for using his jokes without permission. In the apology, the producers acknowledged that the show contained jokes from 'various sources.' They offered to pay 10,000 yuan ($1,569) in compensation for every 1,000 Chinese characters of material. One of the actors on iPartment, Chen He, defended the show Friday in a report in the Shanghai Evening Post, saying the episodes were an homage to the American TV series. (Chen 2012)

The detailed chronicling of this specific case is beyond the scope of this book; however, it is interesting to explore the line of argument of the creative personnel involved in the production of *iPartment*. It seems that basing the main characters on the *Friends* ensemble or drawing on its set design are, or can be, considered as paying homage, but clearly, copying the same jokes and comedic situations is not and cannot. However, as Michael Keane notes, a lack of engagement with copyright and intellectual property 'surrounds format "borrowing" in many parts of Asia' (2004, 10), which is linked to the fact that 'ideological constraints on fictional forms and expression coupled with changing demands from a domestic market being transformed by commercialization have prompted Chinese producers to look elsewhere for materials' (Huang 2008, 106). This suggests that *iPartment*'s problematic discourse is the result of a more structural dynamic rooted in a specific production culture. Addressing a similar case, for instance, Ya-chin Huang (2008) pays attention to how 'pink drama' *Falling in Love* borrows closely from *Sex and the City*.

However, as Jean K. Chalaby has pointed out, 'any scripted adaptation must go beyond copycat television and reactualize the script for a new audience' (2016, 6), especially if the adaptation is to achieve a degree of longevity, and our analysis has shown that *Eshgh Ta'til Nist* and *iPartment* have to be considered as more than just a mere copy of *Friends* (or other American sitcoms), because both exhibit some interesting creative choices. What is particularly noteworthy about *iPartment* is that it brings together notions of the 'cinematic' (single-camera production for location shooting) and the theatrical (the laugh track), and furthermore combines this with interior scenes drawing on multi-camera aesthetics. In this way, it is marked by a distinct 'intermedial texture' (see Pethő 2011). Moreover, *iPartment*, like all format adaptations, negotiates a complex set of national and transnational influences and practices, with *I Love my Family* (1993–1994), Ying Da's landmark sitcom, constituting a particularly noteworthy point of reference.

In recent years, a growing number of scholars have paid more in-depth attention to the distinct challenges of a discourse they have called 'creative borrowing' (Chalaby 2012; Esser 2013). Moran and Malbon claim that infringement occurs when a 'substantial part' of a television format is copied and that in a number of common law countries, the definition of what exactly constitutes a 'substantial part' is determined by a qualitative rather than a quantitative test, hence, 'the mere copying of another copyright work is not in itself an infringement' (2006, 138). One approach has been the establishment of national and international regulatory bodies such as the Format Recognition and Protection Association (FRAPA), founded in 2000 and based in Germany, where television formats can be registered, and their development and adaptation processes are monitored, providing consultancy and legal aids, if necessary. However, the reach and impact of such regulatory institutions is limited both because of their often privatised structure and voluntary nature of membership. As such, more scholars have argued for another approach in which a reconfiguration of 'creative borrowing' and a 'more intensive and multidirectional flow of ideas' (Shahaf 2016, 252) can take centre stage. In his study on the copyright infringements during the problematic adaptation of *Stromberg*, the German version of *The Office*, Kai Hanno Schwind concludes:

what is required and what future research could draw on, might be a shift of focus by both scholars and law-makers – away from various, often either too exclusive or too generalising conceptualisations of 'format', towards a more precise triangulation of the concepts 'originality', 'creativity' and 'authorship'. (2018, 203)

As our analyses of *iPartment* and *Eshgh Ta'til Nist* have shown, 'universally' successful sitcom formats, such as *Friends*, are in fact authored texts. However, they are authored in the sense that originality and creative property do not exclusively extend to narrative concepts, scripts and individual jokes, but also to achievements in, for instance, performance and set design. As such, the cast of *Eshgh Ta'til Nist* interacts in the emulated warmth and intimacy of an Iranian version of Monica's apartment, just as *iPartment*'s Hu Yifei bosses her friends around as the Chinese counterpart to Monica's wedding planner in 'The One with Phoebe's Wedding' (10.12). These programmes can reconfigure our ideas of television authorship, shifting away from the traditional emphasis on the writer (especially the 'visionary' writer) and towards a more collaborative concept of authorial artistry, including directors, actors and set designers.

Conclusion

This chapter has explored a number of *Friends*' intertextual brethren with a particular focus on the *Joey* spin-off and the failed adaptation of the *Coupling* format to the US market. *Joey* did not connect with audiences because of its proximity to its antecedent, thus struggling with a premise defined by the narrative and comedic absence of the other *Friends* characters, as well as a significant alteration of the character Joey. *Coupling* first expanded and then got lost in its own cultural space (Sanson 2011), finally falling victim to a mismanaged transatlantic dialogue about its adaptation process. By exploring the curious case of *Coupling* we argue that neglecting important questions related to aesthetics, style and tonality have been equally responsible for the eventual failure of the show in the USA, as was not addressing important issues concerning representation in the casting. The show looked and felt dated even before it started.

Furthermore, we have considered the reception of *Friends* around the world, by exploring the different approaches to 'making sense' of the series in India and Egypt via Olson's (1999) narrative transparency theory, as well as by looking at the German dubbed version. Here, the appropriations of the cultural specificities of the series' humour is both a necessity and a challenge and the lack of nuanced dubbing performances has contributed to the significant alterations of the comedic sensibility of *Friends* in German and had some effect on its popularity with German viewers. The ways in which *Friends* has been appropriated and adapted in those transcultural contexts speak to the universality of the show, but there are problematic boundaries that, when crossed, result in counteracting the inclusive humour of the show and risk undermining its strategy of intimacy, which, as we have shown in our analyses in the preceding chapters in this book, are crucial for the universal appeal to be facilitated in the first place. Thus, where Indian and Egyptian viewers were laughing with *Friends*, German audiences might have been laughing at it.

Finally, we have considered the effects of *Friends* on international sitcom productions, in particular unofficial remakes. These instances of quoting, copying or 'paying homage' point to the universal appeal and socio-cultural flexibility of the show, yet they illustrate to what extent the dynamics of international format flow, the discourses of creative borrowing and the culturally specific relationships of industry and genre call for more nuanced case studies and refined industry practices and standards.

In conclusion, *Friends*' global journey as a sitcom carrying or signposting a specifically American ideology is not easy to chart. Kevin S. Bright has stressed the specifically 'unpolitical approach' of the show in terms of the absence of references to politicians, political events or a clearly readable political agenda. However, *Friends*' liberal stance on certain issues, for instance relating to LGTBQ+ representations and a positive representation of blended families, makes the show highly political in certain cultural contexts. This is of particular relevance in the cultural sphere of Russia where American sitcoms did not arrive before the fall of the Soviet Union in the early 1990s. As the case studies of Russian sitcoms by Dana Heller (2003) and Jeffrey Brassard (2017) suggest, an initial lack of familiarity and scepticism towards the peculiarities of the sitcom genre, such as the laugh track, were quickly overcome by the increasing professionalisation and commodification of the Russian television industry. Heller, in particular, shows how the critical dismissal of American sitcoms as programmes characterised by superficiality and an 'astounding idiocy' (2003, 62) gained in popularity and to what extent *Friends* played an important role in the reversal of such views. As Heller and other scholars (e.g. Remnick 1996) have argued, the former Soviet Union was a particularly receptive cultural space for this new life, propagating more or less subtle showcases for the joys (and at times also sorrows) of capitalism, as here 'the very question of what constitutes "a national element" or "cultural identity" has become fragile and fraught with contradiction' (Heller 2003, 64). However, we suggest once more that the universal appeal of *Friends*, facilitated by its multi-pronged strategy of intimacy as well as the high quality of its craft, might have made it easier for Russian and other global audiences to open up and appreciate the generic conventions of sitcom and, eventually, paved the way for many more successful American sitcoms to come.

Recalling our introductory reflections on the notion of failure which prefaced our explorations of *Friends*' impact on global television production, we feel a rekindled confidence in the object of our analysis when encountering the different shortcomings, misjudgements and, indeed, failures that the recent critical backlash has so exhaustively catalogued. The multiplatform engagement by fans from around the world, with daily posts on Facebook and Instagram, numerous fan-made YouTube compilations as well as the outpouring of affection for the show's main cast whenever they appear on the global media circuit, attest to the ongoing success of *Friends*. This ongoing success certainly points to there being something about the show which managed to capture 'lightning in a bottle', as Marta Kauffman put it to us, and which is reflexively illuminated by *Friends*' intertextual brethren and their relative failures (and successes). For what they illustrate is the exceptional cultural and personal space the show is occupying and looks set to continue to do so.

Bibliography

Adamou, Christina, and Simone Knox. 2011. Transforming Television Drama Through Dubbing and Subtitling: *Sex and the Cities*. Critical Studies in Television 6 (1): 1–21. https://doi.org/10.7227/CST.6.1.3.

Banham, Mark. 2006. NBC Cancel 'Friends' Spin-Off Joey. Campaign. https://www.campaignlive.co.uk/article/nbc-cancels-friends-spin-off-joey/559312?src_site=brandrepublic. Accessed 25 March 2019.

Becker, Christine. 2007. From High Culture to Hip Culture: Transforming the BBC into BBC America. In *Anglo-American Media Interactions, 1850–2000*, ed. Joel Wiener and Mark Hampton, 275–294. New York: Palgrave Macmillan.

Bore, Inger-Lise Kalviknes. 2011. Laughing Together? TV Comedy Audiences and the Laugh Track. *The Velvet Light Trap* 68: 24–34. https://doi.org/10.1353/vlt.2011.0011.

Brassard, Jeffrey. 2017. Russian Sitcoms: From Post-Soviet Copycats to Aspiring Global Players. *Palabra Clave* 20 (3): 702–721. https://doi.org/10.5294/pacla.2017.20.3.6.

Carlson, Jen. 2012. Has This Chinese Sitcom Been Lifting Scenes from "Friends" and "How I Met Your Mother"? Gothamist. http://gothamist.com/2012/08/07/chinese_friends_under_fire.php. Accessed 25 April 2019.

Chalaby, Jean K. 2012. At the Origin of a Global Industry: The TV Format Trade as an Anglo-American Invention. *Media, Culture and Society* 34 (1): 36–52. https://doi.org/10.1177/0163443711427198.

Chalaby, Jean K. 2016. Drama Without Drama: The Late Rise of Scripted TV Formats. *Television & New Media* 17 (1): 3–20. https://doi.org/10.1177/1527476414561089.

Chen, Lu. 2012. Netizens Post Evidence of Scene Stealing. *Global Times*. http://www.globaltimes.cn/content/725277.shtml. Accessed 25 April 2019.

Chidester, Phil. 2008. May the Circle Stay Unbroken: *Friends*, The Presence of Absence, and the Rhetorical Reinforcement of Whiteness. *Critical Studies in Mass Communication* 25 (2): 157–174. https://doi.org/10.1080/15295030802031772.

Chitnis, Ketan S., Avinash Thombre, Everett M. Rogers, Arvind Singhal, and Ami Sengupta. 2006. (Dis)Similar Readings: Indian and American Audiences' Interpretation of *Friends*. *The International Communication Gazette* 68 (2): 131–145. https://doi.org/10.1177/1748048506062229.

Dillion, Katherine. 2009. *Friends Watching Friends: American Television in Egypt*. Newcastle upon Tyne: Cambridge Scholars Publishing.

Dyer, Richard. 1998. *Stars*, 2nd ed. London: BFI.

Esser, Andrea. 2013. The Format Business: Franchising Television Content. *International Journal of Digital Television* 4 (2): 141–158. https://doi.org/10.1386/jdtv.4.2.141_1.

Gajewski, Ryan. 2017. 'Friends' Creator Talks 'Joey' Spinoff Failure Amid 'Young Sheldon' Success: Stuff Just Happened. The Wrap. https://www.thewrap.com/httpswww-thewrap-comfriends-creator-joey-spinoff-matt-leblanc/. Accessed 25 March 2019.

Gitlin, Todd. 2000 [1983]. *Inside Prime Time*. Berkeley, Los Angeles, and London: University of California Press.

Heller, Dana. 2003. Russian 'Sitkom' Adaptation: The Pushkin Principle. *Journal of Popular Film and Television* 31 (2): 60–72. https://doi.org/10.1080/01956050309603667.

Herbst, Thomas. 1994. *Linguistische Aspekte der Synchronisation von Fernsehserien – Phonetik, Textlinguistik, Übersetzungstheorie*. Tübingen: Max Niemeyer Verlag.

Hogg, Christopher. 2013. Cracking the USA? Interpreting UK-to-US TV Drama Translations. *New Review of Film and Television Studies* 11 (2): 111–132. https://doi.org/10.1080/17400309.2012.708266.

Holzer, Daniela. 1999. *Die deutsche Sitcom: Format – Konzeption – Drehbuch – Umsetzung*. Bergisch Gladbach: Lübbe Verlagsgruppe.

Huang, Ya-chien. 2008. Pink Dramas: Reconciling Consumer Modernity and Confucian Womanhood. In *TV Drama in China*, ed. Ying Zhu, Michael Keane, and Ruoyun Bai, 103–114. Hong Kong: Hong Kong University Press.

Hutcheon, Linda. 2012. *A Theory of Adaptation*, 2nd ed. New York: Routledge.

Jaggi, Ruchi Kher. 2018. Indian TV Studies and the Soap Opera. Keynote Paper at the State of Play: Television Scholarship in 'TVIV' *Critical Studies in Television* conference, Ormskirk, 5 September 2018.

Jenner, Mareike. 2018. *Netflix and The Re-Invention of Television*. London: Palgrave Macmillan.

Keane, Michael. 2004. Asia: New Growth Areas. In *Television Across Asia: Television Industries, Programme Formats and Globalization*, ed. Albert Moran and Michael Keane, 9–20. London and New York: Routledge.

Keinonen, Heidi. 2016. Television Format as Cultural Negotiation: Studying Format Appropriation Through a Synthesizing Approach. *View: Journal of European Television History and Culture* 5 (9): 1–12. https://doi.org/10.18146/2213-0969.2016.jethc103.

Knox, Simone. 2013. Reflection iii: Transnationalisation, Television Formats and the Universal. *Critical Studies in Television* 8 (2): 103–105. https://doi.org/10.7227/CST.8.2.10.

Knox, Simone. 2018. *Shameless*, the Push-Pull of Transatlantic Fiction Format Adaptation, and Star Casting. *New Review of Film and Television Studies* 16 (3): 1–29. https://doi.org/10.1080/17400309.2018.1487130.

Knox, Simone. 2019. The Unwitting Pioneer of Transatlantic Format Adaptation: Beryl Vertue. *Historical Journal of Film, Radio and Television*. https://doi.org/10.1080/01439685.2018.1522790.

Knox, Simone, and Gary Cassidy. 2019. Game of Thrones: Investigating British Acting. In *Transatlantic Television Drama: Industries, Programs, & Fans*, ed. Matt Hills, Michele Hilmes, and Roberta Pearson, 181–200. Oxford: Oxford University Press.

Kurz, Christopher. 2006. *Filmsynchronisation aus Übersetzungswissenschaftlicher Sicht. Eine kontrastive Synchronisationsanalyse des Kinofilms "Lock, Stock and Two Smoking Barrels"*. Hamburg: Dr. Kovac.

Lavigne, Carlen, and Heather Marcovitch. 2011. Introduction. In *American Remakes of British Television: Transformations and Mistranslations*, ed. Carlen Lavigne and Heather Marcovitch, ix–xvii. Lanham: Lexington Books.

Lorenzo, Lourdes. 2003. The Simpsons/Los Simpsons. *The Translator* 9 (2): 269–291. https://doi.org/10.1080/13556509.2003.10799157.

Mikos, Lothar. 2015. *From The Office* to *Stromberg*: Adaptation Strategies in German Television. *Continuum: Journal of Media & Cultural Studies* 29 (5): 694–705. https://doi.org/10.1080/10304312.2015.1068727.

Mittell, Jason. 2009. The Aesthetics of Failure. *The Velvet Light Trap* 64 (1): 76–77. https://doi.org/10.1353/vlt.0.0044.

Mojo. 2014. Top 10 Worst American TV Remakes. YouTube. https://www.youtube.com/watch?v=AF_7LhE_Hs0. Accessed 23 April 2019.

Moran, Albert. 1998. *Copycat TV: Globalisation, Program Formats and Cultural Identity*. Luton: University of Luton Press.

Moran, Albert. 2009. *TV Formats Worldwide*. Bristol: Intellect.

Moran, Albert, and Justin Malbon. 2006. *Understanding the Global TV Format*. Bristol: Intellect.

Müntefering, Matthias. 2002. Dubbing in Deutschland: Cultural and Industrial Considerations. *Language International* 14 (2): 14–16.

Newman, Michael Z., and Elana Levine. 2012. *Legitimating Television: Media Convergence and Cultural Status*. New York and London: Routledge.

Olson, Scott Robert. 1999. *Hollywood Planet: Global Media and the Competitive Advantage of Narrative Transparency*. Mahwah: Lawrence Erlbaum.

Paine, Andre. 2003. Creator of British TV Hit Slams 'US Backstabbing'. *The Evening Standard*. 11 November.

Pedersen, Jan. 2007. How Is Culture Rendered in Subtitles? In *Proceedings of the Marie Curie Euroconferences MuTra: Challenges of Multidimensional Translation*. Saarbrücken: 1–18.

Pethő, Ágnes. 2011. *Cinema and Intermediality: The Passion for the In-Between*. Cambridge: Cambridge Scholars Publishing.

Phillips, Tom. 2012. Chinese Sitcom Accused of Scene Stealing from Cult American TV Series. *The Telegraph*. https://www.telegraph.co.uk/news/worldnews/asia/china/9455776/Chinese-sitcom-accused-of-scene-stealing-from-cult-American-TV-series.html. Accessed 20 April 2019.

Phillips, Tom. 2013. China's Villages Vanish Amid Rush for the Cities. *The Telegraph*. https://www.telegraph.co.uk/news/worldnews/asia/china/10470077/Chinas-villages-vanish-amid-rush-for-the-cities.html. Accessed 3 June 2019.

Pile, Stephen. 2004. The Last Laugh? *The Telegraph*. https://www.telegraph.co.uk/culture/tvandradio/3610803/The-last-laugh.html. Accessed 30 May 2019.

Remnick, David. 1996. *Lenin's Tomb: The Last Days of the Soviet Empire*. New York: Vintage.

Rice, Lynette. 2006. 'Joey' Faces Cancellation. *Entertainment Weekly*. https://ew.com/article/2006/03/17/joey-faces-cancellation/. Accessed 28 March 2019.

Rogers, Mark C., Michael Epstein, and Jimmie L. Reeves. 2002. The Sopranos as HBO Brand Equity: The Art of Commerce in the Age of Digital Reproduction. In *This Thing of Ours: Investigating The Sopranos*, ed. David Lavery, 42–57. London: Wallflower.

Roof, Judith. 2018. *The Comic Event: Comedic Performance from the 1950s to the Present*. New York: Bloomsbury.

Sanson, Kevin. 2011. We Don't Want Your Must-See TV: Transatlantic Television and the Failed 'Coupling' Format. *Popular Communication: The International Journal of Media and Culture* 9 (1): 39–54. https://doi.org/10.1080/15405702.2011.538256.

Schiller, Herbert I. 1969. *Mass Communications and American Empire*. Boston: Beacon Press.

Schwind, Kai Hanno. 2014. 'Chilled-Out Entertainers': Multi-layered Sitcom Performances in the British and American Version of *The Office*. *Comedy Studies* 5 (1): 20–32. https://doi.org/10.1080/2040610X.2014.905094.

Schwind, Kai Hanno. 2015. Like Watching a Motorway Crash: Exploring the Embarrassment Humor of *The Office*. *HUMOR—International Journal of Humour Research* 28 (1): 49–70. https://doi.org/10.1515/humor-2014-0145.

Schwind, Kai Hanno. 2018. 'It's Not Like the Germans to Take Something that Wasn't Theirs': Exploring Issues of Ownership and Creative Borrowing as a Challenge for Transnational Format Adaptation Through *Stromberg*. *Critical Studies in Television* 13 (2): 188–206. https://doi.org/10.1177/1749602018763690.

Scovell, Nell. 2018. *Just the Funny Parts: … And a Few Hard Truths About Sneaking into the Hollywood Boys' Club*. New York: Dey Street.

Shahaf, Sharon. 2016. Decentring Innovation: The Israeli Television Industry and the Format-driven Transnational Turn in Content Development. In *New Patterns in Global Television Formats*, ed. Karina Aveyard, Albert Moran and Pia Majbritt Jensen, 247–261. Chicago: Intellect.

Shannon, Sarah. 2003. No Laughs, Please, We're British. *The Independent*. https://www.independent.co.uk/news/media/no-laughs-please-were-british-99150.html. Accessed 23 March 2019.

Sinclair, John, Elizabeth Jacka, and Stuart Cunningham. 1996. *New Patterns in Global Television: Peripheral Vision*. Oxford: Oxford University Press.

Stanley, Alessandra. 2003. Two Nations Split by a Sense of Humor. *The New York Times*. 25 September.

Straubhaar, Joseph. 1991. Beyond Media Imperialism: Assymetrical Interdependence and Cultural Proximity. *Critical Studies in Mass Communication* 8 (1): 39–59. https://doi.org/10.1080/15295039109366779.

Straubhaar, Joseph. 2007. *World Television: From Global to Local*. Thousand Oaks: Sage.

Thauer, Martin. 2008. *Synchronisation einer Sitcom: Eine situationskomische Fernsehserie durch die Augen eines Übersetzers*. München: Grin Verlag Gmbh.

The Editors. 2009. Dossier: Perspectives on Failure. *The Velvet Light Trap* 64 (1): 76. https://doi.org/10.1353/vlt.0.0043.

Thomas, Matthew. 2019. Joey: 20 Wild Details Behind the Making of the Friends Spinoff. Screen Rant. https://screenrant.com/joey-friend-spinoff-tv-behind-scenes-trivia/. Accessed 23 March 2019.

Todd, Anne Marie. 2011. Saying Goodbye to *Friends*: Fan Culture as Lived Experience. *The Journal of Popular Culture* 44 (4): 854–871. https://doi.org/10.1111/j.1540-5931.2011.00866.x.

Vierrether, Tanja. 2017. Cultural and Linguistic Issues of Sitcom Dubbing: An Analysis of 'Friends'. Master's dissertation, Bowling Green State University.

Walters, Ben. 2005. *The Office*. London: BFI.

Weissmann, Elke. 2012. *Transnational Television Drama. Special Relations and Mutual Influences between the US and UK*. Basingstoke: Macmillan.

Zabalbeascoa, Patrick. 1997. Dubbing and the Nonverbal Dimension of Translation. In *Nonverbal Communication and Translation*, ed. Fernando Poyatos, 327–342. Amsterdam and Philadelphia: John Benjamins Publishing.

Television

Arrested Development (2003–2006, 2013–present), USA: Fox, Netflix.
Beacon Hill (1975), USA: CBS.
Charmed (1998–2006, 2018), USA: The WB, The CW.
Cheers (1982–1993), USA: NBC.
Coupling (2000–2004), UK: BBC2.
Coupling (2003), USA: NBC.
Cracker (1993–2006), UK: Granada Television.
Cracker (1997–1998), USA: ABC.
Curb Your Enthusiasm (2000–present), USA: HBO.
Days of Our Lives (1965–present). USA: NBC.
Die Harald Schmidt Show (1995–2003, 2011–2014), GER: Sat1, SKY.
Die 2 (1972–1989), Germany: ZDF.
Episodes (2011–2017), USA, UK: Showtime, BBC Two.
Eshgh Ta'til Nist (عشق تعطیل نیست, 2015), Iran: شبکه مناخشی خانگی / Home Broadcasting Media.
Falling in Love (情有可缘, 2007), Singapore, Malaysia: MediaCorp TV, NTV7.
Frasier (1993–2004), USA: NBC.
Friends (1994–2004), USA: NBC.
How I Met Your Mother (2005–2014), USA: CBS.
I Love my Family (我爱我家, 1993–1994), China: Beijing TV Broadcast Centre.

iPartment (爱情公寓, 2009–2014), USA: Jiangxi TV, Dragon TV.
Joey (2004–2006), USA: NBC.
Late Show with David Letterman (1993–2015), USA: CBS.
Mad About You (1992–1999), USA: NBC.
Man with a Plan (2016–present), USA: CBS.
Married … with Children (1987–1997, 2002), USA: Fox.
Murphy Brown (1988–1998, 2018–2019), USA: CBS.
Roseanne (1988–1997, 2018), USA: ABC.
Sabrina the Teenage Witch (1996–2000, 2000–2003), USA: ABC, The WB.
Seinfeld (1989–1998), USA: NBC.
Sex and the City (1998–2004), USA: HBO.
Shameless (2011–present), USA: Showtime.
Sherlock (2010–present), UK: BBC One.
Stromberg (2004–2012), Germany: ProSieben.
Terrace House (2012–present), Japan: Fuji Television, Netflix.
The Big Bang Theory (2007–2019), USA: CBS.
The Golden Girls (1985–1992), USA: NBC.
The Office—An American Workplace (2005–2013), USA: NBC.
The Office (2001–2003), UK: BBC Two.
The Persuaders! (1971–1972), UK: ITV.
The Simpsons (1989–present), USA: Fox.
The X-Files (1993–2002, 2016–2018), USA: Fox.
Two and a Half Men (2003–2015), USA: CBS.
Upstairs, Downstairs (1971–1975), UK: ITV.
Who's the Boss? (1984–1992), USA: ABC.

7

Conclusion: The One where They'll Still Be There for You—Reflections on *Friends'* Place in Television Culture for Its 25th Anniversary

In the episode 'Unwomen' (2.2) of dystopian thriller *The Handmaid's Tale* (Hulu, 2017–present), protagonist June (played by Elisabeth Moss) spends time in an abandoned newspaper headquarters, in hiding from the forces of the oppressive Gilead regime. Alone, her successful escape highly uncertain, she finds a DVD and watches it on a portable player. Framed against a nondescript grey wall and, to the far right of the screen, the cold colour scheme and empty space underline her isolation and the harshness of her situation (see Fig. 7.1). But, in a rare moment for the show, June smiles, with her head leaning back against the wall as a further sign of her relaxation. What is giving her this brief moment of joy? Of course, it is *Friends*, and specifically the well-remembered scene in which Monica teaches Chandler about female erogenous zones (4.11). The poignancy of this moment in *The Handmaid's Tale* serves as a useful starting point for offering our final reflections, seeing as it encapsulates so much about *Friends*.

The contrast between the cold, harsh, bare *mise-en-scène* of *The Handmaid's Tale* and the warm, inviting space of Monica's apartment—as Fig. 7.2 shows, in the relevant moment in *Friends*, Monica is surrounded by several colours, fabrics and textures—as well as between June's isolation and the emphasis on supportive friendship, is very

© The Author(s) 2019
S. Knox and K. H. Schwind, *Friends*,
https://doi.org/10.1007/978-3-030-25429-2_7

Figs. 7.1 and 7.2 June (Elisabeth Moss) in *The Handmaid's Tale* ('Unwomen', 2.2) enjoys Monica (Courteney Cox) in 'The One with Phoebe's Uterus' (4.11)

evident. It reflexively highlights the strategy of intimacy that, as the previous chapters have demonstrated, marks *Friends* on a number of levels. Published 20 years before the first broadcast of a show reaching its 25th anniversary in 2019, Horace Newcomb's (1974) argument concerning the significance and productiveness of the notion of intimacy for understanding television has lost none of its relevance. Even as the contexts of industry and consumption, which he sees as shaping the notion of intimacy, have significantly changed, *Friends* is clearly a show that developed 'the idea of intimacy as a conceptual tool' (ibid., 250) and continues to be marked by feelings of closeness, familiarity, attachment and warmth across a changed television landscape. In doing so, the series further points to the continuing relevance of Roger Silverstone's (1994) understanding of television as a medium of considerable emotional significance and consequently aligns the discussion in this book with broader debates concerning the significance of emotion and affect for television, especially those that understand 'emotion […] as an aesthetic quality' (Gorton 2006, 74) and engage with programmes' relevant 'expressive qualities' (ibid.).

What is worth considering here is that the notion of intimacy and the multi-camera sitcom would not make natural bedfellows within the predominant understanding of the latter in established scholarly debates. However, there are no such reservations about multi-camera aesthetics to be found with the creative practitioners that have shaped *Friends*. None of our interviewees expressed any concern that the multi-camera style might not be suited to fostering intimacy; on the contrary, they articulated in different ways that the multi-camera style, as Kevin S. Bright puts it, 'can really lend itself to making it more intimate'. Having worked with single-camera production—Bright collaborated with Marta Kauffman and David Crane on *Dream On* (1990–1996), co-created by Kauffman and Crane—the core creative team was, as Bright confirmed to us, attracted to working with multi-camera, which resonated with Kauffman's and Crane's background in theatre. Marta Kauffman commented that 'we first thought it would be a single-camera show', but then realised 'that this was about living with the six [main characters], that we were invited to be part of their lives'. Significantly, the core creative team sees multi-camera as 'theatrical', but does not equate this with artificiality. As Bright reflects when we asked him about the potential aesthetic benefits of this style:

> The decision was early on that this show is going to have a style that would be better played out in front of an audience. We realised the energy coming from the audience could make it better. […] Multi-camera brought a sense of us really being inside these people's lives, […] making the show more intimate, making you feel like you're in the room observing rather than on the outside watching. I think the multi-camera format really lends itself to that, to bringing you in.

Similarly, James Burrows shows a recognition of the strong potential for intimacy within multi-camera sitcoms, commenting that theatre audiences are 'deeply moved in the theatre', regardless of the absence of features readily associated with intimacy—as Burrows comments, 'there is no close-up in the theatre'—or the 'artificiality' of the performance context. A further parallel between Bright's and Burrows's views can also be found in their repeated highlighting of the importance of the live audience: Burrows sees the live audience not so much as a means to an end, but the end product as effectively a palimpsest marked by a significant energy exchange between the performers and the live audience (as well as across the performers), which we suggest further informs multi-camera's potential for intimacy.

Returning to *Friends*' appearance in *The Handmaid's Tale*—which was facilitated by Warren Littlefield, executive producer for the latter and president of NBC Entertainment in the 1990s—this moment captures not only something about the textual sensibility of the show, but also its broader contexts and historical place. The chosen *Friends* moment's insistent emphasis on female sexual pleasure—'SEVEN! SEVEN! SEVEN! SEVEN! SEVEN! SEVEN! SEVEN! SEVEN! SEVEN!'—and suggestion of male cluelessness (but willingness to learn) speaks to the series' approach to gender dynamics, starkly contrasting with the lack of sexual and reproductive rights in *The Handmaid's Tale*. As we have reflected in the introduction to this book, while *Friends* has a degree of timelessness, it is also linked to the current cultural nostalgia for the 1990s, whereby the programme becomes symptomatic of a (supposedly) more innocent time, in which the global recession, neoliberal precarity, the War on Terror, the climate crisis, the rise of nationalism and the Trump administration had yet to take place and/or to fully make their mark. Referencing the show and this particular moment helps to ground *The Handmaid's Tale* dystopic vision in a recognisable recent past and socio-cultural discourse, implying how quickly a sense of normality (where women joyfully give advice to men about erogenous zones) can slide into a totalitarian nightmare (where women are treated as breeding cattle, made harder to watch in the context of contemporary attacks on reproductive rights in the USA).

The One with Continuity and Transformation

So, the intertextual encounter discussed above concerns a show of the age of TVIV (Jenner 2016) referencing a show of the age of TVIII (Rogers et al. 2002), but, of course, *Friends* is a TVIII show that, as we have discussed earlier in this book, occupies a central place in TVIV and contemporary socio-cultural discourses. In this way, the programme interestingly complicates notions of the 'then and now' and discourses of continuation and transformation. Long-term viewers may, for example, watch *Friends* now and reflect back on their first experiences of watching it—where, in a pre-binge-watching age, they may have spent more time reflecting and anticipating between episodes—mapping their life trajectories against the show and milestones within its story world. Younger viewers such as millennials may be attracted to the programme because of the 'innocent times' it depicts. (The supposed innocence of these times is facilitated by the show's lack of engagement with politics, noted in the introduction to this book, which informs the programme's strategy of intimacy. Here, a link may be drawn to philosophical criticisms of intimacy as 'a retreat from worldliness' [Boym 1998, 500].) Both millennial and post-millennial demographics—a 2019 Childwise survey found that *Friends* is the most popular programme with 5–16 year olds in the UK (Coughlan 2019)—may also be drawn by the absence of digital technology within its fictional world: *Friends* offers depictions of friendships where companions communicate by talking in person, not by sending text or FaceTiming/Skyping, and of dating where romantic interests meet in random encounters and not via the swipe of a thumb in an app. (It is here worth noting that the programme, which uses frequent interstitial shots of Manhattan and the NYC skyline, also played a part in the shift of the broader cultural image of New York, which 'has evolved as the pre-eminent and most memorable location adopted by the Hollywood rom-com' [Jermyn 2009, 10].) This may be attractive to viewers who have grown up with digital technology, whose supposed connectivity has led to selfie culture, where unmediated experiences can be supplanted by a careful construction and performance for social media, and gazes often remained fixed downwards on the small screens carried in people's hands. Kevin S. Bright comments, 'the friends are almost cavemen around a fire', and we would agree, not on the basis of any notion of 'primitiveness', but in the sense that a sense of connected togetherness (and warmth) underpins the intimacy that marks *Friends*.

As far as discourses of continuity and transformation are concerned, the series has strong connotations of continuity in terms of its oft-repeated and (to many viewers) very familiar content. Long-term fans may have gleaned ontological security (Silverstone 1994) from watching the show over the years, which can help viewers cope with social change. However, this very familiar content is not entirely continuous: improvements in the image quality of reception technology make more of the textual detail of the programme visible than it was on (average) television sets in the 1990s. There are also (albeit minor) discrepancies between *Friends* as it appears on Netflix (UK) and the 2009 DVD box set. For example, the sequence from 'The One with the Prom Video' (2.14) that we discuss in depth in Chapter 4 contains a different shot on the streaming platform. (This is part of a trajectory that further includes the other DVD box sets, the Blu-ray box set and how *Friends* has been re-versioned for syndication.) Furthermore, there are not only regular online efforts to highlight spatial and other inconsistencies, but also to make the programme's content more significantly 'strange' still, most notably by highlighting the presence of stand-in actors (e.g. Hooton 2016) that have become detectible in the change of aspect ratio from the original 4:3 to widescreen (16:9) on Netflix. Netflix furthermore offers viewers transformation in terms of distribution

7 Conclusion: The One where They'll Still Be There for You ...

and consumption through the instant availability and possibility for binge-watching; but there is continuity here too in that viewers can also still stumble across repeats of the programme when flicking through channels (e.g. in 2019, Comedy Central and Channel 5 in the UK, TV Fem in Norway, and Comedy Central in India), like they might have done a decade or so ago. As visits to different countries in recent years and friends in different parts of the world confirm, *Friends* is still a regular presence on linear television, still *on all the time*.

Such discursive tensions already suggest that engaging with *Friends* offers television scholarship opportunities for meaningful engagement with not only the programme itself—which is important, worthwhile and overdue—but also past, current and future television culture more broadly. In particular, we argue that engagement with *Friends* helps with identifying certain blind spots and opportunities for intervention into established arguments. Overall, in the book's chapters, we have been concerned to make a substantial contribution to scholarly understanding of one of the most significant programmes in television history, helping to illuminate the programme's enduring appeal and status as one of the few global, cross-generational reference shows. *Friends* is, in many ways, a show about intimacy, and it is also a show about humour, about performance and about style. So, in the chapters, we have also sought to offer productive interventions into existing debates on sitcom (and, at times, also beyond the genre). In particular, Chapter 2 offers a typology of the six main characters, illustrating how they are constructed as comedic types, interact with each other and form the basis of the show's comedic sensibility. This strikes us as a unique approach not offered elsewhere in scholarship engaging with *Friends* or other sitcoms. Providing a 'blue print' that establishes in detail how the humour works both in terms of individual characters and more collectively, we invite other scholars and practitioners to utilise this approach in future work. Chapter 3 works to open up existing debates on comedic performance to more nuanced, in-depth engagement with the intricacies and challenges involved when actors work—successfully or not—with multi-camera production. Addressing established arguments about multi-camera sitcom style, Chapter 4 is intended to help redress 'the lack of work on *other* ways [beyond examination of the 'cinematic'] in which the visual aspects of television can be thought about' (Mills 2013, 64, emphasis in original). Chapter 5 demonstrates the usefulness of engaging with issues of tone (Pye 2007) when exploring television representations. Through its exploration of the 'failures' of the *Joey* spin-off and other format adaptations, Chapter 6 expands the scope of scholarly research by providing new insights with regards to the question of what characterises a monumental global success and universal appeal within an increasingly competitive and crowded international television market. Through these interventions, we hope that the book will signpost productive directions for future scholarship on *Friends*, sitcom and television more broadly.

The One where They Look Ahead

As we have noted in the introduction to this book, our analysis cannot possibly cover all the interesting discussions to be had about the series. For example, there is more to be said about issues of representation, such as that of transgender identity, as well as the writing process. *Friends* also contains a noteworthy meta-commentary about other genres (particularly soap opera) and media (film and especially theatre), in ways that at times uphold, playfully address and challenge established discourses of legitimation (Newman and Levine 2012). There is also scope for a detailed study of the show's fandom that builds on Todd (2011) but explores significant ongoing fan practices, such as attending the Friendsfest or themed quiz nights noted in the introduction to this book, as well as the fan art circulating on social media. For example, there are the Gladys and Glynnis party costumes that recreate Phoebe's disturbing paintings from 10.6, complete with picture frame for the full 3D effect. Teater Pappvin's touring improvisation-performances based on translated *Friends* scripts also deserve more consideration than we could give it in the introduction to this book.

However, concerned with critical depth over scope, we have worked to capture and articulate the (comedic, performance, stylistic and representational) sensibility of the show. In doing so, we have been struck by how much there is to be discovered about *Friends*, not so much in terms of sheer mass (we were very aware of this from the beginning of our research), but in terms of the complexity of the programme's construction. When starting close analysis of selected scenes, we realised quickly that there is nothing simple or straightforward about how this programme works, with camera, editing, space, performances and humour working together in intricate ways. There are precise details, rich textures and diachronic layers that offer 'interpretive richness and endurance (i.e. the capacity to sustain repeated viewings and concomitant interpretive revisions)' (Cardwell 2007, 34). (This links to the above noted rediscoverability of the show for long-term viewers enabled by digital technology, as certain details of set design and performance were not available to us when we first watched the series in the 1990s.) In this way, *Friends* is both representative of multi-camera sitcom—more multi-camera shows deserve more in-depth scrutiny that may reveal their complexity—and also exceptional, with a remarkable degree of creative skill and expert craft collaboratively invested in it by both the above-the-line and below-the-line talent. *Friends* shows not only that multi-camera conventions are not necessarily inherent limitations but also—and crucially—that these conventions need to be reconceptualised and re-evaluated.

The US broadcast of *Friends*' final episode on 6 May 2004 was, as Anne Marie Todd has explored, 'an intertextual media event' (2011, 857) and 'a significant site of fan discourse' (ibid.). The 25-year anniversary in September 2019 of the show's first ever broadcast will be both of these, only more so. As it is, in recent years a striking space of the landscape of participatory culture—which is, as Elizabeth Ellcessor (2012, 49–50) points out, marked by different types of connection, including social, thematic, spatial, temporal and/or conversational—has been devoted to a programme that depicts the beginnings in an episode late in its penultimate season (9.17). The anniversary will see countless conversations and commentaries online, including on social media, by those who have formed an intimate bond of connection with *Friends* (this will most likely play out on Facebook and Instagram) and those who have not and/or take issue with its politics of representation (this will be strongly articulated on Twitter).

The anniversary celebrations are bound to involve a strong desire by fans to obtain 'behind the scenes' insights into the show, which is furthered by the fact that not much 'making of' material exists. This is possibly linked to a desire to keep the diegetic illusion as intact as possible, but 'making of' material can facilitate an intimate bond of connection extra-textually. Fans' desire to extend their intimate connection with the series shows itself in the frequent circulation on social media of trivia facts (e.g. that James Michael Tyler bleached his hair for ten years to play Gunther, or that the break-up scene in episode 3.16 emotionally affected David Schwimmer and Jennifer Aniston) and their enthusiastic responses to the circulation of personal photographs on Instagram. For example, Courteney Cox's posted snapshot of the six main actors on the plane trip to Las Vegas before the programme first aired—a key milestone in fan lore—received more than 1 million likes on Instagram in less than 20 hours in May 2019. As Fig. 7.3 shows, social media such as Instagram may (literally) reframe such older artefacts, offering a joint space of reflection for those directly involved (here, Cox and Lisa Kudrow, who comments on Cox's post) and fans.

Fig. 7.3 Courteney Cox's Instagram snapshot (May 2019): the *Friends* cast on the plane trip to Las Vegas before the pilot aired (1994)

This fan desire further encompasses blooper outtakes, which take on a similar function to the 'on the set' Instagram videos by actors in TVIV shows, in that we see the actors out of character—crucially, still being funny and enjoying themselves—as well as interactions between cast and crew, and the presence of the apparatus that is usually hidden (not only the cameras, but also the shooting script). Some of the blooper clips, such as the much-circulated one of the 'Pivot!' scene (from 5.15, 'The One with the Cop'), in which David Schwimmer corpses and screams 'Pivot!' ever more shrilly, are indeed explicitly framed in such a way, promising to take viewers 'behind the scenes of PIVOT' and expand the scope of the series' comedic sensibility. Such materials indicate an interest to engage with the details of a fictional world that, while, as noted in the introduction to this book, was built on some specificity, was not marked by an intention to build a hyperdiegesis, in other words, 'a vast and detailed narrative space, only a fraction of which is ever directly seen or encountered within the text, but which nonetheless appears to operate according to principles of internal logic and extension' (Hills 2002, 137). This and the occasional spatial and narrative inconsistencies notwithstanding, *Friends* fans show a desire for immersion in this fictional world that is not diminishing, and indeed, if anything, seems to be facilitated by developments in digital technology, as the *Sims* model of Monica's apartment (Romano 2014) vividly attests. The 25th anniversary celebrations look set to spark a fresh wave of such immersive engagement, and it only remains to be seen what future fan practices may emerge on social media (or elsewhere).

The 25th and further *Friends* anniversaries will see a plethora of think pieces and commentary (as well as more of the persistent rumours concerning a reunion or reboot, which have been stoked by the recent revivals of *Will & Grace*, *Roseanne* and *Murphy Brown*). We hope that the backlash against the show is going to be inflected with more nuanced and reflexive debates, where it is okay to suggest certain ideas and to ask certain questions, and that the current debates on comedy and creative risk-taking (noted in Chapter 5) will lead to productive outcomes. Our discussion in this book is intended to help towards the former, and we hope that it will also offer productive insights for practitioners in the creative industries. Here, our reflections on the notions of 'universality' and 'failure' may be especially relevant, because, as we suggest in Chapter 6, 'failure' is indeed the default mode in television production, a discourse characterised and—at times—traumatised by a mode of production which is constantly forced to reconcile a profit-oriented and hierarchical apparatus of production and distribution with the imaginative skills of and precarious conditions for its creative labourers. As our analysis has shown, supported by our conversations with the creative personnel involved, *Friends* can serve as a case study in effective collaborative production between above-the-line and below-the-line talent. (Here, Marta Kauffman points out the importance of hiring 'heads of departments who share your sensibility'.)

A quarter of a century after the first broadcast of 'just another sitcom' (Tucker 1994), *Friends* continues to be highly influential on sitcom production in the USA and beyond, and to shape the lived engagement with the socio-cultural world of people across the globe. Its legacy and place in past, present and future television culture seems assured—as does the place of multi-camera sitcom more broadly. As James Burrows commented in his closing reflections in our interview with him:

> It's relevant. It's a form that is certainly funnier than single-camera, because in single-camera, you only have to make the writer laugh. In multi-camera, you have to make the audience laugh. And I've attended the 'funeral' of the multi-camera sitcom about four or five times, and it always seems to come back.

Friends' intimate bond with viewers certainly shows no signs of dying off. A towering presence in television culture for a quarter of a century (and counting), we hope that this book will help to give *Friends* the central place it warrants in television scholarship.

Bibliography

Boym, Svetlana. 1998. On Diasporic Intimacy: Ilya Kabakov's Installations and Immigrant Homes. *Critical Inquiry* 24 (2): 498–524.

Cardwell, Sarah. 2007. Is Quality Television Any Good? Generic Distinctions, Evaluations and the Troubling Matter of Critical Judgement. In *Quality TV: Contemporary American Television and Beyond*, ed. Janet McCabe and Kim Akass, 19–34. London: I.B. Tauris.

Coughlan, Sean. 2019. The One About Friends Still Being Most Popular. BBC News. https://www.bbc.co.uk/news/education-47043831. Accessed 14 May 2019.

Ellcessor, Elizabeth. 2012. Tweeting @feliciaday: Online Social Media, Convergence, and Subcultural Stardom. *Cinema Journal* 51(2): 46–66. https://doi.org/10.1353/cj.2012.0010.

Gorton, Kristyn. 2006. A Sentimental Journey: Television, Meaning and Emotion. *Journal of British Cinema and Television* 3 (1): 72–81. https://doi.org/10.3366/JBCTV.2006.3.1.72.

Hills, Matt. 2002. *Fan Cultures*. London and New York: Routledge.

Hooton, Christopher. 2016. *Friends* Swapped Rachel in an Episode and No-One Noticed. *The Independent*. https://www.independent.co.uk/arts-entertainment/tv/friends-replaced-rachel-in-an-episode-and-noone-noticed-a6732801.html. Accessed 14 May 2019.

Jenner, Mareike. 2016. Is This TVIV? On Netflix, TVIII and Binge-Watching. *New Media & Society* 18 (2): 257–273. https://doi.org/10.1177/1461444814541523.

Jermyn, Deborah. 2009. I ♥ NY: The Rom-Com's Love Affair with New York City. In *Falling in Love Again: Romantic Comedy in Contemporary Cinema*, ed. Stacey Abbott and Deborah Jermyn, 9–24. London and New York: I.B. Tauris.

Mills, Brett. 2013. What Does It Mean to Call Television 'Cinematic'? In *Television Aesthetics and Style*, ed. Jason Jacobs and Steven Peacock, 57–66. London: Bloomsbury.

Newcomb, Horace. 1974. *TV: The Most Popular Art*. Garden City: Anchor Books.

Newman, Michael Z. and Elana Levine. 2012. *Legitimating Television: Media Convergence and Cultural Status*. New York and London: Routledge.

Pye, Douglas. 2007. Movies and Tone. In *Close Up 02*, ed. John Gibbs and Douglas Pye, 1–80. London: Wallflower Press.

Rogers, Mark C., Michael Epstein, and Jimmie L. Reeves. 2002. The Sopranos as HBO Brand Equity: The Art of Commerce in the Age of Digital Reproduction. In *This Thing of Ours: Investigating the Sopranos*, ed. David Lavery, 42–57. London: Wallflower Press.

Romano, Andrea. 2014. Superfan Perfectly Recreates 'Friends' for 'The Sims 4'. MashableUK. https://mashable.com/2014/09/08/friends-in-sims/?europe=true. Accessed 14 May 2019.

Silverstone, Roger. 1994. *Television and Everyday Life*. London and New York: Routledge.

Todd, Anne Marie. 2011. Saying Goodbye to *Friends*: Fan Culture as Lived Experience. *The Journal of Popular Culture* 44 (4): 854–871. https://doi.org/10.1111/j.1540-5931.2011.00866.x.

Tucker, Ken. 1994. TV Show Review: Winning 'Friends'. *Entertainment Weekly*. https://ew.com/article/1994/10/21/tv-show-review-winning-friends/. Accessed 22 April 2019.

Television

Dream On (1990–1996), USA: HBO.
Friends (1994–2004), USA: NBC.
Joey (2004–2006), USA: NBC.
Murphy Brown (1988–1998, 2018–2019), USA: CBS.
Roseanne (1988–1997, 2018), USA: ABC.
The Handmaid's Tale (2017–present), USA: Hulu.
Will & Grace (1998–2006, 2018–present), USA: NBC.

Index

0-9
9/11 18, 149

A
ABC 1, 2
absurdism 55, 72, 231, 247, 256, 263
affect 14, 41, 145, 153, 279
Allen, Woody 77
All in the Family 9, 138
American Dream 183, 187
Anders, Andrea 227
Aniston, Jennifer 12, 23, 48, 49, 61, 69, 86–93, 102–104, 106, 115, 117, 118, 141–143, 146, 155, 157, 184, 286
Ansari, Aziz 172, 173
anti-jokes 256
Applegate, Christina 50, 208
Archer 199
Aristotle 37
Arrested Development 10, 232
aspect ratio 207, 282
authorship 11, 16, 126, 150, 266
 authorial tropes 14

B
backlash 4, 24, 44, 61, 66, 75, 77, 170–173, 176, 224, 268, 287
Ball, Lucille 42, 43, 52
Baxendale, Helen 62, 186, 205
BBC 234, 245
BBC America 234, 240
Bergson, Henri 40
Big Bang Theory, The 12, 15, 16, 134, 139, 144, 162, 243
Birang, Bijan 260
black hair 90
Black-ish 25, 175, 183

Index

blackness. *See* politics of representation
Branagh, Kenneth 35
Bright, Kevin S. 10, 11, 13, 15, 17, 18, 21, 22, 25, 35, 46, 62, 84, 85, 113, 116–118, 131, 135, 136, 147, 150, 154, 171, 179, 188, 193, 195, 199, 211, 223, 227, 231, 267, 279, 280, 282
Bright/Kauffman/Crane Productions 16
Bringing Up Baby 49
Brock Akil, Mara 179
2 Broke Girls 175
Brooklyn Nine-Nine 174
Buffy the Vampire Slayer 8
Burgess, Titus 181
Burrows, James 15, 16, 46, 58, 84, 85, 116, 117, 146, 147, 150, 155, 156, 193, 280, 288

C

Cahill, Eddie 186
Calhoun, Wil 13
Carell, Steve 76
Carmichael, Jerrod 6
casting 22, 65, 83, 84, 102, 108, 174, 188, 225, 240–242, 254, 256–259, 267
CBS 1, 2, 232, 233, 244
Central Perk 3, 14, 46, 48, 49, 60, 66, 67, 129, 139, 140, 149, 151, 152, 202, 204, 208
Channel 5 283
Charmed 226
Cheers 15, 78, 84, 151, 243

Chinese Dream discourse 260
Chinese television 263
Citizen Kane 126
class. *See* politics of representation
clickbait 4, 150, 200, 212
Clooney, George 102
clowning 42, 52, 108
Coates, Ta-Nehisi 180, 181
Cohen, Ted 192
cold open 70, 72, 241
colour-blind casting 183
colourism 188
Columbo 126
Comeback, The 140
comedic types
    Chandler Bing 37, 66
    Joey Tribbiani 51, 62, 110
    Monica Geller 50, 51, 140
    Phoebe Buffay 51, 55
    Rachel Green 47
    Ross Geller 58, 93
comedy 2. *See also* comedic types; humour
    business 41
    comedic moments 36, 47, 48, 52, 53, 55, 60, 94, 103, 119, 256
    comedic persona 37, 48–50, 53, 60, 66, 68, 75, 78, 94, 233, 255
    comedic sensibility 22, 26, 36, 39, 44–46, 49, 50, 54, 58, 60, 63, 66, 68–70, 72, 73, 75–77, 89, 230, 231, 236, 242–244, 248, 254–256, 258, 260, 267, 283, 287
    industry 41
    Vaudevillian strand 42
Comedy Central 2, 130, 131, 283

Community 10
competitiveness 52, 53, 71
controlling images 185. *See also* politics of representation
   Angry Black Woman 186
   Black Lady 190, 191
   Jezebel 185
   Mammy 185
   Sapphire 185
   Strong Black Woman 185
   Welfare Mother 185
   Welfare Queen 185
Coolidge, Jennifer 228
Cosby Show, The 43, 52, 183, 184, 188
Costanzo, Paulo 227, 230
couple dynamics 54, 255
Coupling (UK) 234, 235, 240, 241
Coupling (USA) 234, 235, 238–244
Cox, Courteney 12, 51, 53–55, 69, 71, 75, 76, 84, 85, 91, 118, 119, 184, 207, 278, 286
Cracker (UK) 238
Cracker (USA) 238
Crane, David 12, 13, 46, 49, 52, 57, 61–63, 66, 77, 85, 94, 118, 211, 227, 228, 279
Critchley, Simon 40
cultural proximity 234, 237, 242, 247
Curb Your Enthusiasm 3, 232

D

Dallas 20
David, Larry 13, 200
Days of Our Lives 110, 225
de Matteo, Drea 227, 230
Deutsche Synchron 253
Dharma & Greg 15, 138, 139
dialogue 6, 15, 16, 36, 48, 50, 59, 62, 66, 68, 71, 72, 74, 91, 93, 96, 97, 103, 105, 141, 174, 210, 213, 239, 241, 242, 244, 251, 253–256, 258, 260, 261, 266
Die 2 256
Dream On 279
dubbing 26, 225, 250–254, 256–258, 267
Dunham, Lena 179, 181

E

'Easter eggs' 14, 150
Egypt, *Friends* reception in 247
Ellen 137
ensemble cast 12, 68, 94, 106, 107, 231, 242
Episodes 233, 234
Epps, Sheldon 191
ER 2, 102
Eshgh Ta'til Nist 26, 225, 259, 260, 265, 266
Everybody Loves Raymond 137

F

Facebook 4, 199, 223, 268, 285
failure 25, 54, 55, 60, 62, 86, 197, 225, 226, 228, 231, 232, 234, 235, 239, 244, 245, 249, 250, 252, 254, 268, 284, 288
Falling in Love 264
Family Ties 43, 52
Fat Monica 75, 76
femininity 47, 52. *See also* politics of representation

first scene 22, 46, 48, 51, 56, 60, 62, 63, 66, 75, 94. *See also* pilot episode
format
  copyright 264
  creative borrowing 26, 265, 267
  format adaptation 25, 225, 233–237, 244, 246, 252, 263, 265, 284
  push-pull factor 240
  USA–UK format adaptation 235
Format Recognition and Protection Association (FRAPA) 265
fourth wall 24, 87, 125, 137, 139, 140, 142, 144, 145, 148, 154, 158, 159
Fox 1, 2, 162, 178, 179
Frankfurt School 246
Frasier 15, 134, 145, 178, 243, 252
Fresh Prince of Bel-Air, The 137, 178, 187, 188, 198, 206
Freud, Sigmund 38, 41
Friendsfest 1, 2, 130, 153, 284

G

Geller Cup 53, 71, 140
genre 2, 3, 7–12, 14, 16, 21, 25, 36, 39, 43, 45, 50, 53, 70, 74, 77, 83, 110, 117, 119, 127, 153, 170, 176, 179, 187, 199, 200, 202, 203, 209, 226, 227, 233, 236, 239, 246, 251, 253, 260, 267, 268, 283, 284
German television 252, 257
Girlfriends 179
Girls 170, 172, 179–181
GLAAD Media Award 178
Glover, Donald 180, 181

Goffman, Erving 100, 101
Goldberg, Adam 227, 228
Goldberg-Meehan, Shana 13, 227
Golden Girls, The 256
Good Place, The 174
Grace and Frankie 175
Grande, Greg 131, 133, 149, 161
growing up 49, 70, 100

H

habitus 197
Haddish, Tiffany 6
Hairpin, The 172
Handmaid's Tale, The 26, 277, 278, 280, 281
Happy Endings 12
Harris, Aisha 5
HBO 10, 11, 180, 238, 244, 257
hedonism 64, 227
Hobbes, Thomas 37
Hollywood hegemony 246
Honeymooners, The 126
Howery, Lil Rel 6, 179
How I Met Your Mother 12, 120, 134, 138, 139, 175, 232, 263
Hulu 26, 162, 277
humour 14. *See also* comedy
  behavioural 42
  dad 51, 59
  dated 75
  embarrassment 94, 101
  incongruity theory 37
  mom 52
  relief theory 37, 38
  specificities of 22, 267
  superiority theory 37
  tonality 36, 37, 39, 78
Hyde Pierce, David 243

I

I Love Lucy 42, 43, 52
I Love my Family 265
India 2, 267, 283
    cultural context 26
    television market 246
Insecure 25, 188, 210
Insomnia Café pitch 46
Instagram 4, 223, 268, 285–287
intersectionality 4, 171, 196, 211
intertextuality 12, 78, 223
intimacy 17, 19–21, 38, 39, 45, 48, 58, 68, 128, 129, 137, 147, 149–151, 154–157, 159, 160, 162, 177, 200, 203, 206–208, 211, 229, 232, 234, 236, 241, 243, 248, 258, 266, 279, 280, 283
    strategy of intimacy 21–23, 25, 26, 36, 50, 54, 74, 75, 87, 91, 93, 101, 115, 134, 138, 148, 155, 162, 201, 228, 254, 259, 267, 268, 279, 281
iPartment 26, 225, 260–266
Iranian viewers 260
irony 22, 56, 66, 72, 109, 174

J

James, Kendra 171
Jay-Z 3, 6
Jezebel 172, 200
Joey 25, 62, 149, 223, 225, 227–229, 231–233, 243, 266, 284

K

Kant, Immanuel 37

Kauffman, Marta 12, 13, 15, 21, 22, 45–47, 49, 50, 52, 55, 57, 58, 61–63, 66, 78, 84, 85, 94, 102, 118, 171, 175, 179, 180, 201, 211, 227, 268, 279, 288
Kemper, Ellie 181
Kinnear, Greg 186
Klein, Dana 192
Kudrow, Lisa 12, 51, 56, 57, 105, 118, 119, 207, 257, 263, 286

L

Late Show with David Letterman 252
Latin American telenovelas 237
Law & Order 3, 145
Lear, Norman 9, 126
LeBlanc, Matt 12, 23, 51, 63, 65, 69, 72, 85, 86, 106, 110–115, 118, 225, 228, 230, 232, 233
Lee, Ki Hong 6
LGBTQ+ issues. *See* politics of representation
Littlefield, Warren 84, 116, 280
Living Single 178, 179, 184, 206
Lookingglass Theatre Company 85
Louis, C.K. 77
Lyle, Amaani 5, 191
Lyle v. Warner Brothers Television Productions 5, 6, 173

M

Macpherson, Elle 186
Mad About You 102, 137, 225
Magna Doodle 14, 149, 229

Magnum, P.I. 107
Man with a Plan 233
Married ... with Children 251
Martin 178, 206
Mary Tyler Moore Show, The 9, 12, 43, 137
masculinity 52, 58, 59, 61, 62, 66, 77, 97, 108, 135. See also politics of representation
  hegemonic 8
  toxic 63, 64
*M*A*S*H* 43
Maude 9, 19, 126, 128
McCormack, Eric 84
McLean, Nick 136, 188
#MeToo 6, 24, 170, 172
Miller, Kelsey 5, 6
misogynoir 183, 189
Moesha 206
Moffat, Steven 234, 235, 239, 241, 244
Mom 162
Mondler 55, 91
Moonlight (film) 188
Moonlight (music video) 3, 178, 185
Moss, Elisabeth 277, 278
MTM 9, 126
Müntefering, Matthias 253
Murphy Brown 226, 287
Must-See TV 2, 7, 227, 228, 235

N

narrative transparency theory 247, 248, 267
NBC 1, 2, 7, 9, 11, 13, 85, 95, 102, 137, 174, 180, 182, 201, 225, 227, 228, 232–235, 238–240, 242, 244, 245, 280

Netflix 2, 5, 66, 162, 170, 174, 178, 200, 233, 238, 252, 282
New Adventures of Old Christine, The 126
Newcomb, Horace 19, 128, 155, 202, 279
New Girl 12, 138
New Yorker, The 172
New York Times, The 172, 210
Nietzsche, Friedrich 37
Nussbaum, Emily 171, 172, 175

O

Office, The 242, 265
Office – An American Workplace, The 3, 12, 199, 238, 242
Oldman, Gary 102, 109
One Day at a Time 174, 178
outrage culture 213

P

Parks and Recreation 76
Parsons, Karyn 187
Paskin, Willa 172
Peep Show 3
performance
  acting 83, 84
  acting off the line 92, 93, 106, 109
  being 'in the moment' 109
  body language 48, 89, 108
  cadence 49, 105, 257
  'comic twinkle' 109
  corpsing 105
  determinants of acting 23, 117
  directing 258
  emotional truth 113

illusion of the first time 103, 109, 118
improvisation 3, 284
naturalism 72, 87
objective 94
pitch 49, 106
realism 21, 23, 72, 86, 97, 109, 119, 257, 258
rehearsals 117, 118
slapstick 95
star image 109
super objective 95
truth 110, 114
unit 88
verb 88, 89, 96
Perry, Matthew 12, 51, 53, 55, 66, 69, 91, 107, 111, 118, 142–144, 158, 194, 207
Persuaders!, The 256
Pigulla, Franziska 257
pilot episode 46, 58, 64, 75, 94, 230, 231, 262
pitch. See *Insomnia Café* pitch
Pitt, Brad 23, 86, 102–107, 109, 110, 113
Plato 37
Plowman, Jon 245
politics of representation 7. See also controlling images; femininity; masculinity
  assimilationist discourse 183
  blackness 212
  burden of representation 211
  class 184, 191, 211
  coolness 197, 198
  homophobia 5, 170
  homosexuality 77
  LGBTQ+ 5, 77, 177
  lighting for black skin 188
  normalisation 211
  Otherness 62
  sexuality 171, 185, 186
  transphobia 170
  unruly woman 43, 52
  whiteness 176, 192, 200, 213
Poniewozik, James 171
postfeminism 131
ProSieben 251

quirkiness 55, 67

Racialicious 172
racism 169, 185, 193
  enlightened racism 183
Rae, Issa 6, 25, 198
regime of looking 148, 149, 155
  regime of looking in 24, 153, 154, 156, 159, 160, 209
Reich, Andrew 192
Rhoda 9, 126
Ribeiro, Alfonso 198
Roberts, Julia 107
30 Rock 10
romantic love 68, 262
Roseanne 43, 251
Rosenberg, Alyssa 171
RTL 251
Rudd, Paul 54, 208
rupture 24, 153, 158–160
Russia, sitcom in 268
Ryan, Mo 171

S

Sabrina the Teenage Witch 226
sarcasm 66, 67, 72, 93
Sat1 251, 252
Saturday Night Live 6
scheduling 2, 225, 228, 241, 250, 252
Schiller, Herbert 237
Schopenhauer, Arthur 37
Schwimmer, David 12, 23, 60–62, 72, 84–87, 89, 91–101, 103–107, 115–118, 141–144, 155, 157, 188, 189, 193, 194, 198, 207, 227, 257, 286, 287
Scovell, Nell 226
Scrubs 10, 12, 45, 128, 136, 161
Seinfeld 8, 11, 13, 39, 68, 134, 145, 150, 174, 178, 200, 201, 223, 243, 252
Seinfeld, Jerry 13, 173, 200
Selleck, Tom 53, 107, 108
Sepinwall, Alan 10, 172
set design 6. *See also* style; texture
  the couch 23, 139
  Monica's apartment 23, 125, 128–134, 137, 138, 259, 266
Sex and the City 8, 15, 172, 244, 257, 264
Shaffner, John 13, 15, 16, 21, 24, 131–136, 138, 139, 149, 150, 160, 161, 179
Shameless (USA) 238
Shepherd, Sherri 186
Shondaland 183
Silveri, Scott 13, 227
Simpsons, The 43, 52, 226, 251
sitcom
  cold 39, 53
  conservatism 8, 43, 53
  hybrid 232, 260
  ideology 267
  in-group 186, 201–203, 209
  laugh track 45, 73, 74, 84, 125, 265, 268
  multi-camera 11, 14, 19, 23, 24, 26, 35, 36, 40, 73, 83, 86, 101, 102, 106, 109, 125–128, 131, 137, 139, 142, 148, 149, 151, 153–155, 160–162, 199, 200, 209, 232–234, 243, 244, 279, 280, 283, 285, 288
  non-diegetic laughter 60, 199, 260
  proscenium arch 86, 148
  single-camera 10, 11, 125–127, 144, 161
  studio audience 73, 84, 87
  warm 39
Slate Represent 5
Sopranos, The 8, 10
Spencer, Herbert 38
spin-off 25, 62, 149, 223, 225–228, 232, 243, 266, 284. *See also Joey*
Standards and Practices 13, 65, 95, 180
Stanfield, Lakeith 6, 179
Stanislavski, Constantine 23, 86, 88
stardom. *See* performance
Stewart, Dodai 171
Stewart, Joe 135, 161
straight man 50
Stranger Things 188

Stromberg 265
style 10. *See also* set design; texture
   cinematic 10, 161
   colour 134, 135, 137, 138, 151, 156
      intensified continuity 161
   intermedial 161, 265
   lighting 126, 135–138, 156, 157, 159
   planimetric staging 139, 154
   theatrical 127, 161
   three-headed monster 23, 83, 84, 125
   zero-degree 125, 161
subtitling 250, 251

T

Teater Pappvin 4, 284
television 2. *See also* comedy; format
   emotion 128, 153, 155, 279
   legitimacy, legitimation 9, 14, 94, 117
   linear 2, 223, 283
   peak 24, 179, 200
   pleasure 23, 127
   prestige 9, 11, 23
   Quality TV 9
   televisuality 11, 127, 128
   transnational 213
   TVIII 223, 281
   TVIV 36, 228, 244, 246, 281, 287
texture 23, 24, 68, 106, 129, 133–138, 148, 152, 160, 161, 191, 203, 229, 277, 285
   intermedial texture 265
Thanksgiving 71, 72, 102, 104, 249

Thompson, Tessa 6, 179
Tom, Lauren 91, 180
tone 25, 48, 92, 93, 104, 134, 173–176, 187, 191, 193, 195, 199, 200, 202, 209, 212, 213, 229, 284
Trump administration 24, 281
Tucker, Ken 1, 171, 211, 288
TV Fem 283
Twitter 5, 172, 285
Two and a Half Men 232
Tyler, Aisha 24, 25, 176, 180–191, 193–199, 204, 206–208, 211, 212
Tyler, James Michael 286

U

Ullman, Tracey 172, 173
Unbreakable Kimmy Schmidt 3, 6, 181
Union, Gabrielle 180–182, 184
universality 21, 224, 230, 249, 267, 288

V

Verfremdungseffekt 260
Vertue, Beryl 244
Vertue, Sue 234
von Bentheim, Irina 257

W

Warner Bros 15, 53, 179, 232
What's Up, Doc? 91
whiteness. *See* politics of representation

Will & Grace 8, 15, 84, 138, 150, 162, 287
Williams, Raymond 20, 133
Willis, Bruce 23, 108, 109
Winfrey, Oprah 171
Witherspoon, Reese 50
Wortham, Jenna 172

X-Files, The 257

You've Got Mail 18

Zoller Seitz, Matt 10

GPSR Compliance
The European Union's (EU) General Product Safety Regulation (GPSR) is a set of rules that requires consumer products to be safe and our obligations to ensure this.

If you have any concerns about our products, you can contact us on

ProductSafety@springernature.com

In case Publisher is established outside the EU, the EU authorized representative is:

Springer Nature Customer Service Center GmbH
Europaplatz 3
69115 Heidelberg, Germany

www.ingramcontent.com/pod-product-compliance
Lightning Source LLC
LaVergne TN
LVHW020327260326
834688LV00037B/911